What Happens When People Talk?

How does language treat the sexes unequally?

What are the real reasons for such strategies as slang, puns, riddles, verbal dueling?

What does body language really mean?

What are the strange and entertaining games people play with language?

WORD PLAY

by Peter Farb

"I learned more about American Indians from Farb's previous *Man's Rise to Civilization* than from any non-specialized source in my experience; and he has done a similar service for linguistics, organizing in readable and concise fashion immense quantities of information."

—Robert Taylor, *Boston Globe*

"It's absolutely fascinating and—for an old word-man—chock-full of goodies. Peter Farb is a great elucidator!"

—Stanley Kunitz,
Pulitzer Prize-winning poet

"*Word Play* is an ambitious and enjoyable attempt to make this 'new science' accessible . . . Puns, riddles, jokes and verbal sparring—[Farb's] book is studded with examples of these . . . He strings a lively assortment of oddities [including] a sensible discussion of the most notorious English four-letter word."

—*Newsweek*

WORD PLAY

What Happens When People Talk

PETER FARB

BANTAM BOOKS · TORONTO · NEW YORK · LONDON

For Mark and Tom

RL 9, IL 9-up

WORD PLAY: WHAT HAPPENS WHEN PEOPLE TALK

*A Bantam Book / published by arrangement with
Alfred A. Knopf, Inc.*

PRINTING HISTORY

Knopf edition published January 1974
2nd printing .... April 1974   3rd printing .... May 1974
Saturday Review Book Club edition published April 1974
Time, Inc. Book Club edition published Spring 1974
Macmillan Book Club edition published June 1974
Portions of this book appeared in HORIZON,
A MAGAZINE OF THE ARTS

Bantam edition / March 1975
2nd printing ...... October 1975   4th printing .... August 1977
3rd printing .... November 1976   5th printing .... November 1978

Grateful acknowledgment is made to the following for permission to reprint previously published material: Crown Publishers, Inc.: For an excerpt from A Treasury of Jewish Folklore, edited by Nathan Ausubel. Copyright 1948 by Crown Publishers, Inc. Harcourt Brace Jovanovich, Inc.: For two lines from the poem "Anyone lived in a pretty how town," from Complete Poems 1913–1962, by e.e. cummings. National Council for Social Studies and the authors: For four lines of "The Night Before Christmas" and the anecdote about William A. Stewart from the article "Negro Ghetto Children and Urban Education: A Cultural Solution" by Stephen Baratz and Joan C. Baratz, from Social Education, April, 1969, Vol. 33, Number 4. The M.I.T. Press: For a diagram of one-syllable words from Language, Thought and Reality, by Benjamin L. Whorf. Copyright © 1956 by The M.I.T. Press. Clarkson N. Potter, Inc.: For excerpts from: The Annotated Alice, by Lewis Carroll, with Introduction and Notes by Martin Gardner. Copyright © MCMLX by Martin Gardner. Anne Kaufman Schneider: For material from "The Cocoanuts" by Walter Kaufman. Anne Kaufman Schneider copyright holder. The Society of Authors on behalf of the Bernard Shaw Estate: For an excerpt from Pygmalion, by Bernard Shaw.

ISBN 0–553–12606–7

Published simultaneously in the United States and Canada

PRINTED IN THE UNITED STATES OF AMERICA

CONTENTS

ACKNOWLEDGMENTS

And for ther is so gret diversite
In Englissh, and in writyng of oure tonge,
So prey I God that non myswrite the

Geoffrey Chaucer's prayer in *Troilus and Criseyde* is mine as well. To write about language and also to present a report on the state of linguistic research demanded that I explore many disciplines—linguistics, anthropology, sociology, psychology, ethology, poetics, and so on—and consequently expose myself to the hazards of interdisciplinary points of view. Further, in writing about language I had no alternative but to use the medium of language itself—which is nearly as difficult as lifting oneself by one's bootstraps.

My task has been eased considerably by the generous assistance of many people. I am greatly in the debt of the following scholars who kindly read the sections of the manuscript that fell within their disciplines and who offered valuable suggestions: Joel Sherzer, Department of Anthropology, University of Texas at Austin; Charles Clifton, Department of Psychology, University of Massachusetts at Amherst; James T. Heringer, Linguistics Program, University of Southern California; and Irven DeVore, Department of Psychology and Social Relations, Harvard University. It would be misleading for me to suggest that these readers found themselves in complete agreement with every idea expressed in this book; nor is it likely that consensus could ever be reached in a field so new and controversial as the one this book is about.

In the course of working on the manuscript I have also been the fortunate recipient of advice and kindness from: Roger D. Abrahams, Director of the African and Afro-American Research Institute, University of Texas at Austin; Thomas L. Bernard, Department of Psychology and Education, Mount Holyoke College; Gary H. Gossen, Department of Anthropology, University of California at Santa Cruz; Nancy P. Hickerson, Texas Technological University; Jim Kakumasu, Wycliffe Bible Translators, Equipe Linguistica, Belém, Brazil; Dina Sherzer, Department of English, University of Texas at Austin; Robert Taylor, Dean of Library Sciences, Syracuse University; and Frederick W. Turner III, Department of English, University of Massachusetts at Amherst. I am also grateful to film critic Pauline Kael and to Joe Adamson, of the University of Pennsylvania, for helpful suggestions and material about the Marx Brothers and visual communication.

My expressions of gratitude would be grossly incomplete without mention of the conscientious people at the University of Massachusetts (Amherst) Library—particularly Donald M. Koslow, formerly in charge of the reference section, Gordon Fretwell, director of special services, and their able assistants—who worked wonders in locating inaccessible research materials for me.

Every page of this book reveals borrowings from scholars in many disciplines. I hope that this single, overriding recognition of that fact will express my deep appreciation and admiration for their work. Rather than attempting an invidious listing of some of their names here, let me instead direct the reader to their works cited in the References and Bibliography sections—which proclaim their devotion to their craft more than my mere words could.

Ultimately, of course, I am responsible for whatever errors, inelegant expressions, or tongue-tied explanations persist in this book.

Amherst, Massachusetts   PETER FARB

The Play and the Players

Immediately after the scene in which Hamlet hires players to act out his theory about the murder of his father, Guildenstern attempts to manipulate Hamlet with words. But Hamlet rebukes him:

> Why, look you now, how unworthy a thing you make of me! You would play upon me; you would seem to know my stops; you would pluck out the heart of my mystery; you would sound me from my lowest note to the top of my compass . . . 'Sblood, do you think I am easier to be played on than a pipe? Call me what instrument you will, though you can fret me, you cannot play upon me.

Hamlet fires off a barrage of puns and employs other forms of word play to make it perfectly clear that he has seen through Guildenstern's attempt to play upon him with words. In this passage, and throughout his works, Shakespeare demonstrates that he understood how people play a game with language to achieve certain ends: to cajole or convince, to display their own wisdom to an audience, to win honor or esteem. He often states his thoughts about language with poetic intensity and apt detail—yet they are nonscientific, merely common-sense observations, no matter how artfully they are expressed.

Beginning about 1960, and at an accelerating pace

since then, a scientific approach has replaced common sense in interpreting the way human beings use their various tongues. Some linguists, intrigued by the social and psychological environments in which people manipulate language, have begun to look upon speech behavior as an interaction, a game in which both speakers and listeners unconsciously know the rules of their speech communities and the strategies they may employ. In the same way that every speaker has an intuitive grasp of the grammar of his native language, the speaker also intuitively understands the correct way to use his language in various situations. This approach—which has engaged a number of recently established fields of interest known by such names as sociolinguistics, psycholinguistics, the ethnography of speaking, the sociology of language, and so on—provides a new way to view language, one so new in fact that almost none of the material in this book has previously been available to the reader untutored in linguistics. Recent as this perspective is, it has already gone far toward revealing the remarkable ability of human beings to play upon one another with their speech. It is what this book is about.*

The scene is a southern city in the United States; the speakers are a police officer and Dr. Alvin Poussaint, a black psychiatrist from Harvard. Exactly fifteen words

---

*This will be the only footnote. The References section that begins on page 371 gives the source of quotations, substantiates possibly controversial points, and leads the reader to further knowledge about the ideas introduced here.

It should be made clear at the outset that "linguist" is the name given to the kind of scholar who discovers and then describes the rules that govern individual languages, traces their histories and their links to other languages, studies the ways in which they are used in human societies, and searches for universal rules applicable to languages everywhere. Contrary to common usage, a linguist is not someone who speaks many languages with ease; such a person is best termed a "polyglot." In fact, some linguists are fluent in only one or two languages in addition to their native tongue.

are spoken in an interaction that has long been typical of black-white relations in the South:

"What's your name, boy?" the policeman asked.
"Doctor Poussaint. I'm a physician."
"What's your first name, boy?"
. . . As my heart palpitated, I muttered in profound humiliation: "Alvin."

To most readers, this exchange is simply an obvious insult offered by a white policeman to a black person—but they might find it difficult to describe exactly the mechanism of the insult offered and the subtleties involved.

The explanation resides in the fact that the American speech community, like speech communities in every part of the world, employs a particular set of rules when one person addresses another, especially when that person is a stranger. The speaker may base his form of address on age (such as saying *mister* to an adult, *sonny* or *boy* to a child), on rank (*sir* to someone of equal or higher status, *buddy* or *Jack* to someone of lower status), or professional identity (*doctor* or *father* if it is apparent that the person being addressed is a physician or a priest). The American speech community considers certain other forms of address to be insulting—such as addressing someone on the basis of a visible physical deformity (*gimpy*), race (*nigger*), or national origin (*wop*)—although some speech communities in various parts of the world do not find these forms insulting at all. As a speaker who belongs to the American community, the policeman was expected to use one of the three acceptable selectors: age, rank, or professional identity. Instead he selected race by addressing Doctor Poussaint as *boy*—which, of course, is a southern white man's common form of address to blacks.

Doctor Poussaint replied by reminding the policeman that the formula for professional identity in address in the American speech community is *Doctor* + Last Name. But the policeman treated *Doctor* + Last Name as a failure to reply, as a nonmove in the game of interaction between them. He made no concession at all to the rule, and he failed even to compromise by addressing Doctor Poussaint as *Doc*. Instead he indicated a second time that he intended to play by different rules. He repeated his question, specified that he wanted the first name only, and also repeated the race-selected form of address, *boy*. Only because both the policeman and Doctor Poussaint shared a knowledge of the rules could the policeman's insult and condescension be clear. And Doctor Poussaint felt humiliated because he acquiesced in the policeman's game by agreeing to supply his first name. He collaborated in negating the American rules of address, one of the social cements that is supposed to hold our society together.

Even such a brief interaction illustrates how speakers play with the rules of their speech community. The word "play," however, should not be misinterpreted. Playing with words does not refer solely to entertainments like anagrams or crossword puzzles. Nor is "word play"—which usually refers to riddles, puns, jokes, wise sayings, verbal dueling, and so forth—a trivial pastime. In fact, "play" and "games" are two of life's very serious and complex activities, despite the apparent frivolousness of card games, board games like chess and checkers, sports like baseball. People are in the habit of saying *I'm in the advertising game* or *My game is life insurance,* but such statements do not mean that they look upon their livelihoods as "fun." Rather, the word *game* in these contexts—as well as in others, such as strategic *game plans* or fierce *war games* —refers to an interaction according to well-defined rules, in which something is at stake that both sides are attempting to win.

The language game shares certain characteristics with all other true games. First of all, it has a minimum of two players (the private, incomprehensible speech of a schizophrenic is no more a true game than is solitaire). Second, a person within speaking distance of any stranger can be forced by social pressure to commit himself to play, in the same way that a bystander in the vicinity of any other kind of game may be asked to play or to look on. Third, something must be at stake and both players must strive to win it—whether the reward be a tangible gain like convincing an employer of the need for a raise or an intangible one like the satisfaction of besting someone in an argument. Fourth, a player of any game has a particular style that distinguishes him as well as the ability to shift styles depending upon where the game is played and who the other players are. In the case of the language game, the style might be a preference for certain expressions or a folksy way of speaking, and the style shift might be the bringing into play of different verbal strategies when speaking in the home, at the office, on the street, or in a place of worship.

Variables such as these make the language game unpredictable. Just as a five of hearts may be used in a poker game to make a pair, a straight, a flush, or a full house, so the same word may turn up in many different contexts or environments. The speech situation gives the word meaning, just as the five of hearts has no meaning in itself until it is placed in the environment of other cards in the game. English offers the speaker *automobile, auto, car, buggy, jalopy, wheels,* and so forth as alternative ways to say virtually the same thing. The speaker's choice of one word in place of all the other possibilities is often determined by an array of subtle social and psychological factors. He may, for example, say *buggy* if he wishes to deprecate his new Mercedes or *wheels* if he wants to show that he is with it in rapping with the younger generation.

Finally, the language game is similar to other games in that it is structured by rules, which speakers unconsciously learn simply by belonging to a particular speech community. Although players of the language game command a vast repertory of moves—that is, a virtually infinite number of things that they could possibly say in many grammatical combinations—nevertheless the number of possibilities is severely limited by the situation in which the speaker finds himself. A speaker may no more switch to gibberish in mid-sentence than a poker player may apply the rules of chess in mid-game. The rules exist for the speaker and he must play by them—or else use the strategy of consciously breaking them.

The previous sentence illustrates one of these rules which make many utterances in English appear to result from male chauvinism. Note that I first said "for the speaker" and then "*he* must play." I expressed myself that way because the rules of English dictate that *he* (and not *she* or *it*) must be used to refer back to a sexually ambiguous antecedent. I might have rephrased the sentence to employ *one,* but that is awkward—or even referred to some hypothetical person, but that still would not have solved the problem because an English speaker also uses *he* as the pronoun to signify a hypothetical person. From a strictly linguistic point of view, of course, it would not matter if I used *it,* or *he* or *she,* or even some new word like *shis;* but centuries of social convention have made *he* the acceptable word here. Similarly, throughout this book English has forced me to use other apparently sexist words—*man, mankind,* and *human* (derived ultimately from the Latin *homo,* "man")—when I refer to both sexes of our species, words that appear to ignore the female sex. (The problem of sexist language will be discussed in greater detail in Chapter 7.)

An important thing about rules is that they do more than merely police behavior. The rules of chess do, of course, define who is playing fair—but they also actually create the game. This is borne out by the obvious fact that a chimpanzee might be taught to move chess pieces correctly, but the animal would not really be playing chess any more than a parrot faultlessly repeating an English sentence is really speaking English. The parrot, like the player of chess, must understand the interaction and the options available to express things in alternative ways. And a player, whether of the language game or of chess, must also be committed to the rule of winning—a commitment utterly lacking in the chimpanzee who moves pieces around a board. We show that we unconsciously sense this commitment by our similar disapproval of the player who throws a game and of the player who cheats. These players have broken quite different rules, but we condemn them equally because each has broken, in his own way, the rules of winning. Similarly, we close our ears to the speaker who utters a nonsensical statement as well as to the speaker who calculatingly lies—because both have violated their commitment to use language properly in the speech community.

When I talk about knowing the rules of a language, I do not mean that a speaker is able to state clearly the rules that govern his speech at any particular moment. In fact, unless he is a specialist in the subject of language, he most likely is unaware that he is following various complicated sets of rules which he has unconsciously acquired and internalized. Yet it is clear that he has incorporated such rules, for he recognizes speech that is "wrong"—that is, speech that departs from rules —even though he does not consciously know the rules themselves. Furthermore, when confronted with a need to say something he has never heard before, he unconsciously applies to the new case the same rules that he unconsciously applied to similar previous cases.

For an obvious example of the way speakers unconsciously internalize rules, take the way *linger* and *sing-*

er, anger and *hanger,* and similar pairs of words are pronounced in many dialects of English. Careful listening reveals that speakers often pronounce the words in each pair in quite different ways. Both *linger* and *anger* are pronounced as if they were spelled with an additional hard *g* after the *ng* sound, somewhat like *ling-ger* and *ang-ger.* This additional *g* sound, though, is missing from both *singer* and *hanger.* If we examine many such pairs of words, a rule finally emerges: When a word is formed by the addition of *-er* to a verb, the *g* sound is not present; when the word is not derived from a verb, an additional *g* is pronounced. Probably no native speaker of a dialect of English that recognizes this rule consciously knows it unless he is a linguist or a teacher of speech. Yet, when the native speaker sees the word *bringer,* he automatically pronounces it without the additional *g* because it is derived from the verb *bring.* And when he sees the word *longer,* not derived from a verb, he introduces the hard *g* sound.

Other animals besides humans stand upright, have clever fingers and cunning brains, use tools. But humans alone possess the capacity to speak languages of such richness that linguists are still unable to describe these languages fully. Speech and human first appeared on the planet together, developed together, and when one disappears the other will also. Speech is not merely some improved form of animal communication; it is a different category altogether that separates human beings, inhabiting the far side of an unbridgeable chasm, from the beasts.

No one knows for sure how human beings developed their capacity for language, but speech is the exclusive property of their direct line of ancestry. Even the extinct subspecies of modern humans, the Neanderthals, possibly could not talk, at least not in a recognizably modern way (judging by the structure of their throat and jaw). Nor can any ape or monkey discuss the meaning of a word, analyze the grammatical structure of a sentence, or use minute differences in sounds, such as those between *b* and *p,* as a way to distinguish between pairs of words like *bat–pat* and *bill–pill.* Chimpanzee infants, reared exactly like children in a human household, have been taught to speak a few words; but that bears not the remotest resemblance to the speech system that human children learn so effortlessly. Some recent sophisticated experiments with chimpanzees show that they have communicative abilities closer to human languages than once believed, although they use signals rather than sounds (these experiments will be discussed in Chapter 11). Apes, monkeys, and all other kinds of animals communicate with each other—but only human beings talk.

Healthy children, no matter where on the globe they live or the particular kind of language they speak, learn a native tongue. And they go through the same steps in acquiring their language at approximately the same speed, independently of whether they are deprived children or children brought up by doting parents who drill them in language skills. By about the age of three months, children use intonations similar to those changes in pitch heard in adult exclamations and questions. By about one year, they begin to speak recognizable words, and by the age of four or so they have mastered most of the exceedingly complex and abstract structures of their native tongues. In only a few more years children possess the entire linguistic system that allows them to utter and to understand sentences they have not previously heard. This remarkable accomplishment, most of it concentrated in only several years of development, is the birthright of every normal child. In contrast to this orderly development, which comes as a matter of course, many children have difficulty with reading, arithmetic, and swimming, even though they might receive considerable instruction. The child acquires his language merely by hearing it spoken in his native speech community. Yet his language is so complex that pages of diagrams, formulas, and explanatory notes are necessary to analyze even a brief statement made in it. (This complexity will be demonstrated in Chapters 13 and 14.) For the rest of his life the child will speak sentences he has never before heard, and when he thinks or reads, he will still literally talk to himself. He can never escape from speech.

And from speech flow all the other hallmarks of our humanity: those arts, sciences, laws, morals, customs, political and economic systems, and religious faiths that collectively are known as "culture." Culture could not exist without language. Even specialists in nonverbal communication—painters, sculptors, musicians, dancers, and mathematicians—must at some time talk about their craft, and they probably think about it in terms of speech. The noted photographer and teacher Minor White has complained that

> people in our culture *talk* photographs rather than experience them visually. Whatever is being looked at, photographs or anything else, the input is visual while the tagging is verbal. So for most of us words, words, words, overwhelm and warp any significance appropriate and becoming to visual perception. Some students even claim, that unless they name it—until they name it—the thing seen has no meaning!

No society can plan ahead to gather food, to undertake public works, or to prepare for an afterlife without the capacity for expressing a future tense. Nor can it prohibit or encourage behavior which it is unable to name. Who is permitted to marry whom in any society is determined by blood relationships or by membership in various clans and castes—rules which can be transmitted only by language.

The statement made a few paragraphs ago that only

human beings have the capacity to play the language game refers to all members of our species. Despite what many people still believe, no such thing as a "primitive" language has yet been discovered. Every language communicates what its native speakers need to communicate in their kind of society. An Aranda aborigine of central Australia who ekes out a primitive existence and who can carry all of his material possessions on his back nevertheless carries in his head a language of unbelievable complexity and richness. Aranda verb stems, for example, can take about a thousand combinations of suffixes—as if, in English, the verb *go* could be converted into a thousand variants like *going* and *gone*. Moreover, just one. of these suffixes can so subtly change the original verb that often an entire sentence is needed in an English translation to express the different shade of meaning. And so rich is the Aranda vocabulary that many archaic words, absent from everyday speech, have been preserved and are used on formal occasions, much as if a speaker of English today could switch suddenly to the Old English of *Beowulf* or to the Middle English of Chaucer.

Linguists have intensively studied several thousand languages, most of them spoken by isolated peoples who live at the periphery of world events. Yet no language system ever discovered is so primitive that its speakers must rely heavily upon gestures as substitutes for words. Nor does any known language lack a highly organized system of sounds selected from the vast array human beings are capable of making, that does not combine these sounds into meaningful words and sentences by means of strict rules, that fails to demand of its speakers the appropriate use of language in different speech situations. All languages possess pronouns, methods of counting, ways to deal with space and time, a vocabulary that includes abstract words, and the capacity for full esthetic and intellectual expression. In short, the most impoverished aborigine can be contrasted in many ways with the industrialist in his grand exurban estate—but no reliable way exists to determine that the aborigine's language is more "primitive" than the industrialist's.

Aboriginal man in North and South America, at the time of the discovery of the New World, spoke some 2,200 languages, more than were spoken in Europe and Asia combined at that time. The Indians communicated a rich tradition of poetry, oratory, drama, and strategies for the use of speech, yet the explorers of the New World often dismissed the native languages as little more than grunts and gestures. So perceptive an observer as Charles Darwin concluded that the speech of the Indians at the southern tip of South America was barely human; but a more recent study of one of these peoples, the Yahgan of Tierra del Fuego, revealed a vocabulary of about 30,000 words. The Aztecs of Mexico had a lexicon of at least 27,000 words, the Sioux of the North American Plains some 20,000—and undoubtedly linguists overlooked many other words. A typical Yahgan, Aztec, or Sioux speaker probably used nearly 10,000 words in everyday speech, which is of much the same magnitude as the 7,000 different words used in the King James Bible. Vocabulary, though, is only one way to evaluate a language. It represents the least durable part of any language system; most of today's slang and other colloquial expressions are destined to be forgotten in a few years. The underlying sound system and the grammar are much more important—and in these respects the language spoken by a band of primitive hunters may be even more complex than the language of an industrialized society.

Language is both a system of grammar and a human behavior which can be analyzed according to theories of interaction, play, and games. It also can be viewed as a shared system of rules and conventions mutually intelligible to all members of a particular community, yet a system which nevertheless offers freedom and creativity in its use. Further, only human beings—no matter the language they speak or the simplicity of their culture—have the capacity to play the language game because all human beings are born to speak. These are the foundations on which the material in this book rests.

Each section of the book poses, and attempts to answer, basic questions about what happens when people talk. The chapters in the first section, for example, revolve around the question: What are the ground rules for the interactions that take place between a speaker and the total environment of his speech community, his particular language, his audience, and the situation in which he speaks? The next question to be answered is: What strategies are available to speakers? Among those discussed in this second section are "talking dirty," dueling verbally, using slang and jargon, playing with words, and lying. Emphasis is placed on the strategies used out of necessity by oppressed peoples— blacks, women, and speakers of low-prestige tongues or minority languages. Is the language game a fair one, or are we all fated to play a "fixed" game because of inherent flaws in language?—that is the problem posed in the third section. After that, questions are asked about the ways in which human beings developed their skills in language, and the book concludes with an attempt to discover how the language game has changed with the passage of time. Throughout, one question is paramount, and it lurks behind all of the material in the book: How do we explain the language behavior unique to our species, *Homo loquens,* Man the Talker?

I

THE GAME

I

The Ecology of Language

Toward the end of the last century people began to speak of languages as being "born," producing "daughter" languages, and eventually "dying"—undoubtedly because the metaphor of a living organism came naturally to a generation that had recently learned about Darwinian evolution. Some languages were also thought to "give birth" to weak mutations, in which case euthanasia could always be practiced upon them by the eternally vigilant guardians of correct usage. The metaphor of language as a living organism persists to this day, but it is inherently false. A language does not live or die. And unless it is to be considered merely a code to be broken (like Egyptian or Mayan hieroglyphics) or an intellectual pastime (like speaking Latin), a language has no life apart from the lives of the people who speak it.

Today a more fitting metaphor might be the "ecology" of language—the web formed by strands uniting the kind of language spoken, its history, the social conventions of the community in which it is spoken, the influence of neighboring languages, and even the physical environment in which the language is spoken. This metaphor emphasizes that the function of language is to relate its speakers to one another and to the world they live in. Eskimo, for example, is a language whose grammar makes it difficult to express certain ideas but

17

very easy to say other things. It is spoken in the particular physical environment of the Arctic Circle, which makes it understandable that this language should have a large vocabulary for describing different kinds of snow and seals. Its vocabulary has also been influenced by the presence of neighboring Indian tribes and of Europeans. And the strategies for using the language are unconscious conventions of the social environment into which native speakers are born—a speech community with its own ideas about the "rightness" or "wrongness" of whatever is said.

An Eskimo's language affords him a tremendous, possibly infinite, number of ways to communicate whatever he wishes to say—whether it be to impart information, to convince someone of the rightness of his cause, or just to be sociable. But in actuality his choice of exactly what he will say at any particular moment is much more limited because his environment severely restricts the strategies he can use. He will express the same thought differently in the igloo than he will on a hunt. And he will unconsciously be influenced by his relationship to his listener, the role he intends to play in his society, whether or not an audience is present, and so on—with the result that out of the many possible things he might say, only a few choices are acceptable at the moment. Everything I have stated about the Eskimo holds true for speakers of other languages any place on earth.

Speakers who share with other speakers the knowledge of such social constraints placed upon them are said to belong to the same speech community. A speech community is not simply a group of people who have a language in common; it is also a community of people in daily interaction and who therefore share rules for the exact conditions under which different kinds of speech will be used. I can understand what is said to me in certain communities that use the English language, but the full import of the message may escape me if I do not belong to the particular speech community. How something is said is an important part of what is said. Americans of Italian ancestry in New York and Americans of Scots-Irish ancestry in the southern Appalachian Mountains both speak English —but they do not belong to the same speech community. I am a member of neither of these communities and if I enter one or the other I will be ignorant of the rules of their language game. I will not know when sarcasm was intended or when I have been insulted; I may misconstrue silence as hostility and talkativeness as warmth; I may consider the speech in one community too flat, the speech in the other too boisterous. Until I become a full participant in a speech community, I have no way of knowing which particular language game is being played or what the rules of play are.

Similarly, blacks and whites are in close physical contact in many northern cities, yet certain linguistic elements have failed to cross the barrier between the two communities. Some black slang—such words as *dig, cool,* and *groovy*—has passed into the white community, but much of the vocabulary, grammar, and speech behavior of the black community is unknown to the white. As the equivalent to the white *common sense,* a black speaker may say *mother wit,* a term which whites are likely to regard as literary or archaic and which is not ordinarily in their vocabulary. A black speaker is likely to use *it* instead of *there* when he utters sentences like *It's no one home*—but few whites understand this construction, despite their frequent contact with black speakers. And whites usually are ignorant of, and often fearful of, black hyperbole, which addresses a wide audience rather than a specific listener, or of the range of vocal effects, such as growling or falsetto, in which utterances are made. For their part, blacks are often bewildered by the pretentious way in which most whites phrase even simple statements— and angered by the inability of the white social worker to communicate without resorting to a Latinate vocabulary.

And so it is apparent that no member of a speech community can say anything he wants to, in any form he cares to use, on any occasion, even though he may be fluent in the sound system and the grammar of the particular language he is speaking. And no visitor to a foreign speech community—regardless of the amount of instruction he has received in the grammar of its language—is ever prepared for the countless subtleties he will find in the way the language is used by its native speakers. Even a child born into that foreign speech community, and who thereby acquires his native tongue effortlessly, nevertheless still has not learned the appropriate use of his language in all situations. By the age of five, the child can utter a wide repertory of grammatical sentences, but he is still learning which of these sentences to use at a given time. Only as he matures within his speech community does he acquire the ability to make statements appropriate for any situation and to judge the appropriateness of statements made by others.

The problem of exactly what to say, and where and when to say it, is extremely complex, and it is further complicated because the choices vary from speech community to speech community. Native speakers in most, but by no means all, American speech communities know that they should avoid *ain't* in formal situations and that they should not employ highfalutin circumlocutions in everyday conversation. Most speech communities make a similar distinction between "formal" and "informal" situations—but each community, of course, defines the distinction in its own way. The Chiricahua Apaches of southern Arizona emphasized war and raiding, which to them were "formal" occasions. The Apaches started training their males in the rigors of the warpath at about the age of puberty, and the course of instruction included the mastering of a special vocabulary which represented the proper speech while on the warpath. To ask for a drink of water in ceremonial warpath language demanded a statement which translates literally—and inexplicably to speakers of English—as "I begin to swim the spectacular iron ore." "Fire" was not simply fire but "that which tells a story." This kind of formal speech had to be maintained until the war party returned to the camp, at which time conversation switched back to everyday language.

Entering any speech community entails learning the rules of the language games the community plays as well as learning the grammar of the language it speaks. Imagine that an American visitor fluent in an African language asks in it the exact equivalent of the English question "How many children do you have?" If he is answered by the husband, he may obtain the number "three"—but if he is answered by the wife, a different number, perhaps "five." That is because in this speech community a man counts only the number of sons ("three") and a woman only the number of daughters ("five"). If the American finally figures out the reason for the different answers and rephrases the question to "What is the total number of children you both have?" he may be surprised to find that the answer is more than the total of the three sons and the five daughters. The explanation is that in this speech community the "total number" of offspring includes living sons and daughters plus those children who have died. Eventually, after many more questions and answers, the American visitor may figure that out also. But if he had been a member of this speech community he would have known unconsciously that the way to phrase his original question was "What is the number of your sons and daughters now alive?"

The snares that can entrap a visitor to a foreign speech community are clearly demonstrated in the close study of the Rundi community, in the small African country of Burundi, made by Ethel M. Albert, of Northwestern University. She discovered that the Rundi attitude toward speech is directly related to their view of the universe and their particular kind of society. They see the world as a hierarchy with a high god at the top followed by the king, princes, nobles, herders, farmer-peasants, and finally the lowborn pariahs. In the upper part of this hierarchy, personal power and free choice are at their maximum, and the element of chance is negligible. But the lower down in the hierarchy a person is born, the less power and free choice he has, and his fate becomes increasingly subject to the whims of his superiors. To the people in the lower ranks of the Rundi speech community, no event can therefore be predicted. Yet they feel that all is not lost. Their universe can be manipulated by speech, so long as it is done cleverly and esthetically, to win gifts, to obtain protection from a superior, to defend oneself against accusations of wrongdoing, or to oust a rival.

It is no wonder that the Rundi speech community places great emphasis upon *imfura,* "speaking well," as an instrument of daily life. Eloquence is highly valued and abundant opportunities exist for it to be displayed in arguments, negotiations, winning favors, in fact in all interactions. The Rundi language offers its speakers a rich vocabulary by which they can minutely analyze and describe speech—and the people spend a great deal of time simply talking about speech and its strategies. Says Albert:

A cool head counts for more than a high I.Q. in realizing the practical-esthetic-emotive values of effective speech. Everyone knows the rules. Everyone plays the game of matching wits through verbal parry and thrust. Differences of individual skills, the likelihood of fortuitous circumstances, and the inherent instability of emotions make it certain that there will be few dull moments. Uncertainty of the outcomes of verbal manipulation of one's affairs is built into the system and is part of the game, enjoyed when the outcome is favorable, lamented when it is not.

To the Rundi the key to the manipulation of the environment through language is *ubgenge,* which means something like "successful cleverness." Therefore, more poetry than truth is heard among them—not only because falsehood is likely to bring success but also because the elegant and poetic expression is most likely to lead to the greatest success. A speaker displays his *ubgenge* when he obtains the gift of a cow from an overlord in reward for virtues he does not possess, when he manipulates the elders in councils, or when he successfully accuses someone else of his own misdeeds. A man in rags does not beg a new pair of shoes from a superior by simply stating that he needs money to replace the shoes that anyone can see are torn to shreds. Instead, he employs *ubgenge* and he says: "One does not hide one's misfortunes; if one tries to hide them, they will nevertheless soon be revealed. Now, I know a poor old man, broken in health and ill; there is a spear stuck in his body and he cannot be saved." The beggar then directs attention toward his ragged shoes, one of which is held together by a "spear"—that is, a safety pin. Clearly, a United Nations technical expert, a Peace Corps worker, or a missionary who has learned Rundi at a language school but has not lived in its speech community could never understand how skillfully the beggar employed the rules of *imfura* and the strategy of *ubgenge* to win out over chance in the game of life. And hearing the beggar's utterance, the foreigner would no doubt consider it florid and meaningless, even though he understood the translated "meaning" of every word.

In the Rundi speech community, and in fact in every other speech community, language fulfills a number of functions. The predominant one, obviously, is what has been called the "referential" function: the verbal structure of the message itself. The "expressive" function is the speaker's attitude toward what he is talking about, whether his emotion is an honest one or is feigned. The "conative" function focuses on who is being addressed —whether it be a human listener, a deity, or a supernatural force (as in "Sun, stand thou still upon Gibeon" from the Biblical book of Joshua). Other "ritualized" functions of language often make speech appear to be devoid of content, but they actually establish or prolong communication, or check whether a channel of communication is open (as when a speaker on the telephone says *Hello! Hello! Can you hear me?*).

Should a person from Burundi visit a speech community that uses one of the European languages, he would undoubtedly note that speakers seem to waste much breath each day on such ritualized functions. He would hear matter-of-fact inquiries made about the state of mind of passers-by (*How you doing?*), vague observations spoken to strangers about the weather (*Nice day*), and self-evident facts expressed (*It's raining hard*). Such empty phrases do not inform, and they certainly do not offer listeners any new thoughts. In these cases the speakers, of course, are using words not for communication but for maneuvering in various social situations. Such utterances identify relationships, express the speaker's role in society, and probe other people's personalities by forcing them into a situation where they must reply. Stereotyped phrases, which nevertheless offer important social benefits, are found in one form or another in speech communities around the world—as the anthropologist Bronislaw Malinowski pointed out half a century ago. He gave the name "phatic communion" (derived from Greek and Latin words that mean "verbal togetherness") to speech that is used as a social cement. And he defined it as "a type of speech in which ties of union are created by a mere exchange of words."

Phatic communion may be empty of content, but it nevertheless functions as an important strategy in the language game. Imagine that I am passing my acquaintance John Smith on the street; I am too busy to stop and chat but nevertheless I utter the phatic communication *How you doing, John?* My stereotyped question has reassured John Smith of my continued high regard for him as an acquaintance. By substituting *Mister Smith* for *John* in the above greeting, I convey no additional information, but I undoubtedly will unsettle John Smith, who will wonder why I am being so formal. He may think that he has offended me in some way and that I am sulking. And if I utter no greeting at all, that is still a phatic communication that says much about the present state of my relationship to John Smith. Such a silent communication of resentment against Smith offers him only two alternatives—refusing to speak also or the humiliation of speaking first and in that way admitting his need for the social relationship that speech represents. *John, Mister Smith,* and Silence can serve equally as phatic communications directed toward a particular person at a particular time and place. But, they are obviously not synonymous in the context of the social game I am playing, with the rules common to both of us in the environment of our mutual speech community.

Any transaction between two human beings—an exchange of words, silence, or a mutually intelligible gesture such as a wave of the hand—conforms to rules and conventions understood by all the members of that speech community. To have no firm rules at all is to have no language game at all. But to have the rules and to break them by lying or cheating confirms the very existence of such rules. The Marx Brothers were the masters of such an anarchic attack upon the rules of language, and most of the humor in their films is derived from their assault upon the conventions of their speech community.

Each brother inhabits a well-defined territory as a specialist in a different kind of language game. Groucho is the fast-talking sharpie, the dueler who employs the pointed wit of speech. Chico's habitat lies on the fringes of language. He is the speaker of a phony-Italian dialect who misconstrues both the meanings and the manners of the "foreign" American speech community in which he finds himself. Finally, the mute Harpo throws language back to the level of the beasts; instead of speech, he employs animal-like signaling systems, such as whistling or charades that substitute for words. Interacting with the verbal, dialectal, and animal systems of the three brothers is the imposing dowager Margaret Dumont, who steadfastly defends the narrow-minded rules and conventions of the American speech community.

The methodology of the Marx Brothers is clearly displayed in their first film, *The Cocoanuts* (1929), which set the pattern for their future films. Groucho owns the incredibly mismanaged Hotel de Cocoanuts in Florida, and the opening scene shows him accosted by rebellious bellboys who clamor for their unpaid wages. Groucho listens to them in apparent incomprehension, as if they were complaining in some foreign tongue. Finally he appears to understand: "Oh, you want your *money?*" They affirm they indeed want to be paid their wages. Groucho replies, "So you want *my* money?"—a mere change of a pronoun plus a shift in the stressed word, which entirely alters the meaning. He continues: "Is that fair? Do I want *your* money? No, my friends, no. Money will never make you happy. And happy will never make you money." Groucho has switched "money" and "happy" as subjects and objects of the two sentences, thereby eliminating the dividing line between a noun and an adjective and making a logical shambles of the sentence.

Soon the bellboys' prospects are enhanced by the arrival of a telegram that makes a bizarre reservation for two floors and three ceilings. "Must be mice," concludes Groucho. Audiences usually are convulsed by this line because they intuitively sense that Groucho has performed linguistic sleight-of-hand, although they may not be certain exactly what it is. One cause for laughter is that space, such as "a room" or "floor space," and not boundaries is what is generally reserved in the English language (although it is just the opposite in the language of the Hopi Indians of Arizona, which has no word for "room" but does for "ceiling"). In English the reservation of two rooms implies the reservation also of three ceilings to enclose those two spaces. Once Groucho has committed himself to accepting the telegram on its literal terms, he must then explain what kind of guest would be interested in the three boundaries of the ceilings rather than in the two spaces for living. Unflagging logic leads him to the one inevitable conclusion—the guests must be mice.

Groucho, with practically every word, directs attention to how unreliable a vehicle language can be for communication. He fires off so many allusions and suggestions, tying them all together with such rapid shifts in usage or emphasis, that it is often difficult to determine exactly what causes the laughter. He misapplies clichés, thereby exposing them as the tricks of language they usually are. He uses strings of unlikely words to construct false analogies and false syllogisms, in that way showing how easy it is to bedevil the most innocent statements. When, later in the film, Margaret Dumont protests that Groucho is repeating what he already told her about Florida real estate, Groucho explains that he repeats himself because he left out a comma the last time. He thus doubly assaults the logic of language because the omission of a comma is irrelevant in speech and also because the omission is insufficient justification to repeat the entire sales pitch.

Enter the senders of the telegram, Chico and Harpo. Chico says, "We sent-a you telegram. We make reservash." Chico's use of "reservation" without the final syllable and his phony-Italian accent give warning of how freely he will play with the English language. His verbal play shows the improbability of words—in contrast to Groucho's puns, which cleverly enlist words to attack conventions. Chico does battle against the language of Shakespeare and Milton armed with only one weapon: unyielding literalness.

In a later scene, Chico demonstrates how formidable this weapon can be. Groucho attempts to employ him as a shill in a scheme to auction off worthless real estate:

GROUCHO: If we're successful in disposing of these lots, I'll see that you get a nice commission.

CHICO: How about some money?

"Commission" versus "money," both having approximately the same meaning in this context, dramatizes the historic conflict in English between the genteel and the plain vocabularies, between the Latinate upper-class speech and the Anglo-Saxon of the common people— the same sort of contrast as heard when a judge asks, "Did you apprehend the miscreant?" and the witness replies, "Yeah, I caught the chiseler!"

The brothers unite in their attacks upon cultural and linguistic decorum, as personified by the wealthy dowager Margaret Dumont. Through all of the confusion, she remains unruffled, protected by her faith that the rules and conventions will ultimately win out over anarchy. She innocently asks Chico when he sits down to perform at the piano, "What is the title of your first number?" Chico holds up one finger and replies, sticking to the point with relentless logic, "Number one!" A further example is the scene in which Groucho plays up to her with the object of financially rewarding matrimony:

GROUCHO: Ah, if we could find a little bungalow. Eh? Of course I know we could find one, but maybe the people wouldn't get out. But if we could find a nice little empty bungalow just for me and you, where we could bill and cow—no—where we could bull and cow.

Groucho's mispronunication of "coo" leads him, when he repeats the cliché in its second and even more distorted variation, to reduce the convention of romantic love to animal sex.

Scenes such as these, in film after film, show the Marx Brothers playing havoc with the conventions of the American speech community. They give the cliché, entrenched by generations of stubborn use, a new vitality. They impale words and ideas, then hold them aloft to show that they are stuffed with straw rather than sinew and muscle. The sound system of the English language meets its match in Chico's Italian-dialect distortions. Many of the conventional gestures and facial expressions that normally accompany speech or sometimes substitute for it become rude and barbaric. But the very recognition of distortion and lying and playing with language means that the brothers and their audience agree on one thing: Rules underlie the use of language in the American speech community. Since an anarchist can flourish only where institutions exist to be toppled, the anarchic Marx Brothers emphasize the presence of rules and conventions in language.

Nevertheless, the importance of rules has occasionally been exaggerated and the conventions too slavishly observed. In writing of Lemuel Gulliver's third voyage to the flying island of Laputa, Swift pokes fun at those people who believe an intimate connection exists between words and things. He describes a scheme to abolish words:

> . . . and this was urged as a great advantage in point of health as well as brevity. For it is plain that every word we speak is, in some degree, a diminution of our lungs by corrosion, and consequently contributes to the shortening of our lives. An expedient was therefore offered that since words are only names for things, it would be more convenient for all men to carry about them such things as were necessary to express a particular business they are to discourse on. . . . Many of the most learned and wise adhere to the new scheme of expressing themselves by things, which has only this inconvenience attending it, that if a man's business be very great, and of various kinds, he must be obliged, in proportion, to carry a greater bundle of things upon his back, unless he can afford one or two strong servants to attend him. I have often beheld two of these sages almost sinking under the weight of their packs, like peddlers among us; who, when they meet in the street, would lay down their loads, open their packs, hold conversation for an hour, and then put up their implements, help each other to resume their burdens, and take their leave.

Many people still take seriously what Swift ridiculed —but the only connection that exists between a word and the thing it stands for is whatever association the speech community has decided to make. The speech community arbitrarily arranges consonants and vowels to signify particular objects or ideas; the exact arrangement does not matter, so long as its association with its meaning is understood by all speakers and listeners.

In the speech situation of a busy luncheonette, a

waitress might call out to a cook a rapid-fire series of orders:

Two burgers without . . . B.L.T. rye . . . ham and—
white . . . barbeef fries . . . three green T.I. . . .
boil five . . . a bowl

In this particular speech situation, abbreviated utter-ances are essential for the speedy transmission of mes-sages. The waitress and the cook have arbitrarily agreed upon their own linguistic system which translates the above orders as:

"Two hamburgers without onions . . . bacon, lettuce, and tomato sandwich on rye bread . . . ham and egg sandwich on white bread . . . barbecued beef sandwich with french fried potatoes . . . three salads with Thousand Island dressing . . . an egg boiled for five minutes . . . one soup of the day"

The waitress and the cook have devised a system in which certain words arbitrarily signify certain things, such as *B.L.T.* for "bacon, lettuce, and tomato sand-wich," a relationship that has little significance for someone who does not speak their particular jargon. To produce the jargon, the waitress and the cook have altered the traditional rule in the English speech com-munity for ordering food—Quantity + Name + De-scriber (as in "two hamburgers without onions")—by eliminating at least one of the three terms. Sometimes Quantity is dropped, usually when the order refers to a single item (in *B.L.T. white* the Quantity *one* is un-derstood). Sometimes the Describer noun is dropped, although the functor words like *and* or *without* may be preserved (as in *two burgers without*). This abbre-viated communications system also involves the loss of segments of words (*ham* dropped from *hamburger*), the use of initials to stand for entire words (*B.L.T.* and

T.I.), naming the preparation needed for an item rather than the item itself (*boil* instead of *egg*), and asking for the container rather than its contents (*a bowl* rather than *soup of the day*).

Free as the waitress and cook were to devise their own system, they could not be completely arbitrary. Unless they were willing to risk confusion during the noisy lunch-hour rush, they could not employ words difficult to tell apart, nor could they use a system in which *ham* was a shortened form for both "hamburger" and "ham sandwich." Conventional language systems similarly appear arbitrary, yet they offer the speaker a somewhat limited array of choices. The animal everyone in the English speech community knows by the arrangement of vowels and consonants that produces *horse* is known to be a *Pferd* in the German speech community, a *caballo* in the Spanish, a *farasi* in the Swahili, and an *uma* in the Japanese. Even though *horse* is an arbitrary English word for a certain kind of animal, speakers did not have complete free choice in creating it. They could not, for example, have called it a *bnug,* because such a combination of sounds does not exist in English, although it does in other languages. Nor would they arbitrarily have assigned the word *checken* to it, since that word is too close to the name of another animal (and in some English dialects both *chicken* and *checken* would be pronounced alike). For similar reasons, Spanish could not have designated the horse a *cdello,* which is an impossible sequence of sounds in that language, or a *cabello,* whose use had already been pre-empted to mean "hair."

The vocabulary of English encompasses several hundred thousand words—and every one of them was created out of only some three dozen sounds selected from the vast number that the human voice is capable of making. The sounds a particular language uses and the ways in which they are combined into words are significant to speakers of that language, but very likely they are not significant to speakers of other languages. For example, a speaker of English immediately detects a difference in the sounds of *law* and *raw* and would never confuse the two words. But a speaker of Japanese usually cannot detect any difference at all—not because his hearing differs from that of a speaker of English, but because his own language does not recognize a distinction between *l* and *r*. An English speaker, in turn, would fail to note distinctions that the Japanese find crucial in their language. Japanese speakers use different pronunciations for their words *to,* meaning "door," and *too,* meaning "ten"—both of which sounds are also words, of course with different meanings, that speakers of English pronounce in exactly the same way. Speakers of both Japanese and English have assented to the convention that certain arbitrary arrangements of sounds signify certain things. No special purpose, though, is served when English makes an arbitrary distinction between *l* and *r* but not between the Japanese *o* and *oo*—and no benefits accrue to the speakers of languages that make them or fail to make them. As Shakespeare observed long before the science of linguistics: "What's in a name? That which we call a rose by any other name would smell as sweet."

Another point should be apparent, yet a misconception exists to this day. No speech community gives birth to children with some special construction of the lips, tongue, nose, mouth, or larynx that enables them to speak the more "difficult" languages. An American child flawlessly utters the sounds of Japanese if he is reared in Japan or the clicks of the Bushman language if he is brought up in that speech community.

The literate peoples of the world have placed deep faith in the written word, yet writing is an imperfect communication system, a pale reflection of the speech it is supposed to substitute for. All human beings speak, but comparatively few attempt to transcribe complex speech into an inherently inexact written form. Unlettered people, however, have not been hindered in the creation of stories, poetry, drama, or oratory. Here, for example, is a tale told by a Hausa of Nigeria:

This is about the Chief of Lies and the Chief of Truth who started off on a journey together. They came to a large town, and lo, the Mother of the King of this town had just died, and the whole town was mourning. Then the Chief of Lies said, "What is making you cry?" And they replied, "The King's mother is dead." Then he said, "You go and tell the King that his mother shall arise." In the evening, the Chief of Lies went and caught a Wasp, the kind of Insect which makes a noise like *Kurururu,* and he put it in a small tin. No sooner had the people departed from the grave, the Chief of Lies opened the mouth of the grave slightly, he brought the Wasp and put it in, and then closed the mouth as before. Then he sent for the King, and said that he was to come and put his ear to the grave—meanwhile this Insect was buzzing—and when the King had come, the Chief of Lies said, "Do you hear your mother talking?" Then the King arose, he chose a horse and gave it to the Chief of Lies, he brought Women and gave them to him, and the whole town began to rejoice because the King's Mother was going to rise again. Then the Chief of Lies asked the King if it was true that his Father was dead also, and the King replied, "Yes, he is dead." So the Chief of Lies said, "Well, your father is holding your mother down in the grave and they are quarreling." And he continued, "Your father, if he comes out, will take away the kingdom from you," and he said that his Father would also kill him. When the King told the people this, they piled up stones on the grave, and the King said, "Here, Chief of Lies, go away. I give you these horses." Certainly falsehood is more profitable than truth in this world.

Some readers may consider this story charming, others may find it somewhat unimaginative. Whatever the judgment, the reader is responding to the story's written form, not to an actual performance of it delivered as a speech event in a particular speech community. Oral narrative depends completely upon a living speaker who has formulated his rendition of a story for a specific occasion and whose performance is influenced by feedback from an audience—in contrast to written literature, where the work has an independent existence once it has left the author's hands. In oral narrative the speech cannot be separated from the speaker.

This Hausa story has not been captured merely by writing it down. In fact, almost all of it has escaped, except for the hollow words emptied of their significance in the environment in which the story was originally told. Neither punctuation marks, italics, nor personification by use of capital letters can reproduce the tremendous variations of emphasis, stress, pauses, and tone of voice that exist in the spoken utterance. In an actual performance of this story, the dead husks of words would be enlivened by the kind of audience that is listening, by the recent events in the community that account for why this story was told at a particular time and place, by the performer's dramatic use of pauses and rhythms, gestures and facial expressions. These things are not embellishments added to an existing literary work; rather they are integral parts of the story's very conception.

Readers of transcribed "folk" stories often complain that the characters lack depth. In actual performance, though, the characters in this Hausa tale are not crude depictions but are brought to life by the speaker's full repertory of the techniques of sound and sight. As the speaker moves within the circle of his listeners, he vividly suggests the fullness of his characters through intonation and exaggeration of volume and tone. No written version of the Hausa story could possibly convey the different voices used to characterize the King and the Chief of Lies for the audience, the inflections that indicate surprise at the Mother's rebirth or horror at the imminent return of the Father, and the repetition of key phrases. The imitation of the wasp's *Kurururu* would be sung, perhaps in falsetto but certainly with a nasal twang for full humorous effect. The Hausa story-teller also commands visual resources that enhance the impact of his story. Gestures, eye movements, facial expressions, even the dress and ornamentation the teller wears—all emphasize aspects of the story that cannot possibly appear on the printed page.

Furthermore, the participation of the audience is essential. The teller constantly observes the audience's reactions so that he can adjust his performance. The audience, in turn, is expected to contribute to the tale by laughing and also by emitting spontaneous exclamations, repeating the teller's words, and asking questions. Most published versions of African stories omit the songs that usually are essential parts of the narration, even though the singing of choruses by both speaker and audience at significant places in the narration may take up more time than the actual plot of the story.

This Hausa story might have been repeated immediately after the above transcription was taken down, but it would have represented a completely different performance. That is because the speaker's motivation for telling this story, his exact visual and verbal techniques, the composition of the audience and its mood—all of these things would have changed. Obviously, the telling of a story goes far beyond the mere grammar of the sentences used. It is the focal point for the total sociology and psychology of a people at a certain time and place, their accumulated beliefs, assumptions, and customs. Contrary to what most people learned in school, oral literature is not something simply "passed on" from generation to generation. What is passed on is only a tattered message that has been ripped out of its communicative context. Never to be retrieved is the entire aura of the speech event, the unique behavior of interacting human beings. Those fortunate enough to have heard storytelling at its finest —that is, by a "primitive" in his own community and with his familiars around him—can never again look down on unlettered man.

Linguists have made numerous attempts to examine verbal communication in slow motion, to break down the speech act into small pieces so that each could be examined separately. Traditionally, the elements of the language game have been the varying relationships between the speaker, the listener, and the topic being spoken about—but nowadays more sophisticated analysis of speech acts makes it apparent that such a simple division is very inadequate. Investigations of speech in many communities around the world show that about sixteen or seventeen components should be distinguished. Dell Hymes, of the University of Pennsylvania, who originated the phrase "ethnography of speaking" and who has been a prime mover in the recent interest in language behavior, has grouped these components in such a way that their first letters spell the easily remembered acronym S–P–E–A–K–I–N–G. A shift in any of the components of S–P–E–A–K–I–N–G—such as the arrival or departure of a participant, a change from playful conversation to serious talk, an alteration in the tone of voice—indicates that a new level of interaction has become operative or that a shift in strategy has taken place.

S—*for Setting and Scene.* Every speech act takes place at a particular time and place and in a certain physical setting. It also takes place in a specific psychological setting: formal or informal, serious or festive.

P—for Participants. The participants are often the speaker, the listener, and the audience, but the principals may vary because people in different speech communities have their own ways of defining who participates in a speech act. Europeans usually speak as if children or servants were absent, even though these listeners are physically present and obviously hear what is being said. Or they speak in a place of worship as if a certain participant, the deity, were present, even though he is physically absent. The Chinook Indians of the Pacific Northwest may state that the participants at a ceremony are the chief, a spokesman who repeats the chief's words, and an audience. But the chief may be absent and the audience may consist only of the spirits of the land and waters, leaving in reality the spokesman as the sole participant.

E—for Ends. When people speak, they do so in the expectation that a certain outcome—an exchange of information, the obtaining of something, an expression of their status, and so on—will result. From the viewpoint of the entire community, though, other ends may exist which are not necessarily identical to the ends of those who do the speaking. Each side in a litigation speaks in an attempt to win a favorable settlement, but for the community as a whole the strategies of the participants are less important than the arrival at some sort of peaceful settlement.

A—for Act Sequence. A speech act is made up of both form and content; in other words, how something is said is part of what is said. When speaking to family or close friends, our speech is apt to be sloppy, unspecific, and ambiguous to outsiders. That is because the speakers and listeners know one another so well and the contexts of what is being talked about are so familiar that a verbal shorthand can be used. But in communicating the same content to strangers, pronunciation unconsciously improves and it becomes necessary to be precise about the specific names of things, people, and places.

K—for Key. Two speech acts may be exactly the same in Setting, Participants, Ends, and Act Sequence, yet differ solely because one is uttered in a serious key and the other in an ironic. Every speech act is delivered in a certain tone, manner, or spirit, although actual words are sometimes unnecessary to provide the key; a wink, a gesture, even posture may convey it. So important is key that it can negate the verbal content of a message. A sarcastic rendering of *I was hoping you'd stop by* to a neighbor who drops in at a late hour overrides the polite greeting implicit in the content of the utterance.

I—for Instrumentalities. Speakers in the southern United States, the Yorkshire county of England, Jamaica in the Caribbean, India, Australia, Hong Kong, and elsewhere share with me the instrument that is historically known as "English." But my dialect of English is a considerably different instrument from that possessed by these other speakers—and in fact none of us would be able to understand one another at all times, even though we supposedly speak the same English language.

N—for Norms. Communities attach certain norms to the speech act. In some speech communities a listener should not interrupt a speaker, while in others he may do so at will. In the American community a speaker whispers in a place of worship, speaks at medium volume in a store, and shouts a greeting to a friend across the street. Such norms are quite the exception in other communities where people vie with each other to see who can speak the loudest during a religious ceremony or greet close friends with a whisper in the ear. Relations between speech communities are often affected by misunderstanding of each other's norms. When a white middle-class speaker hesitates in his speech, he often fills the pause with an *uh;* a lower-class black instead usually returns to the beginning of his sentence and starts all over again. Many white speakers do not regard a black's repetition as simply different; rather they tend to judge it as deficient.

G—for Genres. Communities recognize a great range of genres or categories into which speech acts may fall—greetings, farewells, questions, speeches, prayers, jokes, proverbs, myths, and so on. *Ladies and gentlemen* signals the beginning of a speech, *Did you hear the one about* the start of a joke.

This book is concerned with both speaking and S–P–E–A–K–I–N–G—that is, with the way we construct words and sentences and also with the way the components of S–P–E–A–K–I–N–G operate in the interactions of the language game. Speakers are constrained by the ecology of language, the rules and conventions of the total environment in which speech is uttered; yet even simple speech acts entail major variables, with a wide range of possibilities under each variable. But no contradiction exists. Rules for language assuredly are operative, as are rules for any kind of human behavior, whether it be politics, sports, or sex. But such rules, of course, are always subject to a tremendous number of choices by speakers in various speech situations.

2

Speech Situations

Every speech community has definite ideas about the situations in which various topics can be broached, particular words employed or even pronounced, and certain tones of voice used. Members of the American speech community know that a formal speech situation, such as a public address, demands a different set of rules than an exchange of jokes. But the problem of when and how to say what is usually much more subtle than that. English normally makes a clear distinction in usage between *you must* (which imposes an obligation upon the listener), *you should* (which offers advice to a listener, who is free to ignore it), and *you may* (which gives approval for something the listener already wants to do). In most situations *you may* is the most polite and *you must* the most rude. But a foreign speaker of English usually does not know that in certain speech situations just the opposite is true, and he may be insulted at what seems to him to be rudeness when actually politeness was intended. Imagine a situation in which he visits the home of an American for dinner and his hosts offer him a very special dish prepared in his honor, saying *You must try some of this.* The foreign speaker who knows his English grammar but not his speech situations might consider this statement boorish, because he thinks *you must* is a rude order for him to do something. The American hosts would know, of course, that if they had said *You should try some of this,* they would be speaking with less rather than more politeness—and that *You may try some of this* would be a very rude remark in this speech situation, even though grammatically it would seem to the foreigner to be the most polite alternative.

Every speech situation is made up of a series of briefer speech events which are clearly separated from one another by the employment of different strategies, by a change in social interactions, or by a switch to a different topic of conversation. To a native speaker of a language, these shifts from one speech event to another are so inconspicuous that he rarely is aware of them. He does not detect his unconscious alteration of tone of voice and vocabulary when he interrupts a conversation with a close friend to greet someone with whom he is not on equally close terms. Such a transition, however, is easily detected in those communities where two language systems exist side by side and are used interchangeably, influenced by very subtle social factors. Bilingualism is common in the Caribbean islands, where an official language like English, French, or Dutch exists alongside an informal creole language. The decision to use either the official language or the creole is unconscious on the part of native speakers, but to an outsider the switch from one language to another clearly marks the boundaries of speech events. A bus driver bringing country people to market usually gossips in the creole and then unconsciously switches to the official language when the bus reaches the outskirts of the market city. A social superior asserts his condescension toward a subordinate by beginning a conversation in the creole; the subordinate, however, tries to enhance his dignity by responding in the official language. After initial jockeying to establish roles, the information-exchange portion of the conversation is usually carried on in the creole.

The existence of speech situations and speech events

demonstrates why no one can adequately learn a foreign language by instruction. A course of study teaches merely the vocabulary and grammar, not the appropriate situations in which to use the alternative ways of saying something that every language offers. Dead languages like Greek and Latin are forever dead because no speaker today can experience the way these languages were used by native speakers when Greece and Rome were living cultures. No matter how fluently a scholar speaks or writes Greek and Latin today, he can know them only as sterile codes, severed from the speech communities that gave them life.

An American who requests a cocktail at a party or a bar utters a simple statement like *I'll have scotch and water, please.* The same American probably would assume that asking for a drink in a foreign culture presents no problems either, once he has learned to speak the language. But the problems can be tremendous, and they go far beyond merely learning the correct words. If, for example, the American visited the Subanun—an agricultural tribe which occupies the mountainous interior of Mindanao in the Philippines—he would have to become intimately involved in their speech community to receive a drink of rice beer. Subanun culture appears exceedingly uncomplicated because of the absence of political, economic, and judicial systems; the only official position is that of the religious specialist, but he lacks any authority beyond the theological sphere. No human group, however, can survive without some sort of leadership—people to settle disputes, to arrange marriages, to make decisions about the apportionment of resources. The Subanun do have positions of leadership, but they are not filled by people who were appointed or elected to them or even inherited them. Instead, these roles are filled by leaders who have demonstrated their verbal skills within the context of a particular speech situation, a drinking bout.

The bout consists of three stages, each rigidly ruled by conventions and each the setting for certain kinds of speech. A drinker who attempts to elevate his status and achieve a high, decision-making role must prove that he can manipulate his language during the three stages. He must show himself off as a person of authority, not only in the proper manner of drinking but especially in the speech acts characteristic of the stages.

The first stage of the bout, tasting, begins when the owner of a large jar of beer asks someone to drink with him. The invitation signals that the invited person is the one to whom, at least initially, the provider of the jar will offer the greatest deference. After the owner has asked several more people to drink, but before anyone has actually drunk, the first person invited squats in front of the jar. He turns to the other drinkers to request permission to taste the beer; the order in which he does so and the terms of address he uses with each drinker are further ways in which roles are defined at the outset. Preparations are now completed for the bout proper. Participants have been brought together and a tentative lineup of statuses has been recognized. During this stage, convention prescribes that all speech be limited to polite phrases. No unsettling statements are to be made, no weighty matters discussed, no information communicated beyond the subtle definitions of status.

The next stage, competitive drinking, begins after all the participants have had the opportunity to sample the beer. The speaker who initiates a round sets the pace for consumption and high speed; those who follow try to equal his performance, and a careful mental score is kept. Speech at first is limited strictly to small talk, or "jar talk," as it is called. Comments are made about the strength of the beer and the drinking performances of the participants. Although the conversation sounds trivial, speech is nevertheless being used as a tool to manipulate behavior. Each speaker attempts to provoke from the other drinkers as many responses as possible to his jar talk, in that way making himself the center of attention. After a while some drinkers realize that they are receiving few responses and they drop out.

Eventually only a half dozen or so drinkers remain in competition. Now the conversation becomes less and less predictable. Gossip of various kinds is exchanged; subjects of community interest are talked about; useful information is passed from one family to another. Only after such topics have been exhausted is it appropriate to discuss arguments between families. Because the Subanun lack law courts, disputes must be handled as speech events to influence opinion at the drinking bout. The various sides state their cases and the other drinkers evaluate the points raised. But the real contest is not between the litigants; it is between the drinkers who compete to display their wisdom in settling the dispute. If the litigants finally agree on a settlement, the drinker who proposed it is elevated in everyone's estimation. He has clearly displayed his prowess in verbal combat in an area essential to the welfare of the Subanun. He has peacefully settled a dispute that might otherwise have led to feuding and violence between families.

Finally, after all disputes have been settled in this way, the bout enters the last stage, known as game drinking. The drinker who achieved high status because of his wisdom in settling disputes during the competitive-drinking stage must now defend his advantage. He must disply his artistry in songs and other verbal play which, together with drinking games like the American chugalug, assure that the bout will conclude on a note of good will. Those drinkers who lost their cases or who may have been demeaned during the earlier stages are singled out for special friendliness.

The Subanun method of selecting leaders might appear foolish to people in Western cultures who are accustomed to filling such roles by election, appointment, or inheritance. But the Subanun method really is not much different from many of the speech interactions that take place in more complex societies. A similar sort of interaction can be seen at a meeting of a local Democratic or Republican political club, for example. As the meeting opens, deference usually is paid to the local boss. At first only trivial matters are discussed, but then an insurgent may subtly hurl a challenge by casually mentioning a recent failure of the boss's strategy. Various members speak to impress the others with the great value of their statements; those who note that they have no support soon stop talking. As the meeting continues, the verbal strategies may become more pointed and words may begin to hurt. Finally, a peacemaker emerges and a consensus is arrived at, followed by efforts to placate the losers. The peacemaker undoubtedly emerges from the evening's discussion with a higher status. He is regarded as a potential leader and an eye will be kept on him in the future. And much the same sort of verbal manipulation occurs at company picnics, at executive cocktail parties, at meetings of professional societies and trade associations—in fact, at any sort of gathering where leadership positions can be filled by the artful use of words.

*

Regardless of the speech situation in which I find myself, my English language provides me with abundant ways to speak in grammatical utterances. But between the grammar of my language and its expression in audible speech lies the filter of the social system in which I live. I am not permitted to address anyone in any manner I care to, even if my grammar is appropriate. Imagine a medical doctor, John Smith, walking down the street of his town and being spoken to by various people. Those who know him, but have no special relationship to him, usually address him by the formula of the American speech community: Professional Identity + Last Name (*Doctor Smith*). A more familiar form of address, by a patient of long standing, by someone of equally high professional rank in the town such as a lawyer, or perhaps even by a garage mechanic, is *Doc*. Another doctor in the town with whom he has not yet established a friendly relationship might address him simply as *Smith*. Someone younger than he who accidentally bumps into him on the street is likely to address him in an apology as *sir*. A construction worker who stops him to ask the time might say *Mac* or *buddy;* a close friend would probably use *John* or *Smitty* or some other nickname; his parents, wife, or children might employ various terms of endearment like *sonny, dear,* and *pop*. These forms of address are not interchangeable. Each fills a particular function in an exact speech situation, and each is related to a host of factors, among them inferior or superior status, the respective ages of Doctor Smith and whoever is addressing him, and the formality or informality of the occasion. And once a speaker has selected a level of address, the rest of his utterance will most likely maintain it. A construction worker who chose *buddy* would not be likely to say *Hey, buddy, hast thou the time of day?*

The American system of address is complicated by the fact that it attempts to do two things at the same time: indicate relative status and also the degree of intimacy felt for the person being addressed. *Doctor Smith* indicates both that the person addressing him is not a close friend and that the doctor has a higher status due to his age or profession. Such a system can present problems, as in the case of a doctor, equal in status to Doctor Smith but considerably younger, who has just joined Doctor Smith's hospital. If the young doctor uses *Doctor Smith* out of respect for age, that would appear to give Smith a higher status, which is not the case. But the use of Smith's first name would imply an intimacy that has not developed as yet. By adroit wording of his sentences, though, the new doctor can manage to avoid using any terms of address at all, thus dodging the problem of status until such time as intimacy with Doctor Smith has been established.

Speakers of Javanese have no such option. Every situation requires the speaker to make the most exacting discriminations about his attitude toward the listener's status. Before a Javanese speaks to someone, he must immediately choose one of the three basic styles of his language: the plain, the fancy, or the elegant. Then he has to decide whether or not he will employ special terms known as "honorifics," which allow him to boost his style of speech in careful gradations without raising it an entire notch, somewhat like playing a sharp on the piano instead of the next higher white key. Both the topmost elegant style and the lowest plain style take honorifics, with the further complication that the plain style employs two kinds of honorifics. As a result, a Javanese cannot escape from choosing one of six styles whenever he speaks to someone. He has no choice but to inform his listener exactly what he thinks of him—because the style he selects reveals whether he considers the listener worthy of low speech, the middle-ground fancy speech, or elegant speech, with or without honorifics.

As an example, Javanese lacks a single word for "now" that can be used in any social context, whether speaking to a peasant or to an aristocrat. Instead, different words exist for each of the three basic styles:

1 Plain style: *saiki*
2 Fancy style: *saniki*
3 Elegant style: *samenika*

No honorifics are used with the words for "now," but other words in a sentence in which "now" appears will undoubtedly take them and thereby announce precisely which of the six possible styles is being used. For example, here are the words by which a Javanese says "to eat" in each of the six styles:

1	Plain style with no honorifics:	*mangan*
1A	Plain style with low honorifics:	*neda*
1B	Plain style with high honorifics:	*dahar*
2	Fancy style with no honorifics:	*neda*
3	Elegant style without honorifics:	*neda*
3A	Elegant style with high honorifics:	*dahar*

Further complications in the use of Javanese show up in this list. Certain words appear several times at different levels: *neda* at the levels 1A, 2, and 3; *dahar* at levels 1B and 3A. However, a listener hearing the word *neda* spoken to him will know whether he is being addressed in the plain style with low honorifics (1A), the fancy style (2), or the elegant style without honorifics (3) because of the other words used in the same sentence. That becomes apparent when the two tables for "now" and "to eat" are combined to show the various ways a Javanese can say "to eat now":

LEVEL	"to eat"	"now"	COMPLETE PHRASE
1	*mangan*	*saiki*	*mangan saiki*
1A	*neda*	*saiki*	*neda saiki*
1B	*dahar*	*saiki*	*dahar saiki*
2	*neda*	*saniki*	*neda saniki*
3	*neda*	*samenika*	*neda samenika*
3A	*dahar*	*samenika*	*dahar samenika*

The Javanese is thus presented with six clear choices whenever he wants to utter the simple phrase "to eat now." And once he begins to speak to someone at the level he has chosen, he necessarily must maintain that kind of speech throughout his entire utterance. If a tradesman asks a high official, "Are you going to eat now?" he probably will speak at the elegant level without honorifics (level 3): *Menapa sampejan bade neda samenika?* But if he asks a peasant the same question, he most likely would use the plain style without honorifics (level 1): *Apa kowe arep mangan saiki?* Or, wishing to flatter a peasant in order to sell him something, the tradesman might ask the same question at level 1B, the plain style with high honorifics: *Apa pandjenengan arep dahar saiki?*

So whenever a Javanese speaks, he cannot escape from conveying the content of a message as well as his attitude toward the listener. Often the selection of the proper level is quite easy, as in the above examples of the tradesman speaking to a high official or to a peasant. Other stereotyped situations also call for the conventional use of particular styles. The plain style without honorifics is usually used by peasants when they speak to one another, by an upper-class person when he speaks to someone greatly inferior in status, or by two close friends belonging to the upper class who want to display their frankness toward each other. The middle, fancy style is the highest that most peasants master, and they use it only to address their social superiors. The elegant levels are rarely spoken in the villages; these are reserved for use by aristocrats among themselves or by an educated townsman when he addresses an aristocrat. The selection of the appropriate level, though, is seldom so simple. Influencing the choice are the relative ages of the speaker and listener, whether or not they are close friends, their occupations, education, wealth, ancestry, whether or not flattery is intended, and so forth.

When Java became part of the nation of Indonesia, the problem of which level to use became further complicated. Modern times have brought election campaigning to Java, with the result that politicians often must address rallies made up of mixed audiences. The politician finds it impossible to speak at a level appropriate for everyone. If aristocrats are present on the podium and the politician wishes to honor them for their support, he should, of course, use the elegant style with high honorifics—but most of his audience would not understand that level. The middle, fancy style might at first appear to be a suitable compromise, but many of the peasants in the audience would have difficulty understanding it and would consider the plain style with high honorifics much more appropriate. Because of the imperative of the Javanese language to select and maintain a single level of speech, the politician's problem is insoluble—if he tries to deliver his speech in Javanese. But he has another alternative. He can use the new national language, Indonesian, which lacks the many levels of Javanese. Actually, the increasing use of Indonesian for such difficult speech situations solves nothing. It has become yet another choice, a seventh level in Java that is appropriate in certain speech situations.

Many languages, particularly those of the Far East, oblige a speaker to employ honorifics to indicate when he is being polite to a listener. In Japanese, for example, -san is often added to a personal name to increase the status of the person being spoken to. The speaker may in reality be of lower status than the listener and therefore it is fitting that he use -san—but often he is of equal status and uses honorifics merely as a subtle way to flatter. The ignorance of speakers of European languages about the use of honorifics has resulted in the stereotype of the "polite" Japanese or Chinese. In fact, Hollywood dialogue typically endows the speech of Orientals not only with honorifics but also with debasing dishonorifics, as when in a 1930s movie Charlie Chan says, "Honorable inspector is welcome to humble abode." But such a translation distorts the use of honorifics and dishonorifics. What in the Oriental language was a subtle suggestion of esteem is made ludicrous by crassly converting a grammatical device into unsubtle adjectives like *honorable* and *humble*.

All languages require a speaker to address himself differently to various listeners, and in addition most languages make at least some distinction when the sexes speak. Sometimes the distinction is in pronunciation, as when the Chukchi men of Siberia pronounce their word for "people" *ramkichhin* and the women pronounce it *tsamkitstsin*. The pattern whereby women substitute *ts* for the men's *r* and *tsts* for their *chh* remains consistent in the pronunciation of all words that contain these sounds. Or sometimes the distinction is in vocabulary. Among the Yana of northern California, the male's *auna,* "fire," and *yana,* "people," correspond to the female's words *au* and *ya.*

But most often the difference is in the speech habits of the sexes. Among the Vakinankaratra of Madagascar, for example, both males and females will tell a visiting linguist that the ideal speech behavior avoids confrontations—but only males live up to that ideal. They subtly use speech to encourage easy relations, to hide sentiments rather than to express them. Females, though, are expected to express their emotions directly in face-to-face interactions. Both the men and the women in this speech community agree that a woman has *lavalela,* "a long tongue," but neither acknowledges the extent to which men manipulate the straight-forward speech of women. When verbal confrontations between men sometimes become necessary, the men incite their female relations to speak the harsh words in their behalf, and then the men delicately patch up any hurt feelings that may have resulted. So it is no surprise that women do all of the haggling in the market place, both as buyers and as sellers, since bargaining represents a verbal confrontation; the men buy and sell only those items that have a fixed price. Men also leave to women other kinds of encounters, such as reprimanding children or expressing disapproval of the behavior of kinsmen. The division of responsibilities in speech situations, therefore, is quite clear. Women dominate in situations where directness and unpleasantness are called for, men in situations where indirectness and discretion are valued.

So many exotic languages clearly display male and female sex differences in pronunciation, vocabulary, grammar, and the use of speech in certain situations that a thorough analysis of European languages would no doubt show that such distinctions exist in them also. Very little research has been done, though, and most native speakers merely have the intuitive feeling that the differences do exist. People in English-speaking communities often feel that certain women have "sexy" voices, although these listeners find it very difficult to explain what accounts for that impression. Some men, on the other hand, are said to sound "effeminate," and the explanation usually given is that they lisp. Actually, the impression of an effeminate voice in English-speaking males is due to other factors. Usually the effeminate voice has a wider pitch than normal for men; it uses glissando or sliding effects between stressed syllables, more "breathiness" in voice quality, and an occasional switch to a higher register; and it frequently employs complex tones otherwise rare in English, such as the rise-fall and fall-rise more typical of a tonal language like Chinese. This definition of what constitutes effeminate speech applies, of course, only to the English speech community; other communities undoubtedly have their own intuitive feelings about what represents male or female speech characteristics. Among the Mohave Indians of southern California, for example, a man who imitates a woman or an effeminate male does not switch to a higher register or use complex tones but rather chooses his vocabulary from words typical of women's speech.

Sex differences in English probably were much more marked in the past than they are now, simply because the social lives of men and women were more separated. As early as the sixteenth century, a male grammarian in England complained that women were changing the vowels of the language. For example, at that time men pronounced the word *dainty* as if it were spelled *dinety* —but women pronounced it *danety,* which has now become the standard pronunciation. In vocabulary nowadays, expressions like *goodness gracious* and *dear me* are usually considered women's speech, as are the intensifiers *so, such,* and *vastly* in expressions like *It's so lovely!* A similar excessive use of intensifiers by females has been noted in several other European languages, among them German, Danish, French, and Russian.

The very existence of male and female speech implies, of course, that language, like other kinds of human behavior, recognizes the different categories of male and female. And at some previous time in the history of the languages that show marked sex differences, this distinction must have been considered important, for languages are basically conservative instruments that are not affected by meddling for trivial reasons. Clues from languages around the world and from the history of English point to this conclusion: Sexual distinctions in speech arose as assertions of male superiority. The men's language spoken by the Chiquito Indians of Bolivia, for example, recognizes two genders of nouns —masculine nouns that refer to gods, demons, and males; feminine nouns that designate animals of any sex, women, and everything else. The gender of the nouns affects the entire sentence, with the result that quite different utterances are made when a masculine noun appears in a sentence than when a feminine noun is used. The women's language makes no such distinction, and it uses the feminine construction in all cases, regardless of the gender of the nouns in the sentence.

The inferior social status of Japanese women apparently explains why men and women in Japan use the particle *yo* differently. Japanese speakers, both male and female, can attach *yo* to a sentence to indicate to the listener that the normal rules of grammar are being suspended. If a Japanese man adds *yo* to a sentence that translates as "Jack went up the hill," he has transformed a simple declarative sentence into an order with a meaning something like, "I'm telling you that Jack went up the hill, and you had better believe it!" *Yo* implies both the higher status of the speaker and a demand for the listener to reply in terms that indicate compliance. Japanese women, because of their inferior role, are unlikely to attempt to imply either of these things. So when a Japanese woman uses a *yo* sentence, her meaning is quite different from the same sentence uttered by a man. When she says "Jack went up the hill *yo*," her statement translates as a mild request rather than as an imperative: "I pray that you will believe me when I tell you that Jack has gone up the hill."

Support for the theory that sexual distinctions in language arose because of the male's assertion of dominance is that differences disappear as the social status of women becomes more nearly equal to that of men. The Gros Ventre Indians of Montana once made a sharp distinction between the appropriate speech for men and for women, but such distinctions are dying out as that tribe becomes increasingly acculturated into modern American life. Similarly, in the previous century upperclass American women were insulated against the raw sights and sounds of life. A man might curse and tell "dirty" stories, but a proper lady was expected to swoon if she heard the taboo word *leg* instead of the more appropriate *limb;* pianos were even draped with cloth pantalets to conceal from feminine eyes those obscene supports which are now unblushingly called *piano legs*. Because of the taboo on *leg* and *breast* in America, the custom arose of referring to the parts of a chicken as *dark meat* and *white meat*. But in our generation women are no longer so insulated, and that is reflected in the fewer distinctions about proper speech for men and women. Nowadays young women use words that were formerly taboo for them with as much freedom as young men use them.

Nevertheless, the explanation for male and female styles of speech is undoubtedly more complicated than the simple question of dominance. Studies of sex differentiation in English strikingly share one conclusion: Women—when compared with men in their age group, social class, or level of education—speak in ways which more closely resemble the prestige way of talking. The explanation for why this is so hinges on several factors. One of them is that women—who hold a less secure position than men in American and British society—are generally more status-conscious and therefore more aware of the variables in speech. Men can be rated by their occupations or by their earning power, but women often must signal their status by other means, especially speech.

The reason why men resist adopting the female's more "refined" speech apparently has to do with a factor that men deny but which shows up in studies. Males in most American and British speech communities unconsciously regard the roughness of working-class speech as displaying desirable masculine attributes. In other words, the tough masculine speech of the lower class is subtly supported by the high value that many males place upon it. A study of urban speech in Norwich, England, revealed that male speakers were very favorably disposed toward nonstandard speech, even though they were not consciously aware of the fact. More than half the men studied claimed they used the rough masculine speech, and sometimes actually heard themselves using it—even when it was clear to linguists that they were not using masculine speech at all. In their public utterances males may inveigh against "bad" speech, but privately they seem more concerned with maintaining the prestige of rough speech among fellow males.

*

Nevertheless, people, whether male or female, who use a substandard or less prestigious form of speech often pay a social penalty for doing so. When a corporation builds a factory in Ohio or in Illinois and imports workers from Appalachia, it has transplanted both human beings and a speech community. The workers and their families can adapt to the customs of Ohio and Illinois, but it is much more difficult for them to change their dialects. Every time they speak they reveal by their strange vocabulary and their pronunciation that they belong to an alien speech community. It does not matter that this speech is in many ways a survival of the noble dialect spoken by Shakespeare and his contemporaries. Today it is a form of speech that marks its users as being from the South and belonging to a social class that is poor and uneducated. Whenever a worker from Appalachia calls a small stream a *branch* or says *I'll carry you home* instead of *I'll take you home,* he has identified himself as a member of a particular social and economic class.

George Bernard Shaw wrote *Pygmalion,* the original of the musical comedy *My Fair Lady,* to publicize his belief that social barriers between the classes will not disappear until linguistic barriers first disappear. In the opening scene Professor Higgins takes linguistic notes on the speech of Eliza, a Cockney flower girl. She defiantly protests that she has the same right to be on the street that the linguist has, but Higgins replies angrily:

A woman who utters such depressing and disgusting sounds has no right to be anywhere—no right to live. Remember that you are a human being with a soul and the divine gift of articulate speech; that your native language is the language of Shakespear and

Milton and The Bible; and dont [sic] sit there crooning like a bilious pigeon. . . . You see this creature with her kerbstone English: the English that will keep her in the gutter to the end of her days.

A Cockney girl can be installed in a West London apartment, clothed fashionably, taught what dishes to order in a restaurant—but she will still be a Cockney because she speaks like one. Change the speech of the Cockney, said Shaw, and her social status will change immediately.

But the precise extent to which listeners unconsciously make assumptions about speakers was not realized until a clever experiment was carried out in Montreal by McGill University researchers. Canadians of English ancestry were asked to listen to tape recordings of the same sentences spoken both in Canadian French and in English—and then to evaluate the speakers. The listeners promptly judged the unseen English speaker to be more intelligent, dependable, kind, and ambitious, even better-looking and taller, than the unseen French speaker. Only after the listeners had expressed their opinions were they told that both recordings were made by the same bilingual speaker.

It might seem that in a similar test French Canadians would show equal prejudice against unseen English speakers. But that was not so. They, too, felt that the very same person was more intelligent, dependable, kind, and so on when he was speaking English. These results imply nothing about the "virtues" of the English and French languages, but much about the dominance of people of English ancestry, who have great social and economic power in Canada, over the French, who lack such power. The experiments indicate how quickly a person is likely to be stereotyped according to the way he speaks, and how the English have been able to instill in French speakers a negative view of their own language. The Canadian results are typical of those obtained from similar studies around the world. In New York City, for example, listeners to tapes of speakers who said *dese* and *dose* instead of *these* and *those* were willing to make judgments about these unseen and anonymous people, including whether or not they were qualified for employment.

Social class is but one strand in a web of influences that determine the way people speak—and the attitudes of listeners toward those speakers. That was demonstrated by a study of the pronunciation of the suffix *-ing*. Nothing intrinsically right or wrong exists in the use of either *-ing* or *-in'*, since one or the other has been the accepted pronunciation at various times in the history of the English language. The absence of the final *g* was more common in Shakespeare's day, and his well-known line from *Macbeth* would have been spoken as:

> it is a tale
> Told by an idiot, full of sound and fury,
> Signifyin' nothin'.

On the other hand, the presence of the final *g* is more common today, or at least it is a goal of more speakers. Almost everyone knows that *goin'* is likely to be heard in certain regions of America and among lower-class speakers, particularly in their casual speech. But most people are unaware that speakers constantly shift back and forth between the two pronunciations depending upon the relationship between the speaker and the listener, the setting in which the conversation is taking place, the topic being discussed, and so on.

A study of the speech of children in a New England town showed that even at less than ten years of age they were already sensitive to the social variables governing the two pronunciations. Apparently the *-ing* pronunciation was regarded as more feminine, since girls used it about twice as often as boys did. The "model" boy who did his schoolwork well and whose conduct was praiseworthy almost always used -ing; he did, however, sometimes switch to -in' during casual conversation. What was being talked about was also a factor in the choice of pronunciation. Both boys and girls used -ing with formal verbs like criticizing or interesting but -in' with verbs they considered informal, such as swimmin' or hittin'. And still another variable was the speech situation. The children at first used -ing very often in talks with the linguist who made this study. Later, when they were at their ease while speaking to him, they increasingly switched to the -in' pronunciation.

A painstaking study of the speech of whites born in New York City has confirmed the common-sense observation that people communicate the class to which they belong by the way they talk, and that they vary their speech habits according to the speech situation. But the study was particularly revealing in what it told about New Yorkers who do or do not pronounce the sound r before a consonant or at the end of a word. Traditional New York speech has omitted the r—with the result that guard and god, bared and bad, source and sauce, are pronounced in the same way. New Yorkers share this speech habit with people in most cities of the Eastern seaboard except Philadelphia, such as the Bostonians who usually pronounce Harvard Yard as Ha'va'd Ya'd and those Charlestonians who say that they hail from South Ca'lina. Pronouncing or not pronouncing the r has nothing whatever to do with "good" English. Its use or its omission is a historical accident that depended on where the early English colonists, who spoke different dialects, happened to settle.

About the time of the Second World War, the r in New York City speech became less a matter of historical accident than a matter of prestige. Perhaps because the war exposed New Yorkers to other dialects of American speech, they decided that it sounded more prestigious to pronounce the *r*. Within a decade or so, the inclusion of *r* in speech was widely recognized as a mark of upper-class speech. That became apparent in visits to three of New York City's department stores patronized largely by people belonging to different classes: Saks Fifth Avenue (upper-middle), Macy's (lower-middle), and Klein's (lower). Salespeople at Saks were heard to pronounce the *r* more often than those at Macy's and those at Macy's more often than those at Klein's.

In most cases, the higher a person's class, the more likely he was to pronounce the *r*, but all classes increasingly pronounced it as speech situations became more formal. Lower-class speakers hardly ever pronounced the *r* in casual speech; in slightly more careful speech situations, they might use it nearly 10 per cent of the time; in extremely careful speech the rate of use rose to about 40 per cent. In contrast, the next higher class pronounced the *r* about 80 per cent of the time in very formal speech situations.

The study plainly showed that the higher classes set the standards for speech and that they regarded the use of *r* as a clear mark of prestige. But one fascinating exception was evident. The lower-middle-class use of *r* surpassed even the upper-middle-class in all situations except casual speech—and it did so by a considerable margin. This fact, as well as some others that emerged from the study, revealed the special role of the lower-middle class. It is the class that is aggressively on the make. Like everyone else in New York, its members are exposed to prestige patterns of speech through television and films—but, surprisingly, lower-middle-class people are rarely influenced by the media. Instead, they adopt the speech patterns of the next higher class, the upper-middle, and they tend to do so largely from personal contact with someone on whose speech they model their own.

As a. result, the lower-middle class usually shows great linguistic insecurity as it switches back and forth between the speech of its birth and the upper-middle-class speech it aspires to. That is why lower-middle-class speakers usually are inconsistent in their pronunciation of words that have traditionally varied in pronunciation from class to class. In the cases of *vase, tomato,* and *aunt,* for example, lower-middle-class speakers regard the broad *a* pronunciation of the upper-middle class as the correct one, but in their own casual speech they often forget and use their lower-middle-class pronunciation. One such linguistically insecure woman unconsciously worked out an accommodation toward the two ways of pronouncing *vases.* She told a linguist who was interviewing her, "These little ones are my *vayses* [rhyming with *mazes*], but these big ones here are my *vahses* [rhyming with *Roz's*]."

Almost all of the people in the study firmly believed that other Americans do not like the sound of New York City speech. As a result, New Yorkers are unusually preoccupied with the correctness of their speech. They try to alter it in one way or another, most often by striving for the pronunciation heard in the northern Midwest. And of all New Yorkers, the lower-middle class works the hardest at its speech. But this class has aimed at an unattainable goal. Its speech patterns were set in early childhood, and lower-middle-class people find it very difficult later in life to adopt the speech of a higher class—which accounts for their switching back and forth between the various pronunciations of *vase, aunt, tomato, guard,* and *source.*

The inhabitants of Martha's Vineyard, off Cape Cod, Massachusetts, also have changed their traditional patterns of speech in recent decades. But, in contrast to New Yorkers, they did not imitate the speech of a higher class or adopt a dialect from some other part of the country. They moved in the opposite direction— by switching to a less prestigious way of speaking. The islanders now pronounce *Harry* as if the name were spelled *hairy, forget* as if it were *forgit, house* almost like *hawse*. Such changes occurred among members of all classes, occupations, and ethnic groups on the island, and at first linguists were unable to find the explanation for them.

Finally, it became apparent that the speech changes represented the solidarity of the natives of Martha's Vineyard against the threat of outside economic domination. Those islanders who switched to what most Americans regard as a less prestigious speech had a history of downward social movement over a long period of time. Their grandfathers and greatgrandfathers had been landowners and ship captains, but each generation saw the islanders falling ever lower on the social scale. They considered themselves exploited by the money and power of mainland Massachusetts; they resented the summer residents who bought the old homes and then employed the natives to work as lowly domestics or handymen. The islanders might have reacted by aping these rich and powerful outsiders. Instead, they stubbornly defended their own identity by reviving an old-fashioned way of speech.

3

Words and Deeds

Speech cannot emerge as an utterance until it has first passed through the filter of a speech situation—and also through the filter of the personality of the speaker, who is himself a composite of beliefs, attitudes, and misconceptions that can distort a message and increase the unpredictability of the language game. We all unconsciously assume that the speaker believes what he is saying and that he bothers to speak because he feels he has something worth communicating. Therefore, a speaker who utters nonsense has violated a basic covenant between speaker and listener (unless, of course, a conspiratorial wink or an ironic tone of voice signals the listener that the speaker is only joking). A speaker who says *I am silent* has uttered an impossible statement. He has broken the covenant and converted speech into nonsense in much the same way that the clowns in the film *Blow-Up* played tennis—without a ball.

Most listeners are amazingly trusting, and their lack of discrimination about a speaker's credibility can be observed at any social gathering. Imagine that a speaker states—in an earnest, conversational tone of voice and with a perfectly straight face—something devoid of any significance in that speech situation, such as *The green seas hastened furiously colorless this morning*. His listeners will undoubtedly be confused about what to make of the statement. They may assume that he is imparting some fascinating natural-history lore or they might think that he is making a witty observation which they are too dense to understand. Whatever the explanations that pass through the minds of the listeners, the point is that they attempt interpretations just because they assume every utterance has significance.

Because listeners so obviously place their trust in speakers, the question might well be asked: To what extent is that faith justified? Several years ago a series of experiments was carried out at Princeton University to examine how reliably speakers conveyed instructions to their listeners. Pairs of five-year-old children were separated from sight of each other by screens and provided with identical sets of building blocks. One child, acting as the speaker, selected a block at random and attempted to describe it to his unseen partner; the other child, acting as the listener, tried to find the described block. The speaker then described a second block to the listener, and so on, until all six blocks had been stacked. The game obviously was a very simple one—except for one factor. The planners of the experiment had intentionally printed intricate designs on the blocks to make them very difficult to describe. Therefore, a listener's ability to build a stack of blocks in the correct sequence depended completely upon his partner's ability to describe what the blocks looked like.

The children—all alert and intelligent students from Princeton nursery schools—failed miserably at this game. Nor did they improve after the game was played several times. The problem was not that the game was too difficult, for the same youngsters did very well when pictures of animals were substituted for the intricate designs. Clearly, the reason for the failure was the inability of the speakers to describe the designs well enough for the listeners to stack the blocks in the correct order. Tape recordings of the children's conversations, made while they tried to stack the blocks, explained the failure. The speakers had described the designs in a private language that was as opaque to their listening partners as the screens that separated the pairs of players. One child, for example, described an intricate design as a *sheet*. When asked by the experimenter what he meant, the child replied, "Have you ever noticed when you get up in the morning the bedsheet is all wrinkled? Well, sometimes it looks like this." The child's description of the design in terms of a rumpled bedsheet had great significance for him—but it was, obviously, totally useless information to his partner, who had no such private association.

Children, of course, are less aware than adults of the limitations of the listener. Adult speakers have learned that the sounds they utter must be clearly understood by the listener, that they must be combined into words which are arranged grammatically in sentences—and that the meaning conveyed must be mutually intelligible. The adult speaker realizes that he is somewhat like a transmitter that broadcasts messages to a listener on a very narrow wavelength, so he tries to send his message in forms of speech that can be received by the listener and decoded without static. But sometimes inconsiderate or neurotic speakers encode their thoughts in a language almost as private as the child's description of an intricate design in terms of a bedsheet. They speak with little regard for the effect the utterance will have on the listener, and thus their speech is nonsocial. The result is utter confusion and a total breakdown in communication.

Some parents might argue that the child who described the design as a bedsheet was using language in a poetic way. Parents often feel pride when they hear their child use a strange metaphor, and they may envision him as the next generation's T. S. Eliot or Ezra Pound. They feel that if the poet Gerard Manley Hopkins could write a line like "sheer plod makes plough down sillion shine," then a child is certainly entitled to describe an intricate design as a bedsheet. The difference between Hopkins and the child, though, is major. Hopkins' line is admittedly obscure, but it resulted directly from his awareness as a craftsman of how an obscure image might trigger an emotion in a perceptive reader, tuned to the restricted wavelength Hopkins was broadcasting on. No one, though, could ever hope to decode the child's description of the intricate design as a bedsheet. It was uttered with no consideration for any listener at all. The child simply emitted a nonsocial statement which could never be more than gibberish to his partner. The same block-stacking experiment, carried out with older children and with college students, showed that increasing age brings increasing accuracy. Apparently, as a child grows older, he learns to put himself into his listener's place and to modify his descriptions accordingly.

In the block-stacking experiment, the blame for failure clearly lay with the speaker. But a breakdown in communication can also be caused by the listener. In the same way that optical illusions distort a picture, auditory illusions distort speech; both kinds of illusions are misjudgments about external reality. Every listener during his waking day compensates for auditory illusions. Consider a conversation carried on at a crowded cocktail party. Someone speaks to a listener through canapés and slurps of a beverage; the listener's attention is diverted by the jostling of people nearby, by noisy laughter and chatter, perhaps by music blaring from a record player. The listener could not possibly hear every syllable uttered by the person speaking to him. Yet he somehow utilizes the syllables that reach him during moments free from interfering noise to put together what he does hear into complete statements.

Ingenious experiments conducted by a psychologist and a zoologist at the University of Wisconsin, Richard and Roslyn Warren, have gone far toward illuminating how such auditory illusions work. The Warrens first recorded on tape the sentence *The state governors met with their respective legislatures convening in the capital city.* Then they carefully snipped out of the tape the syllable *gis* in *legislatures* and substituted a cough. When listeners serving as test subjects heard the altered tapes, they unconsciously blocked out the cough and restored the missing *gis* to *legislatures.* Even when the listeners were afterward told that a syllable had been deleted from the sentence, and the tape was played for them again, they still could not distinguish the missing sound. Apparently the process of listening entails the storage of incomplete information in the memory until the entire statement is heard, after which the listener unconsciously supplies what the context tells him must be a missing element.

The Warrens next experimented with auditory illusions free from context. Instead of dealing with complete and meaningful sentences, they recorded the single word *tress* on a loop of tape so that it was repeated over and over again without pause, 120 times a minute. They anticipated that a listener, after hearing *tresstresstresstress* . . . for a few minutes, would merge the sounds to form an illusory word such as *rest* or *stress.* But they were surprised to discover how much greater the auditory illusions were. One listener heard *tress* distorted into eight illusory forms, among them *stress, dress, Joyce, florist,* and *purse.* The listeners obviously were unwilling to believe that they heard a speaker repeat just a single word—so they unconsciously attempted to organize speech sounds into words and sentences.

Further experiments have shown that auditory illusions are much more common than optical illusions. An optical illusion can occur only in certain ambiguous cases in which line, perspective, light, or color distorts the appearance of an object. Auditory illusions, however, are much more unpredictable. They affect some listeners more than others and they vary from speech situation to speech situation. They can occur with any sound or word and they are not restricted to ambiguous cases—which adds yet another element of chance to the language game.

A listener's appraisal of a speaker is influenced not only by the speaker's way of phrasing the message and the listener's illusions about it but also by the speaker's "tone of voice." No protestation by a speaker that he is uttering the truth is equal to the nonverbal confirmation of his credibility contained in the way he says it. A man who says *I love you* to a woman is using a grammatical utterance to convey an attitude; but the woman, if she has any sense, will pay more attention to the accompanying vocal phenomena than to the words. The array of vocal phenomena that every speaker commands is known as "paralanguage," and it consists of such things as pitch, intensity, stress, tempo, and volume.

Contrary to what many people believe, no listener can judge the emotions expressed by a speaker of an unknown language just by noting his paralanguage. Old jungle movies often included lines like "I can't understand a word the beggars are saying, but I don't like the way they're saying it"—even though such an observation is inherently false because each speech community has its own rules for the expressive use of paralanguage. When an American visitor innocently interprets an Egyptian's paralanguage as signifying mere annoyance, he is seriously underestimating the intensity of the emotion. The Egyptian is most likely signaling that he is vengeful and that the American had better be careful.

Everyday experience seems to indicate a connection between paralanguage and personality, and between paralanguage and occupational roles. Most people are intuitively aware that speakers have "old" or "youthful" voices, that they sound "sad" or "self-satisfied." As soon as people step into their professional capacities they assume stereotyped "tones of voice," as is obvious to anyone who listens carefully to the speech of ministers, lawyers, undertakers, sports commentators, disc jockeys, and street vendors. A minister usually sounds like a minister because of paralanguage traits specific to that calling: a narrow range of pitch, frequent use of monotone, overpreciseness in pronunciation, regular rhythm, fairly slow tempo, and deep resonance of the voice.

Even the simplest statement may convey meanings through paralanguage that a sensitive listener detects without quite realizing how he does it. To examine the meanings often hidden in utterances, a team of linguists and psychiatrists collaborated on a remarkable project—a microscopic analysis of the speech interaction between a young woman and a psychiatrist, the words they used, their tone of voice and stress patterns, their pauses and coughs and hesitations. So detailed was the analysis that only the first five minutes of the interaction filled an entire book. This is what took place in merely the first few seconds:

The scene is a psychiatrist's office. A young woman enters and he says to her, "What brings you here?" The woman hesitates for a moment, then emits a brief, throaty sigh; she drawls her words as she replies, "Everything's wrong. I get so—irritable, tense, depressed."

Since the psychiatrist is trained in the strategies of the language game, presumably his utterances are calculated. When he says *What brings you here?* he apparently intends to evoke a certain kind of response from the young woman. His first statement does indeed set the tone for the interaction. Three of the four words he uses—*what, you,* and *here*—are words that linguists call substitute, or pronominal, forms. They can easily be substituted for other words, and therefore they are basically noncommittal. Instead of these pronominal forms, the psychiatrist might have said *What problems bring you so upset to a psychiatrist's office?* But if he had begun the conversation that way, he would clearly be starting off on the wrong track. He would appear to be saying that he already concluded the woman has problems, that her face plainly reveals the intensity of her emotions, and that she is in an office that treats mentally ill people—which is certainly too much for him to convey before the woman has even spoken. Instead, he chose to use neutral pronominal forms and allow the story to emerge from the woman.

A close look at the stress pattern of the psychiatrist's opening sentence is revealing. He placed stress only on the word *here,* and even that was very slight. If the stress had been very strong—*What brings you HERE?* —he might have appeared to express surprise that the woman was seeing a psychiatrist, which would have been unfitting, since he did not yet know anything about her. If he had chosen to place stress elsewhere in the sentence—such as *WHAT brings you here?* or *What brings YOU here?*—he might have seemed to imply amazement that the woman had the same sort of problems as the disturbed people he treats. The word *you* also is significant. He uses it as the object of the sentence, sympathetically indicating that the woman may have come to him because of external pressures that were victimizing her rather than because of problems in her own personality. If, instead, he had used *you* as the subject of the sentence—such as *Why have you come here?*—he would appear to be blaming the woman for having the leading role in whatever her problems are.

It is now the woman's turn to speak. She hesitates,

emits a sigh, and finally says *Everything's wrong*. She drawls her words slightly, which is not the way someone who speaks spontaneously would utter them. Like most people who visit a psychiatrist for the first time —or who go to an interview for a job, meet with a client or customer, or even testify in a law case—she has rehearsed the opening of her story. She no doubt thinks she is being very clever, but her hesitation, sigh, and drawl have given her away.

Her next sentence confirms that she is dramatizing a conversation opener she has memorized. The way she utters the words *I get so* is particularly important. She clips the *so* by closing her vocal cords, then holds a pause before she speaks the three adjectives that are her symptoms: *irritable, tense, depressed*. The absence of *and* between the last two adjectives is a further indication that she is delivering a prepared speech; spontaneous conversation surely would insert an *and* in a string of adjectives. The psychiatrist's first question had been carefully posed to leave open the possibility that the woman had come to see him because of external pressures rather than because of problems stemming from her own personality. But the woman does not accept this opportunity to appear blameless. Instead of making external forces the subject of her sentence— such as *People make me irritable, tense, depressed*— she acknowledges at least partial responsibility for whatever is troubling her by saying *I get so*.

In only a few seconds and through the utterance of a total of a dozen words, two people have entered fully into a speech interaction. Each has heard the sound of the other's voice. The psychiatrist has shown himself to be open-minded, fair, willing to listen. The woman had come to the office with her mind made up to play a part in a drama she had written in advance, yet she displays a willingness to face up to her problems. The rest of the conversation can now proceed fruitfully, as in fact it did.

The microanalysis made plain that considerable interaction took place between the two speakers beneath the mere surface of the way their sentences were grammatically constructed. But in certain rare cases, speakers apparently disregard grammatical constructions altogether and utter what can be considered either gibberish or divine words, depending upon the listener's religious orientation. The second chapter of the Acts of the Apostles in the New Testament relates that the disciples waited in Jerusalem after the resurrection of Jesus. On the day of Pentecost they joined in prayer, when suddenly

> there came a sound from heaven as of a rushing mighty wind, and it filled all the house where they were sitting.
>
> And there appeared unto them cloven tongues like as of fire, and it sat upon each of them.
>
> And they were all filled with the Holy Ghost and began to speak with other tongues, as the Spirit gave them utterance.

Such extemporaneous utterances of incomprehensible sounds, which listeners often assume to be foreign languages, is known among various Christian sects as "speaking in tongues" and among linguists by the technical term "glossolalia." The important thing about glossolalia in the context of this chapter is that it dramatically reveals the unqualified faith that listeners place in a speaker, no matter how incoherent his utterance may be.

Glossolalia is today an important feature of various Pentecostal denominations, as it has been at one time or another of fundamentalist sects, Mormons, Shakers, Spiritualists, the Catholic Apostolic Church, and others. These sects differ in the details of their creeds, but most believe that a Christian needs a "baptism" in the Holy Spirit, an event made manifest by the sudden ability to utter the divine speech of tongues. Believers consider glossolalia to be a "gift of tongues" because the speaker has been selected by God to make a pronouncement in this strange speech to an assembly of worshipers. Since the speaker's utterance is incomprehensible, other members of the assembly have a different "gift"— that of translating what was said into conventional language.

The Acts of the Apostles further reports that the multitudes who heard the strange tongues came from all over the Roman Empire, and that each listener thought that the disciples were speaking in his own language. The belief that a speaker in tongues utters words in languages unknown to him, languages both living and dead, has persisted to this day, but the cases that have been investigated show the belief to be unfounded. Any resemblance to a foreign language is usually in the mind of the listener, not on the tongue of the speaker. If a speaker in tongues utters a long chain of nonsense syllables, simply by the laws of chance some of these syllables will sound like words in foreign languages. And once a listener thinks he detects a few words from a particular foreign language, he would tend to "hear" many more words resembling those in that language. Actual cases do exist in which a speaker has uttered fragments from real languages he never learned—but these cases stem from a completely different phenomenon, known as "cryptomnesia," or "hidden memory." The English poet Samuel Taylor Coleridge, for example, told of an illiterate maid who, in a delirium, spoke in Latin, Greek, and Hebrew. It was later learned that she had unconsciously assimilated these languages from a former employer who read aloud passages in them.

Several characteristics distinguish glossolalia from other speech phenomena such as gibberish, nonsense rhymes, and disguised languages. Glossolalia is usually a sudden and spontaneous utterance, not something memorized or planned in advance. Unlike the random sounds of gibberish, the utterances of glossolalia are structured and follow many of the rules of the speaker's own language, even though the speaker is not aware of it. For an idea of what speaking in tongues sounds like, here are the first few lines of an utterance by a twenty-year-old New England woman:

yah-muh-nuh kee-tuh see-yuh-nah-yuh-see yah-muh-
nuh kee-tuh see-yuh-nah-yuh-see ah-nuh-kee-yah-nuh
tee-yah-sah-nah-yah ah-nah-kee-yah-tah-nah see-yuh-
nah-yuh-see

At first glance the utterance appears disorganized (except for a number of repetitions), incomprehensible, and even exotic. All the syllables end in vowels that are repeated constantly, which might give an impression of "primitiveness" to those listeners who have learned about exotic languages from the dialogue in Hollywood jungle movies. But a closer look makes several things clear. The utterance uses an extremely limited number of vowels and consonants—*t, k, m, n, s, y, ee, ah,* and *uh*—all of which are familiar sounds in English. Not a single foreign sound can be found, such as the rolled French *r* or the gargle-like German *ch.* And the sounds are combined into extremely simple syllables that occur in numerous English words. In fact, the pattern of the entire utterance, its stresses and intonation, is comparable to what one might hear in a typical English sentence.

It is clear that the woman who spoke in tongues was a native speaker of English. And her pronunciation and other clues reveal that she probably spent most of her life in the area between Hartford, Connecticut, and Springfield, Massachusetts. She was attempting to speak a new language—actually, to create utterances in a religious speech situation—yet the resources at her disposal could never be more than those linguistic habits she had stored up as a native New Englander. Some examples of glossolalia are, of course, more strange than this one, but that proves only that the speaker had a wider exposure to different kinds of languages from which he could unconsciously borrow sounds and syllable patterns. Were an American farmer in Minnesota named Ole Svenson to speak in tongues, we would naturally expect that some of his utterances would be borrowed from Swedish, a language which he no doubt heard his parents or grandparents speak.

If glossolalia were merely some aberration of particular religious sects, or if it were characteristic only of people with neurotic tendencies, then little reason would exist for interest in it. But speech acts similar to speaking in tongues have been discovered around the world in many different kinds of cultures and in many different languages, both modern and ancient. In ancient Egypt magicians were accustomed to utter senseless strings of sounds; four hundred prophets are said to have spoken incoherently before the gates of Samaria in 853 B.C.; similar sorts of speech acts are known to have occurred in ancient India and China, among the American Indians, in much of Africa. Those who speak in tongues, though, probably display no more neurotic tendencies than does the general population. Linguists are interested in glossolalia because it bears directly on a human being's ability to create a new language by distorting his native speech and by employing other kinds of speech he may have consciously or unconsciously learned. Glossolalia emphasizes that human speakers use their sound-making abilities in unconventional ways. Other forms of language play—verbal dueling, nonsense rhymes, children's verses, disguised languages, and so forth (which will be discussed at length in Chapters 5 and 6)—also confirm that people often speak in ways that have no "meaning" but instead serve other functions.

For the moment, though, what is of interest is that certain speech communities allow, and even encourage, speakers to utter nonsense. Furthermore, these communities put a premium on incomprehensible utterances, regarding them as more inspired or supernatural than conventional statements. The fact that glossolalia thrives only in speech communities that approve of it demonstrates the extent to which a speaker requires audience approval. The speaker in tongues gradually learns how to use his new speech within the environment of the speech community of his religious denomination and how to adjust his utterances according to its conventions—just as a child reared in a more traditional denomination learns to say his prayers in a low voice.

A speaker with a firm conviction, who is reinforced by his speech community, is a difficult person to change. So long as he knows that other people exist who approve of what he says, he can encounter the disbelief of the world with unwavering faith in his own statements. A true believer in any cult is unshakable—whether he puts his faith in a miracle diet, a drug, a way to make plants grow by prayer, the teachings of a guru, or a political perspective that sees a Fascist or Communist conspiracy in the most innocent transactions. Quote evidence against his opinions and he will deride its authenticity. Apply the strict rules of logic and he will reply that logic is irrelevant. No matter how devastating the attack upon him, the speaker will successfully protect his opinions—so long as he knows that fellow believers support him.

But what will happen if this speaker commits himself irrevocably to his opinions by staking his livelihood or even his survival on them—and then finally receives undeniable proof that he was wrong? Will he finally come to his senses and stop speaking the way he did previously?

An answer to these questions was accidentally provided some years ago. Psychologists at the University of Minnesota read a newspaper report about a housewife who claimed she had received messages from another planet that foretold destruction by flood at 7:00 A.M. on December 21. Here was a woman who had publicly uttered very controversial opinions and who had assembled a group of fellow believers. She would be forced to commit herself to some kind of action to escape the deluge which she herself foretold—and her opinions would be clearly demonstrated as true or false by whether or not the deluge occurred at the time specified. The Minnesota researchers infiltrated the housewife's group to observe events as they developed; their report is a fascinating study in depth of speakers who are committed to their own utterances.

During the few months before the December 21 deadline, the housewife, Mrs. Keech, attracted a small group of believers in her community of Lake City and elsewhere (all persons and places mentioned in the study were given fictitious names). One of her followers, Dr. Armstrong, was a physician in nearby Collegeville; he spread Mrs. Keech's message among a group of students, known as "The Seekers," who met regularly at his home to discuss spiritual matters. Throughout the fall the Lake City and Collegeville groups held joint meetings to prepare themselves for salvation. They spoke passionately of their convictions; they committed themselves irrevocably to them by giving away their possessions and by resigning from their jobs. As the day of the deluge approached, Mrs. Keech announced that the believers should gather at her house to await a visitor from outer space. He would arrive precisely at midnight on December 20–21, escort them to a flying saucer, and take them to a place safe from the flood.

By late afternoon on December 20, most of the believers had gathered in Mrs. Keech's living room. The only absentees were some of the college students, who had gone home to await the cataclysm with their families during the Christmas vacation. Mrs. Keech instructed the believers in the correct way to greet the visitor and she revealed the passwords that would allow them to board the saucer. As the minute hand approached midnight, the believers sat quietly in the living room, their coats on their laps. The clock chimed midnight, then the hours passed—and nothing happened. The time for salvation had come and gone, the cataclysm was due in a few hours, but no visitor arrived from outer space to save them. The believers discussed the messages received by Mrs. Keech; they re-examined their interpretation of them and offered various explanations for what might have gone wrong. At 4:00 A.M. Mrs. Keech broke down and cried bitterly. Then, three quarters of an hour later she announced that she had just received a new message. The cataclysm had been called off.

The believers stood firm in the face of the utter failure of Mrs. Keech's predictions. They phoned the news media to tell of God's grace in calling off the deluge, and they even increased their efforts to win converts to a belief that had already been demonstrated false. In other words, they attempted to maintain their beliefs by convincing others that the messages really were true; after all, if new believers could be enlisted, then apparently the messages were still believable. In contrast, the students from Collegeville who had gone home to await the deluge with their families acted quite differently. They were in the presence of nonbelievers who ridiculed their opinions. When these students learned of the failure of the prophecy, most reacted by giving up their beliefs completely, and some even concealed their previous association with Mrs. Keech.

The contrasting reactions of the Lake City group and the students demonstrated how vital audience support is for a speaker's expression of his convictions. All conditions were the same for the two groups—with but a single exception. The Lake City group was constantly in the presence of fellow believers when the deluge failed to occur; rather than being shaken from their beliefs, they stuck to them more stubbornly. The students, though, faced the aftermath of December 21 alone. Lacking the support of other believers to reinforce their statements, they stopped uttering them and even denied having made them.

All of his waking day the human chatters, grumbles, argues, mutters, implores, pontificates. He asks questions and furnishes answers when other people ask him questions; he emits pat phrases and clichés; he inquires about people's health and he comments about the weather, although he usually cares about neither. Man the Talker besieges the eardrums with an arsenal of speech—but at no time does he utter random collections of idle words or completely spontaneous statements. No matter what he says, he always had other choices. He might have expressed the same thought in a different way, said something quite different altogether, or even remained silent. In short, every language offers its speakers an array of strategies with which they can play the language game.

II

THE STRATEGIES

4

The Speakable and the Unspeakable

The statement is often heard that people can say anything they want to, in any way they care to, because no such thing as "right" or "wrong" exists in language. This view is partly a reaction against the last century's emphasis on "correct" speech by Miss Fidditch—the linguist's imaginary old-maid schoolteacher who would rather diagram a sentence grammatically than eat. To Miss Fidditch, there is but one Webster, and she is His prophet. Despite the modern linguist's impatience with Miss Fidditch's dictatorial attitudes toward speech, he nevertheless recognizes the existence of different degrees of rules for the use of language.

The first kind of rule applies to the automatic, deep-seated statements that a native speaker makes in his own language. These are the rules that are never violated at all. An example from grammar might be the automatic contraction of *He is here* to *He's here,* but never to *Here he's.* A second category consists of rules that are only rarely violated, and the violation usually is so exceptional that it is talked about. Examples might be the utterance of an obscenity by a minister during a religious service or the pretentious broad *a* pronunciation of *aunt* as *ahnt* by a lower-class speaker in Chicago. The final category is made up of rules that everyone knows should be observed yet which are commonly violated without too much notice being taken of the breach. If a New Yorker pronounces *then* as *den,* he still can be understood, but he might pay a penalty by being socially stigmatized as "uneducated."

One justification sometimes heard for freedom in breaking the rules of the language game is that languages change with time anyway. But that argument is beside the point. Even though the rules may change tomorrow, they still are binding while they are in force today. Whether speakers like it or not, no way exists to escape the rules. Every person on earth is a member of a particular speech community. Someone born into an English-speaking community is born into a world where the rules of English grammar and of appropriate speech in various situations already exist. He can make himself understood and evoke responses only if he abides by the rules of play, although he does, of course, have great latitude in applying strategies. If he does not like the rules, he is free at any time to cancel his membership and join a different speech community. But then he will be forced to learn a foreign language and its appropriate use—which are themselves systems of rules.

Witness the rules of play that anyone must abide by if he wishes to live among the Zuñi Indians of New Mexico. The Zuñi inhabit a pueblo, a very close-knit community with rigid rules of behavior. Deviations from accepted attitudes are immediately known about and discussed, and the transgressor is corrected. Only after many years of rebuke does a Zuñi child, who so easily acquires the grammar of his language, learn the various strategies for its use. Among these strategies is knowing which speech situations call for the conversational, the sacred, or the frivolous levels of usage.

Zuñi sacred terms are used for prayers, songs, tales, traditional sayings, and religious ceremonials. The old people of the Zuñis have the best knowledge of sacred language, and that is one reason why they are accorded high status in that religion-dominated society. Young Zuñis do not, however, usually understand the full implications of the sacred words. They know only that certain terms have been accorded sacred usage and that it is proper to speak them at certain times and places. A young Zuñi learns, for example, that it is particularly bad taste to utter the word *takka,* meaning "frogs," during a ceremony. The proper way for him to say "frogs" in a religious context is to use a string of words that means, literally, "several-are-sitting-in-a-shallow-basin-where-they-are-in-liquid." He does not know why *takka* is an unacceptable word for "frogs" at certain times—and no real reason, in fact, exists apart from the arbitrary conventions of the Zuñi community. Nor is it acceptable to utter the borrowed word *melika,* meaning "white American," in a speech situation in which sacred matters are being discussed. If a Zuñi must refer to a white American in such a situation, he uses words that translate as "a wide hat." A possible explanation for shunning *melika* at these times might be the Zuñi fear of bringing any innovation, whether it be a radio or a borrowed word, into a religious setting.

At the other extreme from sacred language is what the elders regard as frivolous uses of language: slang, punning, tall tales, obscenities, and so on. Such utterances are deplored in the community when spoken by adults. The old people are somewhat more tolerant of frivolous language from the mouths of children and young adults, and they are likely to excuse it as a characteristic of youth which the speaker will eventually grow out of. But if he does not grow out of it at an appropriate age, social pressures of varying degrees —from stern rebukes to fines and even ostracism— will be brought to bear upon him.

To an outsider, no intrinsic explanation can be found in the Zuñi language for why one expression is regarded as sacred and another as slang, or why one word is appropriate in a particular setting but not in another. For example, Zuñi slang uses a word which means "a spring of water" to indicate "a woman"—a shift of meaning, fairly common in Zuñi, that relates thirst to sexual desire. Zuñi disapproval of slang raises the question of why people bother to speak slang at all. It assuredly is troublesome to learn new terms and then to find that many listeners do not understand them. Nor does slang usually fill any void in a language's vocabulary; on the contrary, it often provides a new term when nothing new was needed in the first place. Objections such as these really offer reasons for speaking slang. Contrary to what many people believe, slang is not the naive speech of the common man. It is rather the speech of those who, for one reason or another, consider themselves members of a select or separate group. The common denominator of all slang, whether it be the speech of adolescents or the jive talk of musicians, is that it tests who belongs to the group and who is an intruder. That is because slang is fully intelligible only to the initiated. The select groups that use slang are more severe about standards for its correct usage than Miss Fidditch is about her English grammar; anyone not hip to the latest slang is a square.

Most slang words are heard for a few years and then disappear, usually forever. Some are fated to endure solely as slang without ever being admitted to polite usage, such as *bones* (in the meaning of "dice"), which was first used by Chaucer, and *beat it*, used by Shakespeare. But occasionally some slang words—like *joke, fad, boom, crank,* and *slump*—become respectable items in the vocabulary. The Standard German word for "head," *Kopf,* was once slang, and so also was the French word with the same meaning, *tête,* derived from the Latin *testa,* "earthen pot."

Every human society around the world prohibits certain kinds of behavior and certain categories of words, although those prohibited in one society may turn out to be the norm in another. The word *taboo* has been borrowed from Tongan, a language of Polynesia, to describe the avoidance of particular kinds of behavior, an avoidance which sometimes appears arbitrary and fanciful to an outsider. Not only do taboos prohibit certain acts; usually these acts must not be talked about either.

People living in Western cultures have long looked upon their verbal taboos as hallmarks of their advanced "civilization." Until quite recently, speakers in the genteel tradition of the southern United States avoided the word *bull* in conversations between the sexes; they much preferred to substitute expressions like *he-cow, male beast, brute, sire, critter,* or *the big animal. Privy* entered the English language as a veiled word to replace some previous taboo word—but it also became tainted and nowadays other euphemisms are substituted for it, such as *toilet, restroom, bathroom, lavatory,* or *john.* (Euphemism, by the way, is a compensating strategy in language to skirt the taboo word; the term is derived from Greek and means "good-speak.") Children in English-speaking communities learn early that their communities regard certain words as "dirty" and instead offer euphemisms that usually are of Latin or French derivation. Instead of *prick,* the child is supposed to say *penis,* and he is expected to substitute *vagina* for *cunt*—which leads to Robert Graves's story of the soldier who had been shot in the ass. When a lady visitor to the wards asked where he had been wounded, he replied: "I'm sorry, ma'am, I can't say. I never studied Latin."

Although English has exiled a tremendous number of taboo words, it is not true that their exclusion from polite vocabulary points to any greater degree of refinement in English-speaking communities than among primitive peoples. Verbal taboos exist in all speech communities, and if one wished a particularly good example of them, he might turn to the Nupe of West Africa, among the most prudish people on earth. The Nupe make a very sharp distinction between terms that are acceptable in polite speech situations and those that are not. Indelicate subject matter must be expressed by a circumlocution, by a word borrowed from another language, or by a technical term reserved for use solely by the scholarly class. Nupe lacks any native word for sexual intercourse; instead, its speakers use a word of Arabic derivation that means "to connect." Nor do words exist in the native vocabulary for "defecate," "menstruation," or "semen." Should the need arise to express these things, Arabic technical terms or very involved euphemisms are used. An obscene word for "vagina," *dzuko,* does exist, but it is rarely used; speakers attempt to avoid expressing the thought altogether, but when it is necessary to do so they employ a borrowed word, *kafa,* that means simply "opening." Respect for what they consider standards of good taste is a conscious process among the Nupe. Anthropologists who have studied this tribe report that the Nupe are intensely interested in language and they spend much time talking about its fascinating aspects. When they employ euphemisms, manipulate words to eliminate tasteless connotations, or borrow terms from other languages, they are as fully aware of what they are doing as is any genteel lady from one of the Western cultures.

From an unbiased position as outside observers of the Nupe language, we consider it foolish to make a distinction between *dzuko* and *kafa* to refer to the vagina. But the English language makes distinctions equally foolish. Most American families have their own stores of nursery words which are handed down from generation to generation, usually in the female line. New euphemisms are constantly being invented because after a while even the substituted words become too infected for use in polite society. If two words sound alike and one of them is taboo, then the respectable word often becomes taboo as well. That happened in America to the words for the animals once known as *cock* and *ass* but now usually called *rooster* and *donkey*. In fact, *cock* has in the past been subjected to unremitting attack because it sounds the same as the synonym for *prick*. In some parts of the rural South speakers to this day do not tell *cock and bull tales* but rather *rooster and ox stories* because the *cock*, *bull*, and *tale* (*tail*) of the first utterance are taboo. The last century's relentless attack upon *cock* caused the father of Louisa May Alcott, author of *Little Women*, to change the family name from Alcox.

The habit of creating euphemisms dates back at least to the Norman Conquest of England in 1066. At that time the community began to make a distinction between a genteel and an obscene vocabulary, between the Latinate words of the upper class and the lusty Anglo-Saxon of the lower. That is why a duchess *perspired* and *expectorated* and *menstruated*—while a kitchen maid *sweated* and *spat* and *bled*. The linguistic gulf between Norman-derived and native Anglo-Saxon words remains as wide as ever after nine hundred years. The farmer today still looks after his Anglo-Saxon *cows*, *calves*, *swine*, and *sheep*—but once they are served up appetizingly in a restaurant or supermarket, they become French *beef*, *veal*, *pork*, and *mutton*. And whenever the speech community must discuss anything it deems unpleasant, the discussion is acceptable on the condition that it is carried on in the elegant vocabulary bestowed on English by the Normans.

The unpleasant subject of death has inspired, century after century, whole vocabularies of euphemisms which are replaced periodically as they become tainted. In the United States *undertaker* drove out *mortician* until it, in turn, was replaced by *funeral director* as a result of a public-relations campaign, about 1925, directed toward newspapers and telephone directories. *Coffin* has become *casket,* even though more than a century ago Nathaniel Hawthorne denounced *casket* as "a vile modern phrase which compels a person to shrink from the idea of being buried at all." *Hearses* are now *coaches,* and the *cadavers* they used to transport from the *funeral parlor* are now *the loved ones* escorted from the *chapel*.

This situation would be merely ludicrous if it did not continue to inflict lasting damage on each generation. In schools today, the *educators* (Latin-derived) hold sway over the ordinary *teachers* (Anglo-Saxon). Educators speak a Latinate language, incomprehensible to parents and children alike, which is disparagingly referred to by those within the profession as "Pedaguese" or "Educanto." Someone fluent in Educanto can rattle off such expressions as *empirically validated learning* and *multi-mode curricula.* Report cards carry Latinate comments like *Academic achievement is not commensurate with individual ability,* which means virtually the same thing as the unpleasant-sounding Anglo-Saxon *The child could do better.* Such reports are not simply a florid attempt to impress parents; too many teachers also speak that way in the classroom. A recent National Education Association study revealed that in many classrooms half of the words used by educators are not understood by the pupils—and that 80 per cent of the words the children fail to understand are of Latin or Norman derivation.

The passion for relegating certain words to taboo status and then substituting euphemisms for them—with the inevitable result that some speakers are thereby encouraged to break the rules and use these words—gives considerable insight into the speech communities that emphasize such taboos. All languages, for example, must acknowledge the physical fact of menstruation, since it is a reality for half of the world's population—yet speakers of different languages react differently to that fact. Among the Irish, menstruation is very much a taboo subject and the vocabulary is severely limited. The Irish sometimes describe menstruation as *in season,* thus equating women with animals, or as *monthly flowers,* a quaint archaism dating back to Middle English. In Poland also, menstruation is something not to be spoken about, but when it is, it is equated with a bitch's being in heat. German offers a considerably richer vocabulary, but most words refer to the woman in terms of being "unclean," and two of the more common words, *Schweinerei* and *Säuerei,* stress the filthy aspects of swine.

Of all the European languages, the English spoken in America appears to possess the greatest number of euphemisms or circumlocutions for menstruation. A compilation after the Second World War showed nearly a hundred expressions in common use, most of which fit into five categories:

Illness: *the curse, sick, unwell, cramps, feeling that way, fell off the roof*

Method of sanitary protection: *wearing the rag, covering the waterfront, wearing the manhole cover*

The color red: *flying the red flag, bloody Mary, the Red Sea's in*

The idea of a visit: *little sister's here, entertaining the general, grandma's here from Red Creek*

Sexual unavailability: *ice-boxed, out of this world*

To the credit of today's younger generation, few such euphemisms are in use and college women say simply *I'm having my period.*

So pernicious can the strictures against taboo words be that speakers of minority languages sometimes eliminate from their speech innocent words that resemble the majority language's taboo words. The Creek Indians of Oklahoma avoid their words *fakki,* "earth," and *apissi,* "fat," because the accented syllables in them resemble taboo words that they know speakers of English are not supposed to use. Or the taboo may work in reverse; harmless English words may resemble taboo words in the minority language. In the Nootka Indian language of Vancouver Island, British Columbia, the English word *such* so closely resembles the Nootka word meaning "cunt" that teachers find it very difficult to convince their students to utter the English word in class.

Many scholars have concluded that prohibiting the use of taboo words is not a hallmark of refinement and civilization, but rather a wound in the body of language. When a speech community isolates certain words and designates them as taboo, it debases natural things like sexual intercourse and the bodily functions; it spreads guilt by causing people to repress words and even any references at all to the natural acts of the body these words describe; it encourages the exhibitionist, who then goes out of his way to use the taboo words; and it provides an excuse for low forms of scatological and sexual humor.

A strange thing about taboo words is that often they are the names of animals, only certain of which have been singled out for use as abusive terms. A speaker of English may abuse another by calling him a *son of a bitch* or a *horse's ass,* but he never tries to abuse him as *you squirrel* or *you buffalo.* The British anthropologist Edmund Leach has attempted to explain why English-speaking communities regard certain animals, and not others, as labels for abuse, and why they place taboos upon the use of these terms. He first eliminates certain animals from consideration because their names obviously are similar in pronunciation to already existing taboo words; *fox* is too close to *fucks, cuny* to *cunt,* and *shoat* to *shit.* He then examines the way English-speaking communities categorize animals, and he finds two extremes: the tame-friendly animals (such farm animals as sheep, lambs, and ducks) and the wild-hostile animals (such as grouse, pheasant, deer, and most zoo animals). Animals in both these categories are exempt from use as verbal insults, are not thought of as obscene in any way, and have no taboos placed upon them.

But a number of ambiguous categories exist between the extremes of tame-friendly and wild-hostile. These are the animals used for insult terms and these are the ones that English-speaking communities regard as taboo—for the reason that our community distrusts the ambiguous, whether it be the homosexual in the realm of sex or the separatist in religion. Pets, for example, are ambiguous because they are beasts that are treated like human beings—and that is why *bitch, cat* (as in *cathouse,* "brothel"), *pussy,* and so forth are obscene insult terms. Similarly, certain farm animals are ambiguous because they are regarded affectionately even though they are used for food, and these also furnish insult terms—pigs (*swine*), chickens (*cock*), and so on. Since the fox is a wild animal it should be immune from taboo, but to call a woman a *vixen* used to be regarded as a major insult. The reason is that in England and in the southern United States it has an ambiguous position as a wild animal that is also the subject of a highly ritualized hunt. The only zoo animals that figure in taboo words are the apes and monkeys, undoubtedly because they are ambiguously wild but seemingly human in their behavior. Leach's attempt to systematize animal terms is probably not the entire answer, yet it represents a start in trying to make sense out of the way speech communities set apart certain beasts and then taboo their names as abusive.

The insults spoken by adults are usually more subtle than the simple name-calling used by children, but children's insults make obvious some of the verbal strategies people carry into adult life. Most parents engage in wishful thinking when they regard name-calling as good-natured fun which their children will soon grow out of. Name-calling is not good-natured and children do not grow out of it; as adults they merely become more expert in its use. Nor is it true that "sticks and stones may break my bones, but names will never hurt me." Names can hurt very much because children seek out the victim's true weakness, then jab exactly where the skin is thinnest. Name-calling can have a major impact on a child's feelings about his identity, and it can sometimes be devastating to his psychological development.

Almost all examples of name-calling by children fall into four categories:

1 Names based on physical peculiarities, such as deformities, use of eyeglasses, racial characteristics, and so forth. A child may be called *Flattop* because he was born with a misshapen skull—or, for obvious reasons, *Fat Lips, Gimpy, Four Eyes, Peanuts, Fatso, Kinky,* and so on.
2 Names based on a pun or parody of the child's own name. Children with last names like Fitts, McClure, Duckworth, and Farb usually find them converted to *Shits, Manure, Fuckworth,* and *Fart.*
3 Names based on social relationships. Examples are *Baby* used by a sibling rival or *Chicken Shit* for someone whose courage is questioned by his social group.
4 Names based on mental traits—such as *Clunkhead, Dummy, Jerk,* and *Smartass.*

These four categories were listed in order of decreasing offensiveness to the victims. Children regard names based on physical peculiarities as the most cutting, whereas names based on mental traits are, surprisingly, not usually regarded as very offensive. Most children are very vulnerable to names that play upon the child's rightful name—no doubt because one's name is a precious possession, the mark of a unique identity and one's masculinity or femininity. Those American Indian tribes that had the custom of never revealing true names undoubtedly avoided considerable psychological damage.

Most children want to know the "dirty words" almost as soon as they begin to study another language. An interest in these words continues unabated into adult life, even though the American speech community has placed social sanctions against their use in most public places, particularly those where "ladies" are present. The state of Kansas has even gone so far as to pass a legal stricture against the use of obscenity by faculty members on university property. People in the American speech community "talk dirty" for many reasons. One of them, of course, is to attract attention to the speaker because of the jolting effect of obscenity in places, such as public forums and the media, considered inappropriate. Closely related to this reason is another: to display the speaker's contempt for the standards that his society upholds. Such a speaker often regards civil speech as the behavior of those who uphold the *status quo,* whereas talking dirty is a symbol of "honest" rebellion against the power structure. Further, militants of every persuasion have shown that talking dirty is an effective rhetorical device for verbal aggression, an easy way to provoke confrontations. Finally, talking dirty is a way to sexually mock authority figures—parents, teachers, clergymen, policemen, political leaders—thereby relieving the speaker of his own feelings of inadequacy.

The extremely obscene remark or joke, which is often signaled by an unusually gross and obscene vocabulary, often hides by means of laughter the speaker's anxiety about certain taboo themes in his personality or his culture. Obscenity of this sort is often graphic and detailed about such substances as semen, feces, and urine; or the content of the utterance may concern horrible accidents, mutilations, and genital injury. That is because bodily functions, venereal disease, castration, and homosexuality are often deep-seated anxieties of both men and women in American culture. Jokes on such themes are usually embarrassing to a listener who lacks these anxieties. The jokes often issue from a teller with explosive force, as if he were hurriedly trying to foist off on the listener his own anxieties. Such utterances are sometimes described as "sick," although possibly it is the speech community which places taboos on certain words and ideas that is ailing and not the individual speaker.

Freud long ago pointed out that talking dirty is sometimes employed as a strategy of verbal seduction. Males in particular use speech as a sexual display equivalent to poetry, music, and oratory—which in part accounts for the sexual reputations of poets, tenors, and ministers. An obscene pun or a clever "off-color" remark, either of which relies upon double meanings rather than taboo words, gives the woman the option of rejecting (by not laughing or "not understanding") the verbal approach. But when a man tells a joke to a woman in which he graphically depicts the sexual organs or the sexual act, he has gone beyond verbal seduction—and entered the realm of verbal rape. An insistent display of this sort represents the speaker's preparation by words for a direct physical approach. A woman who agrees to listen to such a joke (or even sometimes tells one of her own) indicates that she is ready to accept such an approach. And once she has shown her willingness, it is very difficult for her later to revert to a pose in which she is shocked by the man's physical behavior. She no longer has the option to reject his approach on moral grounds, since she previously signaled her availability by her willingness to listen to the dirty talk. Instead, her rejection can be only on personal grounds, a confrontation often difficult for a speaker to cope with.

Should a woman show herself unwilling to listen to dirty talk, the speaker can either direct his verbal display to a different woman or become more insistent with the woman who rejected him. If he chooses the latter option, his talk usually becomes increasingly sexual, and sometimes scatological as well. He will tell his jokes which have as their theme the false modesty and inherent wantonness of women, such as this typical one:

A traveling salesman, between trains in Chicago, meets a girl at the railroad station and says, "Look, I've got to catch another train in half an hour so I don't have time to fuck around. Do you screw or don't you?" The girl replies, "Well, I'm not usually that kind of person—but you just talked me into it."

Or he might make a diversionary feint and direct obscene jokes ostensibly to a male third party, but with a volume loud enough for the woman to hear.

Naturally, such an interaction as I have described applies only to some American speech communities and would be quite different in other communities around the world. The reason is that the interaction depends heavily upon traditional social and sexual roles in the American community: males as the "attackers" and females as "submissive." Such strategies are possible only so long as the sexes maintain those roles. If the stereotypes can be removed from the roles, as females in the liberation movement and enlightened males are attempting to do, then obviously this strategy will become inoperative. Which is not to say that talking dirty will thereby cease to exist as a strategy—just that its function in the speech community will be different.

People who talk dirty usually have their own personal styles. They rely heavily on certain taboo words and they structure their statements in habitual ways—but, most important, their utterances often center on one or two themes. They usually laugh uproariously when they hear jokes on their favorite themes, but laugh only politely at equally funny jokes on themes that do not concern them so intimately. Clearly, dirty talkers make unconscious use of joke-telling and similar speech events for verbal relief of their personal anxieties—which is one reason why a speaker's favorite joke is often a key to his personality.

Personal style is somewhat influenced by the styles that predominate in different speech communities. It is, of course, hazardous to generalize about national characteristics because the boundaries of nations often change faster than their languages. Yet many Germans seem so extraordinarily susceptible to scatology that it dominates all other themes when they talk dirty. Says Gershon Legman, who has published scholarly studies of the dirty joke:

> A clever joke teller can bring the usual German audience to quite a high pitch of screaming entertainment, rolling out of their seats, and so forth, just by *preparing* to tell a joke of which the inevitable punchline must include the word "shit" (sometimes built up to the reduplicative *Scheissdreck*), without ever even beginning the joke.

The explanation for the dominance of this theme among German speakers undoubtedly can be found in the social environment in which German speakers grow up. Legman suggests that it may be a reaction against German rigidity in the upbringing of children, particularly in their toilet training. Other speech communities also seem to have their own dominant styles—no doubt also because of social factors in the speech community. French dirty jokes are usually concerned with seduction, adultery, and sexual technique; British with homosexuality and incest; American with oral-genital themes and the debasement of women.

English-speaking communities nowadays regard the pun as a very low form of humor—and they are particularly fearful of the obscene pun, which is a major variety of the form. The obscene pun is dangerous because it cleverly attacks the sacredness of taboo words, and it manages to do so with apparent innocence. A dirty story usually leads up to the punchline by the use of taboo words, but a well-fashioned obscene pun never overtly uses taboo words. Rather, the pun allows two different words, which are pronounced in the same way, to be substituted for each other. Usually one of the two ambiguous words is taboo, but the teller of the pun claims innocence by leaving it up to the listener to connect the innocent and the taboo meanings.

A speaker who says *She was only a fisherman's daughter, but when she saw my rod she reeled* is really launching a sneak attack upon verbal taboos through the use of a pun. This well-known pun has endured probably because of the cleverness of its triple construction. On the level of a matter-of-fact utterance, the speaker could innocently claim that he had made a simple statement about a fisherman's daughter reeling in the line on a fishing rod. Even on the slang level, the speaker could also claim innocence of any obscene intent, because the statement could be interpreted as merely saying that the fisherman's daughter reeled with fright when she saw the *rod* (slang for "gun"). It is up to the listener, of course, to make the obscene interpretation: *rod* as "penis" and *reeled* as "sexually aroused." The nervous laughter that a pun such as this evokes is due to the listener's uncertainty about which of the meanings he should acknowledge. He could interpret the statement on a matter-of-fact or a slang level, but then he would risk being regarded as dense or prudish. If he laughs, that means he has interpreted the pun on the obscene level—and thereby become an accomplice to challenging the taboos of his speech community.

The offering of a choice between two meanings, one innocent and the other taboo, is essential to the obscene pun. Because the taboo word is not expressed directly, the listener is therefore given the option either to accept the ambiguity or not to accept it (signified by his refusal to laugh nervously or by his uttering a deprecating groan). And the obscenity must be clever to be tolerated, as Freud pointed out in *Wit and Its Relation to the Unconscious:*

> The technical means of which it [obscenity] mostly makes use is allusion, i.e. substitution through a trifle, something which is only remotely related, which the listener reconstructs in his imagination as a full-fledged and direct obscenity. The greater the disproportion between what is directly offered in the obscenity and what is necessarily aroused by it in the mind of the listener, the finer is the witticism and the higher it may venture in good society.

All obscene puns have the same underlying construction in that they consist of two elements. The first element sets the stage for the pun by offering seemingly harmless material, such as the title of a book, *The Tiger's Revenge*. But the second element either is obscene in itself or renders the first element obscene, as in the name of the author of *The Tiger's Revenge*— Claude Bawls ("clawed balls"). Any wit that the pun possesses must lie in the surprise presented by the ambiguity of the second element. The two-element structure is adaptable to a great variety of pun forms, such as the Punning Question: "Did you hear about the Arabs who were sitting under a tree eating their dates?" Or the Confucianism, which partakes of the traditional proverb with its pretensions of wisdom, thus adding an extra bite to the humor: "Confucius say, 'Seven days on honeymoon make one whole week.'" Or the eloquence of the Spooneristic Conundrum, which not only poses an unanswerable question but then cleverly replies to it by switching around sounds in the second element to avoid the actual use of an obscene word: "What's the difference between a pygmy village and a women's track team? The pygmy village is a cunning bunch of runts."

English speech communities are not, of course, the only ones to use the strategy of the pun to challenge taboo words. Even the prudish Nupe occasionally tell improper stories, but when they do they tone them down by placing obscene allusions in the ambiguous context of a pun. To understand the following Nupe story, you must know that *eba* means "husband," although it can also have the obscene meaning of "penis."

At one time there was a town where only men lived and another town where only women lived. The king of the Town of Men sent a young man to the Town of Women to obtain wives. The young man did so by a clever plan. He made a beer which the women drank and liked so much that they wanted more. So they followed the young man back to the Town of Men where they were captured and made the wives of the inhabitants. In this fashion the young man brought it about that the men now had wives. He brought it about that the women tasted the sweetness of the *eba.*

"Four-letter words" (itself a euphemistic expression to skirt having to use the words) are more strictly taboo than any others in the English language. Until very recently they were considered too indecent for publication even in scholarly dictionaries; and a study in a linguistics journal several decades ago failed to mention the abhorred word the entire article was about. However, some of the recent dictionaries—among them the new *Supplement to the Oxford English Dictionary* and one which was designed for family and school use, *The American Heritage Dictionary of the English Language*—now acknowledge the obvious fact that the word *fuck* is known by every native speaker of English. The sexual act described by *fuck* refers to standard sexual behavior, and so there is nothing intrinsically "bad" or "dirty" in this word. Any word is an innocent collection of sounds until a community surrounds it with connotations and then decrees that it cannot be used in certain speech situations; this is what happened when the English speech community relegated *fuck* to forbidden status about 1650. Only by the creation of this taboo did the English community create an obscenity where none existed previously. Speaking of *fuck*, Edward Sagarin, who has made a study of obscene words in English, says:

> In the entire language of proscribed words, from slang to profanity, from the mildly unclean to the utterly obscene, including terms relating to concealed parts of the body, to excretion and excrement as well as to sexuality, one word reigns supreme, unchallenged in its preeminence. It sits upon a throne, an absolute monarch, unafraid of any princely offspring still unborn, and by its subjects it is hated, feared, revered and loved, known by all and recognized by none.

Considerable dispute surrounds the derivation of *fuck*. The 1972 *Supplement to the Oxford English Dictionary* states that its derivation is "unknown"— but undaunted philologists have nevertheless attempted to postulate its origins. One, who has examined closely related words in other Germanic languages, believes the original meaning was "to knock"; if so, the meaning has persisted to this day in the American slang term for "made pregnant," *knocked up*. The word possibly can be traced back to the Latin *pungo*, "to prick," and *pugil*, "a boxer." If that is so, then respectable English derivatives of these Latin words—such as *pugilist, pugnacious, puncture,* and *appoint*—are related to the most abominated word in the language.

Whether used as a noun (*a fuck*), verb (*to fuck*), or adjective (*fucking*), it is a full-fledged word and not dialect or slang. Nor can *fuck* even be considered substandard, since it is a part of the linguistic repertory of all speakers of proper English, whether or not they publicly acknowledge the fact. It turns up, for example, in the speech of anaesthetized patients, both male and female, who are among the most respectable citizens in their communities. And it is one of the oldest and most enduring words in the English language. Its first dictionary appearance was in John Florio's *A Worlde of Wordes* (1598), where it was listed with four other words having the same meaning: *jape, sard, swive,* and *occupy.* These other words have disappeared from English usage, except for *occupy,* which was scrubbed clean of its sexual connotations and returned to respectable speech in the early nineteenth century. Yet, *fuck* has persisted and remained vividly alive.

Part of the reason for its persistence—and also a partial explanation for its being taboo—is that *fuck* is unabashedly explicit. Among all the words for the sex act, *fuck* is the only one that has no connotations or usage not related to its primary meaning. The other words are either euphemistic (such as *to sleep with*), metaphorical (*to screw*), technical (*copulate,* which also has other meanings in grammar and in logic), or legal (*fornicate,* which also is an architectural term). Strangely, the euphemisms for *fuck* often describe activities that are quite the opposite of what is meant. A man who *sleeps* with many women certainly is not getting much sleep, and one who *makes love* to her may be performing a sexual act in which no pretense of affection exists. Or if we say that a man or a woman *has many affairs,* we are using a word that describes businesslike rather than sexual activities. The metaphorical word *screw,* obviously derived from the movements of the penis into the vagina, is an objectionable substitute for *fuck,* as Sagarin points out:

> It suggests passivity and resistance by the female, struggle to enter by the male. Sex is something, of course, that a nice girl is not supposed to like, but submits to with reluctance because the male has the devil in his flesh. By appropriating the verb *screw* for sexual description, a society perpetuates this concept, and at the same time permits the conquering warrior male to retain an image of himself as having forced himself upon the reluctant female. The language is a reflection of a society that abhors sex while idolizing the male who obtains it and denouncing the female who offers it.

The explanation for the strong taboo against *fuck* cannot be found in linguistic history alone. At least part of the explanation lies in the domain of psychology, and indeed many psychiatrists have looked into the matter. Freud theorized that obscene speech in general serves as a substitute for aggression—as, for example, the hostility of the expletive *Fuck you!* The nonsexual use of the word in its many forms and combinations shows that it is always employed in speech situations that call for an aggressive vocabulary. When something is *fucked up,* it has been done very badly—and when a speaker says *I got a fucking,* he means that he lost out to someone more aggressive than he is. Freud's disciple Sandor Ferenczi associated obscene words with the childhood period of learning about sex; obscenity, in his view, therefore is the last stronghold of infantile sexual pleasure persisting into an adult world of conventional utterances. Edmund Bergler revised these theories somewhat and emphasized the importance of the oral pleasure an individual receives when he uses obscene words.

More recently, a sociological and linguistic attempt to explain the taboos surrounding *fuck* has been undertaken by Leo Stone, a psychoanalyst. Stone believes that the exaggerated fear of *fuck* is related to its similarity to *suck,* not only in the unconscious impulse toward oral sex but also in the closeness of the two words in spelling and sound. *Fuck* and *suck* are differentiated by only a single letter, and even this slight difference was nullified about the time that *fuck* became taboo, for English typography used to represent the letters *f* and *s* in much the same way. Furthermore, it is well known in psychiatry that both males and females fantasize as a mouth the female's entranceway to the vagina, part of which is, in fact, known as the *labia* or "lips." Stone speculates that the weakening of the taboo against *fuck* in recent years—as demonstrated by the word's inclusion in dictionaries, its use nowadays in literary works and in mass magazines, and its great frequency in the speech of respectable people—parallels a general breakdown in the community's taboos against sexual behavior.

Whatever the correct explanation for the antipathy toward *fuck,* the problem is much greater than just this word. If discussion of a subject is sometimes necessary, then why not allow the use of ordinary words? Prohibiting certain words actually elevates them in a neurotic way by encouraging the strategy of talking dirty; it endows them with titillation, shame, and a vulgarity that the things they stand for do not themselves possess. As long ago as 1934, Allen Walker Read, of the University of Chicago, labeled taboo words "a diseased condition" of our language, and he suggested we get rid of the taboos in a very simple way—by using the words.

When one refrains from using the stigmatized words, one is not ignoring the taboo but is actively abetting it. The solution lies in adjusting oneself to these words without the reaction of shame. The use of them must be unostentatious, in order to avoid inverted taboo, and it must be recalled that language is not the property of any person but that such changes must take place gradually by general consent. A beginning can best be made in the home, so that each of these words will not be a little festering sore in the adolescent's mind.

Now, some forty years later, what Read prescribed has begun to happen.

5

Verbal Dueling

Most speakers unconsciously duel even during seemingly casual conversations, as can often be observed at social gatherings where they show less concern for exchanging information with other guests than for asserting their own dominance. Their verbal dueling often employs very subtle weapons like mumbling, a hostile act which defeats the listener's desire to understand what the speaker claims he is trying to say (but is really not saying because he is mumbling!). Or the verbal dueler may keep talking after someone has passed out of hearing range—which is often an aggressive challenge to the listener to return and acknowledge the dominance of the speaker.

Whenever two people who know each other approach, a duel immediately takes place over who will speak first. The role of the first speaker is almost always determined by cues from eye contact, facial expressions, and gestures rather than from words. And once he has spoken, the conventions of probably all communities decree that the participants will speak in a rhythm that alternates rapidly from one to the other. Although it might appear to an observer of such a conversation that one speaker starts to talk as soon as the other stops, that is not the case. Careful study of recordings of conversations shows that only about one exchange in four takes place without a definite pause between the conclusion of one speaker's utterance and the beginning of the next speaker's. In most cases, an interval of mutual silence is required to transform a speaker into a listener and a listener into a speaker.

A key feature of any conversation is that only one speaker holds the floor at a time, and that while he does so he suppresses, apparently by the mere sound of his voice as well as some visual cues, any simultaneous speech by the other participant. The absence of simultaneous speech appears to be a universal feature of all languages, which may be due to the limited ability of the human nervous system to process information. The neurophysical make-up of our species seems to prevent us from both imparting our own information and decoding someone else's at the same time.

Dialogue, then, is the basic form of human speech—and monologue, in which one speaker is silent for a very long time, exists only in special cases such as theatrical performances, prayers, and ceremonial speeches. The monologue, rather than being simpler than the dialogue, actually is a very complex structure which is unknown in many speech communities. The linguist who visits an exotic people to study its language learns quickly that he is not offering freedom of expression when he asks someone to tell his life's story. In fact, by asking the native speaker to deliver a monologue, the well-intentioned linguist has deprived him of an essential freedom, the security of being able to speak within the structured framework of a dialogue.

The speaker who initiates a dialogue can select a gambit out of a large number of possible utterances. Whichever utterance he chooses, he will convey fundamental assumptions about his speech community and its conventions, his place in this community, and the rights he possesses and the obligations he owes to its other members. The truly amazing thing is that such far-reaching relationships can be established so promptly and by the utterance of so few words. If we disregard antisocial openings such as *Hey, jerk!* all conversations are opened in one of six ways:

1 A request for information, services, or goods. Examples are: *What time is it? Do you have a match? Please pass the sugar.*
2 A request for a social response. *What a slow bus this is! It sure is raining hard.*
3 An offer of information. *Did you hear about the robbery last night? You seem to be lost.*
4 An emotional expression of anger, pain, joy, which often is a strategy to solicit a comment by a listener. *Ouch! Whoopee! Look at this!*
5 Stereotyped statements, such as greetings, apologies, thanks, and so on. *Hello. I'm sorry. Thanks a lot.*
6 A substitute statement to avoid a conversation about a subject the speaker anticipates the listener will broach. An example would be a water-cooler meeting between a boss and a subordinate; the boss anticipates conversation about a raise, so he hurriedly speaks first and uses an avoidance opener: *The traffic sure was heavy this morning.*

Once A has opened a conversation in any of these six ways, he can anticipate a stock reply by B—after which A has the option to make another statement and thus launch a conversation with an ABAB pattern or to break off the conversation. But sometimes the opening utterance can lead to a completely unexpected reply. Witness this example from Jewish folklore of a conversation on the train to Lublin, Poland. A young man chose the first of the six conversation openers and asked a merchant, "Can you tell me the time?"

The merchant looked at him and replied: "Go to hell!"

"What? Why, what's the matter with you! I ask you a civil question in a properly civil way, and you give me such an outrageous answer! What's the idea?"

The merchant looked at him, sighed wearily, and said, "Very well. Sit down and I'll tell you. You ask me a question. I have to give an answer, no? You start a conversation with me—about the weather, politics, business. One thing leads to another. It turns out you're a Jew—I'm a Jew, I live in Lublin—you're a stranger. Out of hospitality, I ask you to my home for dinner. You meet my daughter. She's a beautiful girl—you're a handsome young man. So you go out together a few times—and you fall in love. Finally you come to ask for my daughter's hand in marriage. So why go to all that trouble? Let me tell you right now, young man, I won't let my daughter marry anyone who doesn't even own a watch!"

The humor in this story hinges, of course, upon our unconscious knowledge of the ABAB pattern in conversations. The merchant made an unconventional reply to a stereotyped conversation opener—and he so well understood the ABAB sequence that he was able to anticipate the entire conversation carried to its ultimate conclusion.

The irreducible minimum for any conversation is two participants. And to reduce the conversation to its barest essentials, the two participants would have to be out of sight of each other, in that way eliminating the interference of facial expressions, gestures, posture, attire, and so on. A telephone conversation provides exactly such a situation. Because of the absence in a telephone conversation of the physical cues that determine the first speaker, a convention has arisen that the person who answers the phone is the one to speak first. So unconsciously do people accept this convention that even the obscene caller follows it. He may be a psychopath and a violator of society's rules, but nevertheless he will tend to obey at least this convention and not usually unleash his obscenities until he hears a female speak into the phone.

It is a strange rule that designates the person answering the call to speak first. After all, the caller is the one who possesses all the information. He knows his own identity, the identity of the person whose number he is calling, and what he wishes to convey by the call. The person on the answering end could decide to violate the convention by picking up the receiver and remaining silent. In that case, the caller would probably utter a hesitant *Hello?* as if checking whether or not the phone was working. The person on the answering end would now possess at least some information: a clue to the identification of the caller's voice. Such a strategy, though, violates accepted behavior for the use of the telephone; it irritates the caller and sometimes it prevents a conversation altogether because the caller may simply hang up.

A good reason does exist why the person being called should speak first. The ringing of the telephone can actually be regarded as the first utterance of A, the caller, which represents a direct summons for B to reply to. Some people so unconsciously regard the ringing as an utterance that they hesitate to pick up the phone in the middle of a ring. Instead, they wait until the moment of silence between rings, much as if they did not want to interrupt a human speaker. B replies to the summons of A's ring with *Hello* or *Doctor Smith's office* or some such statement. No matter how B phrases his first utterance, it has the character of a question that implies a request for information about the caller. And whenever anyone makes such a request, he implies an obligation to respond after the information is supplied.

Once these opening AB statements (A's summoning ring of the phone and B's answer) have been made, the stage is set to generate a conversation. A is now obliged to reply to B by supplying information—such as *Hello, this is Joe* or *I'd like to make an appointment with Doctor Smith*. B has already implied an obligation to speak again after receiving some information; he now does so, since he could not very well insult Joe by hanging up after hearing his name or turn down a patient who wants to make an appointment with Doctor Smith. B might say *Hello, Joe, how are you?* or *What time would you like to see Doctor Smith?*—but, whatever the utterance, B has spoken a second time, asked for additional information, and concluded the process of launching a telephone conversation by rounding out the ABAB sequence.

The course that the conversation takes after A's summoning ring and the three subsequent utterances is partly determined by the paralanguage of those utterances. Both speakers will necessarily express attitudes by their tone of voice: friendliness, sincerity, annoyance, haste, expectation, and so on. The tone of B's initial *Hello,* for example, will inform A whether B is rushed or whether he has time to chat. If B does sound rushed, A may simply hang up without identifying himself. Or he might respond in a conciliatory tone that conveys how sorry he is to bother B. Now it is B's turn to reply, and his tone of voice will influence whether or not the conversation will be launched. He might reply in a tone that indicates *Well, I am rushed, but I'm happy to speak anyway,* in which case the conversation proceeds. Or his tone may indicate that the caller should try again later, in which case the conversation ends abruptly.

The simple ringing of a telephone, followed by three very brief utterances, has enabled two people to interact verbally. Each has committed himself, either by placing the call or by answering the phone, to a willingness to talk at this time; each has produced in the other and assumed in himself the obligation to make inquiries and to reply to them; each has tacitly recognized the existence of the ABAB sequence and waits his turn to speak. So obligatory is the relationship established on the phone that most people find it very difficult to break the sequence, even with a stranger. An obvious example is the clerk in the store who interrupts the customer he has been waiting on to answer the phone. Common courtesy demands that the clerk ask the caller to wait while he finishes with the customer, who took the trouble to come to the store in person. But the clerk, like most people, finds it very difficult to extricate himself from the obligations of the ABAB sequence once it is launched. He supplies the information requested by the caller while the customer is forced to wait.

At first thought, the riddle might appear to be an even simpler form of verbal dueling than opening a conversation or beginning a phone call. Indeed, most English-speaking communities attach little significance to riddles and usually regard them as a simple pastime of children. In fact, the majority of American children *are* strikingly punctual in acquiring a repertory of riddles at about age six or seven, and at that age they tell about three times as many joking riddles as jokes in any other form. During the next several years, riddles continue to make up about half of a child's store of jokes, and it is not until about age eleven that they are discarded in favor of anecdotes. A few children between the ages of six and eleven can tell the difference between a joke and a riddle, although most of them will ask a riddle when they are requested to tell a joke.

But the roots of the riddle in the ancient world show that it was rarely used as a humorous diversion for children. Rather, it was a serious adult strategy, as when the Queen of Sheba tested Solomon's wisdom by posing riddles. Often the penalty for a wrong answer was death, and Oedipus staked his life on solving the Sphinx's riddle of what walks on four legs in the morning, on two at midday, and on three in the evening. (The answer, of course, is man, who crawls as an infant, walks upright as an adult, and uses a staff in old age.) When Alexander the Great's armies reached India, they captured a town that, on the advice of ten sages, had dared to offer resistance. The conqueror sent for these ten men; he said that they would die if they answered his riddles incorrectly, and the one who answered worst would die first. Alexander appointed one of the ten sages to serve as the judge, after which he asked such riddles as: Which is the greater, land or sea? Which came first, day or night? Finally, Alexander demanded that the sage who served as judge tell who had answered the worst. The wily judge replied, "Each worse than the other!"—in that way upsetting the plan, for now no one could be killed.

Although riddles asked in speech communities around the world are essentially alike in their underlying structure, the form of the African riddle at first appears to differ from the strict question-and-answer sequence that is familiar in most European riddles. Instead, the "question" in the African riddle usually is a cryptic descriptive statement that refers by analogy to something else. The listener is expected to reflect upon the statement and then to make some kind of reply about what the description refers to—even though he has not been asked in so many words to "guess" anything. African riddles, therefore, often appear much more reflective and poetic than English ones, as is evident in these examples:

STATEMENT: "Invisible."
REPLY: "The wind."

STATEMENT: "Little things that defeat us."
REPLY: "Mosquitoes."

Some African riddles are longer and deeply philosophical, like this one told by the Thonga of southeastern Africa: "Over there smoke goes up, over there smoke goes up." To which the reply, in beautifully balanced rhythm in the original language, is: "Over there they mourn over a chief, over there they mourn over a poor man."

In many parts of southern Africa, "bird riddles" are a competitive game in which statements are exchanged rapidly in front of an audience. A contestant names a bird, then makes a clever analogy which compares the bird with a certain kind of human being. Not only must each contestant demonstrate his familiarity with the birdlife of the region, but he must also display inventiveness both in his analogy and in the way he tests the other contestant. A typical exchange might be:

CHALLENGER: "What bird do you know?"
PROPOSER: "I know the white-necked raven."
CHALLENGER: "What about him?"
PROPOSER: "He is a missionary."
CHALLENGER: "Why so?"
PROPOSER: "Because he wears a white collar and a black cassock and is always looking for dead bodies to bury."

Examples such as these from numerous unrelated languages reveal that the riddle is more complex than a childhood word game. The basic structure of almost all riddles consists of two descriptions of a single object —one literal and the other figurative—and the comparison between them must be searched for. The descriptions are, of course, intentionally obscure, and the listener's task is to identify whatever has been described in such a cryptic way. The audience delights in the riddle because it is momentarily misled—but then, when the answer is given, the audience is led into discovery or rediscovery of a sense of world order. Each riddle also exists on three levels. The first level is its form, the two or more descriptive elements whose relationship is to be guessed or commented upon. This level exists independently of any language or culture and can survive translation. The second level is the content, what the riddle is about. Content usually survives translation, but for full understanding the listener must be a member of the particular speech community in which it is told. Finally, the third level consists of the linguistic devices used in telling the riddle: rhyme, alliteration, onomatopoeia, puns, and so on. These devices are inextricably bound to the language in which the riddle is told and almost never survive translation.

The three levels become apparent in a riddle posed by the Fulani of West Africa: *tiisiinii taasaanaa siradel woogana* ("the gait of a large bird in sand") is replied to by naming a particular kind of pigeon native to that area. The form of this riddle, a statement followed by a reply, exists on the first level and it is easily enough translated into English. But to understand the second level, the listener must belong to the Fulani speech community. Even though the riddle can still be translated at this level, only a Fulani speaker would understand the allusion to this kind of pigeon, its habitat in certain sandy areas, its gait, its connotations in Fulani culture, and so on. The third level—the linguistic devices employed—defies translation. No translation could duplicate the verbal effect of the pigeon's swaying gait achieved through the high tone and closed vowels of *tiisiinii* alternating with the low tone and open vowels of *taasaanaa*. A listener would also have to be a native speaker of Fulani to understand that the drawn-out words, combined with short vowels, represent the pigeon dragging its feet through sand while also making occasional hops.

The prevalence of riddles in speech communities around the world raises the question of why this strategy is so widespread as a language game. Most games pay social benefits in education—yet riddles do not stimulate the imagination as much as some other kinds of word play. They do not, for example, equal proverbs in their capacity to impart practical knowledge; out of three hundred riddles collected in southern Africa by one linguist, only five taught anything of practical value. The proverb, by the way, is closely related to the riddle in that both are metaphorical and both compress thought to express a general truth. But the proverb supplies the answer as well as posing the question.

Instead of offering children and young adults specific instructions for day-to-day living, riddles are a more subtle education for life in general. They are stepping-stones to adulthood because they prepare the child for an important aspect of life in all cultures: interrogation. Part of an adult's adjustment to living in a social group is his recognition of higher and lower roles—as when a parent questions a child, a teacher a pupil, an employer an employee, a judge a defendant, a physician a patient, a highway patrolman a driver, and so on. In all such situations, the role of the interrogator includes the right to pose questions. The person being interrogated, on the other hand, plays a passive role in which he is forced to respond verbally. Apparently the riddle affords excellent preparation for the roles which speakers will assume as adults in their speech communities.

Riddles and proverbs belong to a larger group of strategies that also includes aphorisms, maxims, and other wise sayings—all of which have been given the name "gnomic expressions." Some well-known examples are:

Seeing is believing.
We all have strength enough to endure misfortunes of
    others.
A stitch in time saves nine.
Neither the sun nor death can be looked at steadily.
There is no odor so bad as that which arises from
    goodness tainted.

Just as *Ladies and gentlemen* indicates that a formal speech is about to begin and *Have you heard the one about* that a joke will be told, a gnomic expression is signaled by certain characteristics:

Meaning. Gnomic expressions deal with basic truths about life: health, love, poverty, riches, goodness, and so on. They also give advice and imply strategies to adopt in life. They usually do these things by employing a metaphor—as, in an example above, the association between a real odor and the tainted quality of goodness.

Sound. Gnomic expressions make use of various linguistic devices such as alliteration, assonance, and rhyme (as in *A stitch in time saves nine*).

Vocabulary. Impersonal forms—*one, we, people,* and so forth—are either stated directly or implied. The copula verb form *is* or *are* is frequently used.

Grammar. The verb is almost always in the present tense, which lends the gnomic expression the aura of universal application. Constructions such as parallelism, symmetry, and reversal of the elements in the expression are common.

These characteristics combine to produce a strategy of language manipulation for the particular purposes of teaching, conveying wisdom, and expressing a philosophy.

In probably no part of the world are gnomic expressions so important as in Africa. They abound in almost all languages on that continent, with the possible exception of the Bushmen of southern Africa and some speech communities along the Nile. Proverbs and other wise sayings are central to the African judicial process, and litigants quote them to support their cases in much the same way that lawyers in European cultures cite legal precedents to bolster their arguments. They are used profusely in many kinds of family discussions, as is seen in the following exchange recorded from the Yoruba of West Africa. A mother and father were disagreeing about the extent to which their child should be disciplined. The mother stated that the child was young and foolish, and therefore he should be indulged. The father replied with a proverb that translates roughly as: "Untrained and intractable children would be corrected by outsiders." This proverb in its original language hinged on play between the words translated as "untrained" and "intractable." The proverb allowed the father to maintain that a parent is obliged to train his child and the child is obliged to obey that training; if either the parent or the child fails in his duty, then the child will be corrected by community action.

The child's mother countered with a proverb of her own: "If a man beats a child with his right hand, then he should draw the child to him with his left." She thereby stated that she recognized the attitude conveyed by the father's proverb—but her proverb makes the point that discipline should be combined with parental love. This exchange is typical because it reveals the extent to which Africans command a vast number of proverbs, and also know exactly how to employ them in particular speech situations.

*

Gnomic expressions and their application in specific speech situations represent a creative use of language by human beings that is apparent even in very young children. Before a child has completely learned the grammar of his language, he delights in transforming utterances. Teach him a nursery rhyme and he will soon change it—perhaps by introducing alliteration, as in *Sing a song of sixpence, a socketful of sye,* or by substituting a single vowel for all the other vowels, as in *Jock and Joll wont op the holl.* The child adds rhythm and rhyme to stock utterances and substitutes nonsense words for meaningful ones, as Nathaniel Hawthorne pointed out about little Pearl in *The Scarlet Letter:*

> Pearl mumbled something into his ear, that sounded, indeed, like human language, but was only such gibberish as children may be heard amusing themselves with, by the hour altogether.

Children, regardless of the language they speak, progress rapidly to more sophisticated language games, such as disguised speech. Many American children, for example, learn to speak "pig Latin" sometime during childhood. Instead of saying *Give it to me,* they learn to say *Ivgay itay ootay iymay.* The distortion is easily accomplished, of course, by transferring the first consonant or consonant cluster to the end of the word, and then adding an *ay* sound. Pig Latin is probably the most widespread disguised language in America, although other kinds are also quite common—among them various "op" languages, which insert *op* or some other nonsense sound before every vowel, as in *Gopive opit topo mope.* The use of similar tricks to obscure the meaning of speech seems to be characteristic of children everywhere. For example, the normal way to say "He will give it to me" in Japanese is *Anohito-wa sore-o watashi-ni kureru-deshoo,* but the disguised form becomes *Akanokohikitoko-waka sokoreke-oko wakatakashiki-niki kukurekeruku-dekeshokooko.* The secret, of course, is to place a *k* sound after each vowel and then to repeat that vowel—a simple enough disguise when seen on the printed page but almost unintelligible when heard. Yet another variation is found in the disguised speech of the Cuna Indian children of Panama, who place *ci* before every syllable and then stress the syllables of the normal form. This kind of transformation changes the normal word for "friend," *ai,* into *ciAciI* and the word for "man," *maceret,* into *ciMAciCEciRET.*

Similar examples could be given from many other languages, but the point should already be clear that children are endlessly inventive in creating disguised speech. Children, speaking many kinds of languages and living in both simple and complex societies, have learned that they need use only two or three rules of transformation to produce speech that outsiders find very difficult to understand. In short, children have discovered possibilities in their native speech not exploited by the normal language. Various as these disguised languages are, an interesting thing about them is that they share three traits. First, all disguised speech adds or rearranges sounds that do not provide any additional information but serve only to confuse the uninitiated. Second, the rules introduced to transform the normal language are used consistently while the disguised language is being spoken, which means that disguised speech imposes its own kind of grammar upon the normal grammar of the language. And finally, almost all the transformations are based on the syllable—which is interesting evidence of the importance of the syllable in the structures of most languages.

Disguised speech usually serves to conceal something from adults or other children, although exceptions do exist. Thai children apparently use it to help them improve their skill in speaking. And for the Cuna Indians, the primary purpose appears to be linguistic play for play's sake, pure fun rather than concealment. Whatever the reason for the disguised speech, it does allow its speakers to demonstrate, by the fluent use of a transformed language, that they are members of a select group. The inevitable fate of these languages is that they are useful only for a limited time—until the uninitiated have mastered the transformations. Some disguised speech, though, manages to resist efforts by outsiders to learn it, such as the French *langage à l'envers,* "inverted language," which is based not on normal French but on the argot of adolescent gangs. Thus an outsider would have to make two translations to understand what has been said—first from the disguised speech into the gang's argot and then from the argot into Standard French.

A much more direct form of verbal dueling engaged in by ghetto blacks, almost always adolescent males, is known by such names as "playing the dozens," "sounding," "woofing," "capping," and "signifying." The game begins when one youth "sounds" another to see if he will play. That is done either by "signifying" (hurling a direct insult at the opponent) or by "the dozens" (insulting the opponent's family, particularly the mother). The youth who has been insulted may refuse to duel, in which case he makes a retort like *I laugh, joke, and smoke, but I don't play.* Or he might take up the challenge and reply with a clever slur against the attacker or his family. The retort, of course, leads the attacker to make further verbal jabs—and the insults fly back and forth until everyone becomes bored with the game, until some other subject comes up to interrupt the duel, or, rarely, until one participant hits the other. An audience is essential, both to spur on the two contestants and to prevent the insults from leading to a fight.

An attacker might, for example, sound someone by saying simply *Fuck you!* If the youth who has been insulted wants to duel, he will make a retort like *Man, you ain't even kissed me yet!*—and the game is under way. But the game is more likely to begin when youths are joking on a street corner and the name of someone's mother is mentioned. That provides an opening for one of the youths to say *Your momma eat shit.* The audience now senses the beginning of a game, and someone is likely to prod the youth whose mother has been insulted by asking *You gone let him say that bout your momma?* The insulted youth must now reply, or he will lose status, so he may say something like *Least my momma ain't no railroad track layin' all round the country*—which inevitably prompts a return insult by the attacker.

And so the game continues, as each participant attempts to make a clever retort, often a pun or an unexpected rhyme, although rhyming is not essential. In contrast, when the dozens is played in the West Indies —where the original calypso was a somewhat similar insult contest—rhyme must be used. The audience incites both participants, cheering good hits and ridiculing bad ones, occasionally interpolating insults when the action slows down. The status of a participant is greatly diminished if he answers a verbal insult by fighting. Instead, a loser tries to regain status by sounding someone else in the group whom he considers more vulnerable—and the loser of that round will, in turn, sound someone else, until eventually a pecking order is established.

Although many of the retorts are stereotyped insults, some players achieve real proficiency. They develop the verbal skill to take what their opponents have said and use it in a return attack. Such skill in words is greatly admired in the black community, among both men and women, and "signifying" has taken on the wider meaning of "to top any preceding remark," as in this example recorded by a linguist:

A man coming out of the bathroom forgot to close the zipper on his pants. A group of women watched him and laughed among themselves. The man's friends informed him what they were laughing at. So he went up to one of the women and said, "Hey, baby, did you see my big Cadillac with the full tires, ready to roll into action just for you?" She answered, "No, mother-fucker, but I saw a little gray Volkswagen with two flat tires."

Similar kinds of verbal dueling are found in speech communities around the world—as, for example, in Turkey, where it is part of the life of every teen-age youth. The Turkish duel always deals with homosexuality and virility, and the goal is to force an opponent into a feminine, submissive role. A youth whose family has been insulted must show the manliness to retort—so he parries the thrust by, in turn, attempting to deprive the attacker of his manliness. Most duels, particularly when they are between evenly matched adolescents, consist of long chains of insults hurled from opponent to opponent at a very fast pace. The technique of the duel demands that the retort be linked to the previous insult, either by playing upon a word or by attacking some inadequacy in the previous speaker's thrust, and that it must rhyme—both of which techniques sometimes make the game clever instead of a random collection of sexual insults. The ideal retort is immediate and skillful, and it provides little opportunity for a return insult.

The question naturally arises why certain speech communities encourage the expenditure of so much time and energy on verbal duels. Several attempts have been made to explain duels in psychological terms. For example, Turkish dueling is said to be related to problems of masculinity in Turkish society and to the confusion of youths about their circumcision; dozens is supposedly played because the black youth has grown up in a matriarchy and has not achieved a positive masculine identity. Such psychological explanations, though, do not search deeply enough into language behavior for an explanation. They emphasize the problems of speakers as individuals, not the role of a speaker inside his own speech community.

Nor do they explain name-calling and verbal dueling in cultures other than the Turkish and that of the black ghetto. For example, Eskimo culture does not practice circumcision, as does the Turkish—yet the Eskimo is noted for his skill in verbal dueling. He engages in song duels in which two disputants hurl insults, lampoons, and obscenities at each other, much to the delight of their audience. As verse after verse is exchanged, the audience gradually takes sides; eventually it laughs louder and longer at the insults hurled by one of the participants, thus acknowledging him victor in a bloodless contest. And that is precisely the point of the Eskimo song duel. Two disputants batter each other by the singing of insults rather than by blows, in that way preventing a quarrel from turning into a socially divisive feud.

All such duels—whether they be Eskimo songs, West Indian calypso, or insults exchanged by Turkish or black youths—have several things in common. They are verbal encounters in which words are an alternative to actual fighting. If enmity can be dissipated through songs and insults, then society has profited by the avoidance of bloodshed. A second function of verbal dueling is that it permits children and youths to test their society verbally in order to discover where the boundaries are drawn, how far (but no further) someone's mother can be insulted and how far (but no further) a speaker can go in expressing dominance in his group. These contests therefore are training grounds for adulthood, with appropriate changes in technique as age increases. In the case of black youths in particular, such verbal training has been essential. Virtually powerless in a white world, blacks discovered that one of the few ways they could fight back was verbally. Verbal battle against whites became more important than physical battle, where blacks have been outnumbered and outgunned. The game of the dozens has provided black youths with early opportunities to become proficient in verbal strategies and at the same time to elevate their standing in the group.

Although almost all known examples of verbal dueling are competitive strategies, the duels performed by speakers of Tzotzil, a Mayan language of Chamula, Mexico, are strategies for education in linguistic skills. The Chamulas believe that at one time all people spoke the same language. But eventually they quarreled, with the result that the sun deity divided the single world language into many different kinds to make people learn to live together peacefully in small groups. The Chamulas, however, were fortunate. They were given the Tzotzil language, which they regard as the best and which they refer to as "true language." It is no wonder, then, that they consider correct verbal behavior to be the defining trait of their own identity. They prize skill in the appropriate use of different kinds of speech for such strategies as "Conversational Speech," "Speech for People Whose Hearts Are Heated," "Ancient Speech," "New Speech," "Ritual Speech," and so on.

Verbal dueling is one of the strategies of "Truly Frivolous Talk," which also includes proverbs, riddles, jokes, lies, and insults. The Chamulas look upon all these kinds of verbal behavior as good-natured fun— even though the obscenities and insults expressed in a Chamula duel might lead to violence in many other speech communities. These insults are treated so lightly because they are regarded as training grounds for the skillful use of speech rather than as competitive strategies. The duel is usually engaged in by two friends or relatives, most often adolescent males, who may exchange as many as 250 challenges. As in Turkish and black-ghetto dueling, the players often accuse each other of being effeminate or of having promiscuous female relatives, and an audience is also present to encourage the players with its laughter. But a major difference is that a Chamula duel emphasizes skill in playing with the very strict rules of the language. Each player must not only maintain the obscene or derogatory meaning of his opponent's previous utterance; he must also do so while making his retort as close in sound to the preceding insult as possible. And a truly talented dueler will also display cleverness while employing such devices as alliteration and parallel syntax.

In a typical exchange, Dueler A might say *sec avakik* ("Come on in and give it to her"), to which Dueler B promptly replies, with the change of merely a single vowel, *sec avokik* ("Come on in and break her hymen"). Not to be outdone, Dueler A then makes another minimal change to produce *sec apokik* ("Come on in and give her a washing with your penis"). These exchanges are quoted from an actual duel that continued at a rapid pace for 210 rounds—and in almost every retort only a single vowel or consonant was altered.

Such duels drill the Chamulas to a remarkable degree in linguistic virtuosity. Since they are convinced that they speak the only true language, they must learn to speak it well in all its aspects. Without such skill, no man can hope to become *bankilal* (an almost untranslatable word that refers to "power," "seniority," and "rank" in the Chamula universe). A young man who wages a good verbal duel displays early signs of his understanding of the cultural values of his speech community, as well as signs of his ability to use language and potentially to achieve *bankilal*. A successful dueler is talked about in his community, and he is placed in the ranks of the esteemed, "those who know how to talk well."

6

Playing with Language

People in speech communities everywhere distort their language, manipulating it to create new expressions and to display personal styles. Their efforts range from the apparent frivolity of disguised speech, riddles, and puns to the seriousness of poetry and literature. Whether the intent is serious or frivolous, the result is the same: a creative use of language. While linguistic play may stretch the rules, it does not completely break them; even the nonsense of Lewis Carroll's "Jabberwocky" is only partially nonsense, as Chapter 14 will show. True word play employs linguistic virtuosity while still operating within the general framework of a language's rules. Gibberish and insane ravings are not word play, for the simple reason that the grammatical structures essential to language have been destroyed. The mentally retarded cannot play with language because it demands intelligence and inventiveness to abstract from normal speech, to know how to break the rules in consistent ways.

Most advertising jingles and political slogans, for example, achieve their effect by playing with language. Julius Caesar's victory message—*veni, vidi, vici* ("I came, I saw, I conquered")—is memorable both because of its brevity and because of the symmetry of three two-syllable verbs with the same first consonant and final vowel. The *I like Ike* slogan used during

Eisenhower's campaign for the presidency in 1952 is also a near-perfect expression of the symmetrical use of sound in English. The slogan consists of three mono-syllables, each of which has as its nucleus the same vowel and each of which when spoken aloud is followed by a single consonant. And the last two words form an echo rhyme in which the third word (*Ike*) is fully included in the second (*like*).

Poets often maintain that certain sequences of sounds have a built-in emotional impact, regardless of the dictionary meanings of the words that are used. For example, most poets would probably agree that the sounds in this line from William Butler Yeats's "Byzantium"—"That dolphin-torn, that gong-tormented sea"—express the explosive force of a raging sea, regardless of the meaning of the individual words. Robert Frost made sound symbolism a cornerstone of his beliefs about poetry, and he stated it in this way:

> . . . every meaning has a particular sound-posture, or to put it another way, the sense of every meaning has a particular sound which each individual is instinctively familiar with, and without at all being conscious of the exact words that are being used is able to understand the thought, idea or emotion that is being conveyed. What I am most interested in emphasizing in the application of this belief to art, is the sentence of sound, because to me a sentence is not interesting merely in conveying a meaning of words; it must do something more; it must convey a meaning by sound.

A poet's belief in sound symbolism implies that qualities inherent in certain sounds suggest meanings—which have little to do with their dictionary definitions. Sound symbolism undoubtedly is important in poetry, but considerable dispute exists over whether it has any influence in everyday speech. Few speakers feel that their casual utterances are more or less beautiful because of the arrangement of sounds. Some speakers of English might regard *ermine* as a sonorous arrangement, but they are unlikely to regard as equally sonorous another word with a very similar arrangement, *vermin*. And what is considered beautiful in one language might not be so considered in another. Danish speakers, for example, express the beautiful thought "pretty girls" by saying *smukke piger,* an ugly combination of sounds to most speakers of English.

Yet numerous experiments show that speakers do have strong feelings about certain sounds, and they agree about these feelings with remarkable consistency. In the earliest experiment designed to test attitudes about sound symbolism, the influential anthropologist and linguist Edward Sapir in 1929 made up two words, *mal* and *mil.* He told five hundred subjects, who ranged in age from eleven-year-old children to adults, that one word meant "large table," the other "small table"—and then asked the subjects to tell which word referred to which size table. By the laws of chance, the subjects should have chosen one word or the other in approximately equal numbers; instead, 80 per cent of them agreed that *mal* meant "large table" and *mil* meant "small table." Since the two words differ solely in their vowels, the subjects apparently felt that *a* conveys largeness and *i* smallness. Of course, the results might be suspect because of the resemblance of *mal* to such "large" English words as *maximum, major,* and *large* —and *mil* to such "small" words as *minimum, minor,* and *little.* On the other hand, the reverse could be true, for the vowel of *small* is also like that of *mal* and that of *big* is like that of *mil.*

A few years later another linguist extended Sapir's experimental approach to all the vowels. As a result, he placed vowels in a sequence that, he stated, English speakers feel refers to increasing size: *i* (as in *ill*), *e* (*met*), *ae* (*hat*), *a* (*ah*), *u* (*moon*), *o* (*hole*), and so on. The interesting thing about this sequence is that it

matches both the increasing size of the mouth necessary to pronounce the vowels and the path taken by the
tongue from the front to the back of the mouth. In
other words, the psychological awareness that speakers
of English have about what the vowels convey matches
the anatomical means of producing them.

A much more recent experiment with sound symbolism took a different approach. Subjects were asked
to listen to various kinds of noises made with hammers,
iron weights, cooking pots, chains, wooden balls, and
other objects—and then to make up onomatopoeic
words that seemed to express the sounds they just
heard. Once again the subjects were in remarkable accord as to the characteristics of the words they invented. After hearing a noise that began with an abrupt
sound, most subjects composed words beginning with
p, t, or *k,* consonants which are called "plosives" by
linguists because their sounds begin at peak intensity
and appear to explode upon the eardrums. In contrast,
for a noise that began slowly, the subjects usually made
up a word that began with one of the "spirant" consonants, *s* or *z,* which are speech sounds that begin gradually. If the noise was composed of repeated parts,
such as the rapid striking of a hammer, the invented
words also were composed of many parts or syllables—
and if the noise consisted of just one sound, the words
had only one syllable.

Most psychologists and linguists have long denied
sound symbolism because they doubt connections between hearing and the other senses. Yet here are experiments in which the great majority of the subjects
agree that the sounds they heard could be related to
what they knew from their sense of sight about the
size of objects—and that their feelings about sounds
somehow seem linked to the way the speech organs produce them. Nevertheless, for every experiment that appears to confirm the existence of sound symbolism,
critics can point to other experiments that show no

relationship between sound and meaning or whose results are controversial. The remarkable thing is that such experiments in sound symbolism continue to be carried out with great inventiveness and persistence in the absence of clear-cut results. Perhaps the explanation for this interest is the intuitive feeling of most speakers that a connection between sound and sense does exist—even though no one has yet been able to prove it.

People are correct when they feel that the written poetry of literate societies and the oral poetry of non-literate ones differ considerably from the everyday language spoken in the community. Listeners not only tolerate the strange use of words, rearrangement of word order, assonance, alliteration, rhythm, rhyme, compression of thought, and so on—they actually expect to find these things in poetry and they are disappointed when poetry does not sound "poetic." But those who regard poetry as a different category of language altogether are deaf to the true achievements of the poet. Rather, the poet artfully manipulates the same raw materials of his language as are used in everyday speech; his skill is to find new possibilities in the resources already in the language. In much the same way that people living at the seashore become so accustomed to the sound of waves that they no longer hear it, most of us have become deaf to the flood tide of words, millions of them every day, that besiege our eardrums. One function of poetry is to depict the world with a fresh perception—to make it strange—so that we will listen to language once again. But the successful poet never departs so far into the strange world of language that none of his listeners can follow him. He still remains the communicator, the man of speech—as two prominent literary critics, Cleanth Brooks and Robert Penn Warren, have pointed out:

Wordsworth called the poet a man speaking to men. Poetry is a form of speech, written or spoken. To the person who is not well acquainted with poetry, the differences between poetic speech and other forms may seem to be more important than the similarities, but these differences should not be allowed to obscure the fundamental resemblances, for only by an understanding of the resemblances can one appreciate the meaning of the differences. In poetry, as in all other discourse, one person is saying something to another person.

Most, and perhaps all, speech communities employ the strategy of verse to state ideas and emotions that are important to the community. They usually regard poetry as the suitable vehicle for the expression of holy things, whether it be a hymn to a deity or a magical incantation to ward off evil. Sometimes poetry has little to do with esthetic ends; rather it makes texts easier to remember, as in advertising jingles and in memory rhymes like *Thirty days hath September*. Probably this was the reason that the ancient Hindus wrote their scientific treatises in poetry, as did such Greek and Latin philosophers as Empedocles and Lucretius; and as recently as 1868 the Japanese composed parts of their state documents in verse form.

I emphasize these practical uses of poetry because in recent decades many people have come to think of poetry as an esthetic experience that has little relevance to everyday speech. But such an opinion of poetry is a false one. Poets have always been the teachers, the seers, the sorcerers of their communities. And more often than not, they have been the ones who find new truths through playing with language—as Johan Huizinga emphasized in *Homo Ludens*, his study of the play element in human communities:

> Poetry . . . lies beyond seriousness, on that more primitive and original level where the child, the

animal, the savage and the seer belong, in the region of dream, enchantment, ecstasy, laughter. To understand poetry we must be capable of donning the child's soul like a magic cloak and of forsaking man's wisdom for the child's.

An easy way to don the child's magic cloak is to look closely at the linguistic aspects of some children's verses. The familiar English nursery rhyme is composed of lines with four beats which fall at regular intervals, almost like the steady ticking of a clock, and always upon syllables that are stressed in everyday speech. Such verses disregard the number of unstressed syllables that fall between the beats. Should three or four unstressed syllables occur in a row, they are simply spoken more rapidly so as to maintain the steady beat. Here is a typical example, with the stressed beats marked above the appropriate syllables:

> 1 2 3 4
> Humpty Dumpty sat on a wall,
> 1 2 3 4
> Humpty Dumpty had a great fall.
> 1 2 3 4
> All the king's horses and all the king's men,
> 1 2 3 4
> Couldn't put Humpty together again.

So persistent is the four-beat rhythm that some nursery rhymes maintain it even when a line has only three beats. That is done by requiring the speaker to make an obligatory pause or rest at those places where a beat should normally occur. Speakers deeply feel this obligation to give each line its full allotment of four beats, with the result that they find it extremely difficult to recite a verse with missing beats without allowing for rests:

> 1 2 3 4
> Old King Cole was a merry old soul,
> 1 2 3 4
> And a merry old soul was he; (rest)

He called for his pipe and he called for his bowl,
And he called for his fiddlers three. (rest)

The same four-beat line, which disregards the number
of intervening unstressed syllables, appears in almost all
counting, jump-rope, and clapping games played by
English-speaking children, such as:

One to begin, two to show,
Three to make ready, and four to go!

And "Eeny-Meeny-Miney-Mo" requires the child who
does the counting to mark each beat by pointing at a
different child. The same pattern has also been carried
over from children's verses into adult efforts: popular
songs, incantations (the witches' *double, double toil
and trouble* from *Macbeth*), advertising jingles, senti-
mental songs, and the easily remembered verse that appears in mass publications.

Only recently have some linguists paid attention to
the fact that children who speak unrelated languages
also recite verses that apparently follow the same pattern as the English ones. Chinese children's verse, for
example, is very much like the English verses just
quoted—in content, in the inclusion of large amounts
of nonsense, and also in patterns of rhyme and rhythm.
Like the English children's verses, the Chinese ones
similarly disregard the number of unstressed syllables
between the four stressed beats, consist of stanzas of
four lines, and often substitute rests for beats:

Syau har, syau har shangjing tar
Shwaile ge gentou, jyanle ge chyer

1   2   3   4
You da tsu, you mai yer
1   2   3   4
You chyu syifu, you gwo nyer.

> ("Little child, little child climbs the well platform
> Falls head over heels, picks up a coin
> And vinegar, and buys salt
> And gets married and lives out his years.")

The same kind of children's verse has been dis-covered in so many other unrelated languages—among them Serrano (an Indian language of southern California), Benkula (spoken in Sumatra), Yoruba (Nigeria), Trukese (South Pacific), and Arabic—that it would seem to be a universal pattern of speech behavior. Says Robbins Burling, of the University of Michigan, who recently called attention to the occur-rence of these patterns around the world:

> If these patterns should prove to be universal, I can see no explanation except that of our common humanity. We may simply be the kind of animal that is predestined not only to speak, but also, on certain occasions, to force our language into a recurrent pattern of beats and lines. . . . If we knew more about enough languages, it should be possible to describe the general pan-human features of verse, the features within which our human nature limits us. To these general rules each language could be expected to add its own restrictions, rules that would limit the broader human capacity to the narrower channels of a particular culture and linguistic tradition.

The adult poet also plays with his language and manipulates it in much the same way that children manipulate nonsense verses. But as a self-conscious craftsman the poet possesses an intuitive knowledge of the abstract patterns of his language and a feeling for the extent to which he can use them creatively. Whether he is discovering new and expressive uses for sound, reviving an archaic word, borrowing words from other languages, or forcing old words into novel grammatical structures, he is always exploiting the linguistic resources already in his spoken language.

Nowadays some linguists are confident that they can enhance the understanding of a poet's creative use of language through the new tool offered by generative-transformational grammar (which will be explained more fully in Chapter 14). First of all, this grammar offers a fresh view of what the poet does in that it accounts for all the grammatical sentences in a language and thereby allows us to see in what way he makes certain strings of words differ from ordinary speech. Should a poet write a phrase which appears to break the rules of English grammar—such as *Sincerity loves John*—this grammar makes clear that it does so because a noun with abstract features (*sincerity*) has been used to serve as the subject of a verb with animate features (*loves*). Secondly, this grammar shows that some poetic sentences revise the rules to a greater extent than other poetic sentences do, which makes them seem more strange to the listener. For example, a relaxation of the rules that allows a poetic statement like *thou wild west wind*—in which an inanimate noun (*wind*) substitutes for the animate noun expected after *thou*—is much less drastic than a relaxation which ignores altogether the distinction between nouns and other parts of speech. Of course, when we analyze a poem in this way we cannot really analyze the mysteries of artistic invention, nor can a person become a poet simply by referring to rules of grammar. But we can at least obtain some further understanding of the creative act the poet has achieved.

Compare two phrases by modern poets, both of which creatively exploit the rules of English grammar:

he sang his didn't (from E. E. Cummings' "Anyone lived in a pretty how town") and *a grief ago* (from Dylan Thomas' poem with the same title). Speakers of English intuitively feel that *he sang his didn't* is very ungrammatical, whereas *a grief ago* is much less so. To create *he sang his didn't,* E. E. Cummings radically exploited the grammatical rules for creating sentences of this type. If he had instead written *he sang his song,* he would have created a perfectly grammatical sentence which conforms to the structure of a subject (*he*) followed by a predicate (*sang*) and then an object consisting of a noun phrase (*his song*). But instead E. E. Cummings changed the rules to make a verb (*didn't*) part of a noun phrase. Such a change is a major revision of the rules of English grammar. The consequences would be drastic if the revised rule were admitted to English grammar—because it could generate a tremendous number of similarly ungrammatical sentences, such as *he hoped his gone.*

In contrast, most speakers of English do not feel that *a grief ago* is as drastically ungrammatical. That may be because it sounds close to such grammatical utterances as *a year ago* or *some time ago,* which have the structure of a determiner (*a*) plus noun (*year*) plus adverb (*ago*). All of the nouns used in this kind of structure, however, refer to time, whereas in *a grief ago* the noun *grief* refers to a state of mind. So for English grammar to generate *a grief ago,* the rules have to be relaxed in only one way: Nouns referring to a state of mind, as well as nouns referring to time, would be permissible. The consequences of such a relaxation of the rules would be quite minor and would produce only a small number of slightly ungrammatical utterances like *a happiness ago* or *some sorrow back.*

Most English speakers find meaning in *a grief ago* because they unconsciously think of *grief* as a noun that implies time rather than a state of mind. They feel that Dylan Thomas is really saying, with poetic force and economy, "at some time in the past, a time filled with feelings of grief." But the revision of the rules required to generate E. E. Cummings' *he sang his didn't* is much more drastic for English speakers because it would allow verbs to serve in place of nouns. It might lead to such structures as *he danced his did* and *he went their came,* which are in fact other phrases from the same poem, or such a grotesque structure as *the went grasses a had,* in which the distinction between nouns and verbs is obliterated.

Although poets are acclaimed for their creative use of language, other groups within speech communities also use words uniquely and employ them creatively in various speech situations. The argot of criminals and the jargon of lawyers, doctors, and professors differ from one another and from all other kinds of speech, but they share a similar function: to display in-group solidarity and to maintain a boundary against outsiders. Doctors sometimes use arcane language in prescriptions to be secretive, and lawyers quote Latin phrases because of the traditions of their profession—but in most instances argot and jargon are not secret languages which allow their speakers to talk without being understood by those who do not belong to the group. That is clear from a look at the argot of the confidence man. A novice con man may need several years to master his difficult argot. And once he has learned to speak it fluently, he obviously will not use it when his potential victims, or "lambs," are within earshot, lest they become suspicious. Instead, the argot is the badge that allows one con man to identify another. Like any criminal, the con man knows that he is in constant danger of exposure. The only people he can rely on are his fellow specialists in crime, and his argot provides a way to recognize them as members of this mutually dependent group.

Each specialty within crime—con men, counterfeiters, drug pushers, pickpockets, burglars, and so on—has its distinctive professional argot. The members of each specialty admire one another in proportion to the ability to speak it and they take pride in their own performances. Of all criminals, the quick-witted con men are naturally the most adept at argot, and they coin a constant stream of colorful new expressions. Says David W. Maurer, who studied the lingo of this criminal specialty and reported on it in *The Big Con:*

> They derive a pleasure which is genuinely creative from toying with language. They love to talk and they have markedly original minds, minds which are singularly agile and which see and express rather grotesque relationships in terms of the flickering, vastly connotative metaphor which characterizes their argot. . . . Their proclivity for coining and using argot extends much beyond the necessary technical vocabulary. They like to express all life-situations in argot, to give their sense of humor free play, to revolt against conventional language.

It is indeed metaphorically refreshing when a con man says *to fit the mitt* to mean "to bribe," *get a hard-on* for "pull a gun," and *a push note* to refer to a dollar bill that is used as a come-on in a swindle.

As soon as a group becomes newsworthy, its argot is likely to escape from specialized use and enter the general slang vocabulary of the speech community. Many Americans learned a smattering of criminal words through gangster movies and radio programs like "Gangbusters" during the 1930s and 1940s. (More recently, listeners have been exposed to the argot of Jewish comedians, who regularly appear on television talk shows, and they have been introduced to the argot of the black ghetto through the civil rights and black-liberation movements.) The leakage of the criminal's vocabulary into everyday speech has been going on for thousands of years. Much of the fresh use of language found in the *Satyricon* of Petronius Arbiter stems from the author's use of the argot of the Roman underworld. Shakespeare borrowed freely from the criminal languages of his day, and such writers as Defoe, Fielding, Smollett, and Sterne flavored their literary vocabularies with colorful argot phrases. Once the argot becomes known, though, its value for distinguishing professionals from outsiders is lost—and so new words must constantly be added to keep the in-group vocabulary intact. Nowadays many con-man argot terms reported by Maurer—such as *monicker, bilk, beef, fix,* and even *con game* itself—are general American slang and are no longer in use by the underworld.

Whatever has been said about criminal argot is also true of the jargon of professions like medicine and law and of specialized interests like baseball and beetle-collecting. A baseball fan who says that a player "connected for four RBIs in a twin bill" is just as mystifying as the linguist who writes in a scholarly journal that "nonnuclear constituents may combine to form a discontinuous peripheral immediate constituent." Both the baseball fan and the linguist, by their competence in employing the specialized vocabulary, have signaled to others in their subgroup that they belong.

Probably the most widely known jargon in use today is that spoken by the astronauts and those engaged in aerospace technology. In the same way that the jargon of the astrologers once furnished English with many common words—such as *jovial, mercurial, saturnine,* and *martial*—in the past decade or so aerospace words have seeped out into the general vocabulary. Most Americans are familiar with such aerospace jargon as *countdown, malfunction, hold, systems,* and so forth. Space jargon has several characteristics which immediately mark it as belonging to this profession. First of all, economy of effort in speaking is achieved by using abbreviated versions of longer utterances:

recirc for *recirculation, NASA* for *National Aeronautics and Space Administration,* and *lox* for *liquid oxygen.* Then, as is fitting to such high aspirations, euphemisms have developed for anything that might smack of the ordinary. *Failures* have been turned into *partial successes, a shutdown to find out what went wrong* has become *a hold.* Thirdly, clusters of nouns —such as *stage systems design parameters*—are excused in space jargon apparently because they describe complicated equipment. Finally, space jargon is characterized by needlessly repetitious vocabulary—like *A-OK all systems go*—possibly because the equipment itself has so many back-up systems to prevent partial successes.

Even when no reason exists to use the jargon, as in a nontechnical conversation between an astronaut and ground control, the speech nevertheless clearly belongs to the aerospace age. It is slangy, idiomatic, comradely, and it alternates between wild exaggeration and benighted humility. Nouns are used in structures that demand verbs (*I was an addict to it*), and adjectives are changed into adverbs (*real good*); comic-book expressions are widely used (*pow!*); the personal *I* is avoided in favor of the brotherly *we;* attempts are made to obliterate human emotions (instead of *I was scared,* an astronaut says *I suffered some apprehension*). Despite the continual leakage of many space expressions into our everyday vocabulary, we can anticipate that astronaut speech will become increasingly specialized—until the gap between Technical Aerospace English and Standard English becomes almost unbridgeable.

The argot of the criminal and the jargon of the astronaut represent the "styles" of their speech communities—that is, the habitual use of certain strategies in speech. Several other speech communities discussed

so far—such as the Rundi, Hausa, and Chamula—
possess a style that places a premium on words as a
powerful social force. Most speech communities similarly admire the ability to speak well. The Anang of
Nigeria, whose tribal name means "they who speak
wittily upon any occasion," pride themselves on their
eloquence, and their youths are encouraged from earliest childhood to develop verbal skills. Among the
Iroquois Indians of northeastern North America, a chief
could rise in status through eloquence as easily as he
could through bravery in war.

In contrast to those societies that admire the man of
speech, some put a premium on silence. The Paliyans
of southern India generally speak very little, and by the
time someone reaches the age of forty he is nearly
always silent; voluble people in this speech community
are regarded as abnormal and their behavior as offensive. For different reasons, the Society of Friends
(Quakers) has from its founding in the middle of the
seventeenth century been self-conscious about speech.
The Quakers set themselves apart from the surrounding
social environment in their dress and behavior, and
particularly in their speech. Instead of seeing the positive values in speech that most communities do, the
Quakers from the outset distrusted almost all forms of
speech. They have traditionally looked upon articulate-
ness as a distinguishing mark of the worldly man and
a behavior inappropriate to an inward communion with
God. They believe in direct personal revelation in
which the Spirit of God within oneself will be revealed
if the earthly self can be suppressed. This state of
suppression is known as "silence"—and it refers not
only to verbal silence but by extension to the quieting
of all worldly activities and impulses.

Whether the premium be placed on speech or on
silence, the selection of one over the other represents
the "style" of the entire speech community—although
the individual speaker can always display his creativity

by selecting from a number of alternative strategies his language offers. An example is the style of giving names to children, which in most American speech communities is quite standardized. A child is usually given the first name of a parent or grandparent, the family name of the mother or some ancestor, or one of a limited number of quite common names like *Thomas, Richard, Harold, Jane, Carol,* or *Elizabeth.* But in certain speech communities in the South and Midwest, where most of the members belong to fundamentalist Protestant sects, the style is to bestow curious, folksy, or amusing first names—not as nicknames but as official birth-certificate names. Some fancy first names have been combined with family names to produce *Honey Combs, Pleasant Weathers, Bunker Hill* and *Dill Pickle.* A socialite leader of Houston, Texas, bears the name *Ima Hogg.* Other first names selected at random from the Bible Belt are: *Coeta, LaVoid, Phalla, Buzz Buzz, Nicy, Sugie, Dilly, Skeety, Early Bill, Billye Joe, Lum, Quince, Prince, Queen, Duke, Earl, Rob Roy, Thais, Orlando, Tennessee, Savannah, Odessa, Venice, Paris, Oleander, Girlie, Fawn, Kitty Bit, Charme, Rose Bud.* A possible explanation for such a curious style of child-naming is that the fundamentalist sects to which these people belong do not practice infant baptism. When name-giving is not part of the sacrament of baptism—and consequently a clergyman with a sense of decorum has no say—individual style may run wild, as it often does in areas of the United States where members belonging to these sects are concentrated.

Style is always present, of course, in the utterances of every speaker. Most listeners, after a moment's thought, can probably isolate the stylistic peculiarities of speakers whom they have heard often. Some speakers habitually use slang; others habitually avoid it or else utter a slang word as if quotation marks were placed around it. Some fluently spatter their speech with pomposities, while others hesitate. A close examination of styles of speech reveals a penchant for or an avoidance of the following: adverbs or adjectives, certain tenses of verbs, clauses introduced by *but* or *however,* and so on.

Most readers of novels intuitively feel that their favorite authors have distinctive styles, and some sensitive readers can even attribute passages which they have not read previously to one or another of these authors. Readers usually can make such an identification regardless of the subject matter of the passages—which indicates that style has its own life apart from the content of what is being talked about. In other words, readers unconsciously recognize that the grammatical patterns the authors employ are somehow different from the messages they communicate. Everyone knows that the English language offers the speaker the option to say exactly the same thing in many different ways. *Ernest Hemingway wrote the novel,* for example, can be transformed into other sentences with exactly the same meaning, such as *The novel was written by Ernest Hemingway* and *The writer of the novel was Ernest Hemingway.* When an author habitually chooses two or three transformations out of the vast possibilities offered to him by his language, that choice becomes part of his style—and it is unconsciously recognized by readers.

Look at this brief extract from a complex, 1600-word sentence in William Faulkner's story "The Bear":

the desk and the shelf above it on which rested the letters in which McCaslin recorded the slow outward trickle of food and supplies and equipment which returned each fall as cotton made and ginned and sold

Much of the complexity of this sentence results from Faulkner's reliance primarily upon reduced structures linked by conjunctions and relative pronouns. If these reductions had not been made, the passage would have read this way:

> The desk. The shelf was above it. The letters rested on the shelf. McCaslin recorded in the letters the trickle of food. McCaslin recorded in the letters the trickle of supplies. McCaslin recorded in the letters the trickle of equipment. The trickle was slow. The trickle was outward. The trickle returned each fall as cotton. The cotton was made. The cotton was ginned. The cotton was sold.

The content of the two passages is exactly the same. But in the second passage Faulkner's distinctive style has been completely obliterated. And this obliteration has been accomplished simply by reversing the few grammatical operations that Faulkner relied on so heavily to produce his idiosyncratic style. This example was not intended to render judgment on whether Faulkner was a better or a lesser author because of his habitual use of reduced structures. The aim has been, simply, to show that literature—like everyday speech, nursery rhymes, advertising jingles, and jargon—also takes the resources of a language and then strategically manipulates them to produce desired results.

*

The ultimate way to play with language, of course, is to lie, a strategy that exists in every speech community. Swift attempted to describe a utopian society in which lying does not exist when he wrote about Gulliver's final voyage—to the land in which wise horses, known as Houyhnhnhms, rule over humanlike beasts, Yahoos. Swift, of course, is reversing traditional beliefs by making human beings the unreasoning brutes and brute horses the reasoning animals. Gulliver learns from one of the Houyhnhnhms why they lack words in their language to express falsehoods:

> The use of speech was to make us understand one another and to receive information of facts; now, if anyone said the thing which was not, these ends were defeated, because I cannot properly be said to understand him, and I am so far from receiving information that he leaves me worse than in ignorance, for I am led to believe a thing black when it is white and short when it is long.

A language that cannot be used for lying, however, is a logical impossibility. That fact has been known at least since Epimenides the Cretan said *All Cretans are liars.* Because Epimenides himself was a Cretan, his utterance must have been a lie. And if his utterance was a lie, then all Cretans could not be liars. So if Cretans are not liars, and we already know that Epimenides was a Cretan, then *All Cretans are liars* should be a true utterance. But it could not be true because Epimenides was a Cretan.

The plain fact is that a lie is built into Epimenides' utterance, and no way exists to extract it. Such paradoxes of language were very popular among the ancient Greeks. This kind became known as the Antinomy of the Liar (*antinomy* in Greek means literally "against the law" and it refers to a basic contradiction between two statements that seem equally reasonable). It tormented the ancient logicians and was the delight of the satirists, such as Lucian, who wrote: "I will say in advance this one true thing, to wit, I am going to tell you lies." Its popularity remained high during the Middle Ages, and in this century Bertrand Russell gave it new life by his discovery that its logical structure was identical with that of certain mathematical paradoxes.

Philosophers of language have found numerous variations of the antinomy, such as this one:

> *All sentences*
> *within*
> *this square*
> *are false.*

The statement inside the square obviously is a sentence. If we assume that it is a true statement, then it must be false because it says that all sentences within the square are false—and it is the only sentence to be found there. On the other hand, we cannot assume the statement to be false. It has to be true because it is the only sentence within the square and it does say that it is false.

Other antinomies can become considerably more involved. Imagine, for example, a speaker who utters a statement every minute for sixty minutes. During the first minute he says *The sentence I will speak in the second minute is true.* During the second minute he says *The sentence I will speak in the third minute is true.* And so on until the final minute, when he says *The sentence I spoke during the first minute was false.* If the final utterance is taken to be a true one, then the sentence spoken during the first minute must have been false. If the sentence spoken during the first minute was false, then the one spoken in the second minute had to be false also. And so on until the final statement, which would then have to be assumed false rather than true. Everyday speech acts in which lying occurs, such as tall tales and extended jokes, sometimes follow this pattern. A speaker begins a story with a somewhat unbelievable statement but immediately adds *Now I'll show you why that's so.* He then proceeds to support the first statement with a second apparently untrue sentence, which he bolsters by *I know that sounds peculiar also, but I'll tell you why it's true*. He keeps piling exaggeration upon exaggeration until his final sentence, in which he disowns his very first sentence either by wild hyperbole or by saying *I wasn't exactly accurate the way I began this story*.

Philosophers of language have vacillated between two extremes in their attitude toward the antinomy. Some regard antinomies as mere quirks built into language, somewhat the way every piece of machinery of necessity has vibration built into it. This view regards the antinomy as a harmless game that reveals nothing about language but shows only the cleverness of the people who play it. Other philosophers, though, take the antinomy very seriously—as an essential paradox of language. They are severely troubled that carefully expressed statements, analyzed by rigorous logic, should turn out to be nonsense. This view regards the antinomy as a symptom which may indicate a defect in the body of language.

The existence of rules and conventions about language implies the ability to break such rules and conventions, as Oliver Goldsmith pointed out: "The true use of speech is not so much to express our wants as to conceal them." (Even such an innocuous statement as this, the alert reader will note, might contain an antinomy.) Mark Twain took the pessimistic view that lying could never be eliminated from language. So the only lying that should be condemned, he felt, was lying performed with a lack of artistry:

Lying is universal—we *all* do it; we all *must* do it. Therefore, the wise thing is for us diligently to train ourselves to lie thoughtfully, judiciously; to lie with a good object, and not an evil one; to lie for others' advantage, and not our own; to lie healingly, charitably, humanely, not cruelly, hurtfully, maliciously;

to lie gracefully and graciously, not awkwardly and clumsily; to lie firmly, frankly, squarely, with head erect, not haltingly, tortuously, with pusillanimous mien, as being ashamed of our high calling. Then shall we be rid of the rank and pestilent truth that is rotting the land; then shall we be great and good and beautiful and worthy dwellers in a world where even benign Nature habitually lies, except when she promises execrable weather.

Psychiatrists regard lying as a pathology, whereas members of Liars' Clubs across America think of it as a humorous verbal duel. But the strategy of lying has different implications for those interested in language. They are appalled that language—an edifice of staggering complexity, built up of certain sounds sensitively distinguished from other sounds, mortared into a tremendous number of possible utterances—can be toppled by any dunce who cares to utter a falsehood.

The eighteenth century was assuredly the great century for the liars of Europe who brought back unbelievable—and, as we now know, not worthy of belief—travel accounts from around the world. I do not mean the imaginary voyages such as *Gulliver's Travels,* the fictitious tales like *Robinson Crusoe,* the many varieties of the picaresque such as *Gil Blas, Rasselas,* and *Candide,* nor the easily visible lies of someone like Baron Munchausen. No, I mean those thousands of eighteenth-century travel books and shorter accounts that attempted to foist off as truth statements that the authors obviously knew were false—like Chateaubriand, who convinced people that he had visited what is now the southern United States, although he had not; Jonathan Carver, who printed vocabularies of the languages of Indians he never met and described habits of animals he never saw; Daniel Defoe, who remained comfortably in his London room and hoaxed the reading public with *A New Voyage Round the World;* and all those other travelers who claimed that in Argentina they saw a race of giants, who fabricated tales of a river that connected the Rockies with the Mississippi (in this case truth gave the lie to falsehood with the discovery of the Missouri River), who told of a serpent in Egypt that could rejoin its cut parts and glide away, who described a Louisiana plant that made Indians live more than a hundred years, who lied about the world's newly discovered peoples, geography, plants, and animals with all the grace and frankness that Twain admired.

Why did the eighteenth-century travelers lie? And why was lying particularly prevalent in that century? The second question is the easier to answer. The travelers lied simply because they thought they could get away with it. Since they could not envision the invention of photography in the nineteenth century or the great age of scientific exploration in the late nineteenth and twentieth centuries, they anticipated that no readers would ever see the places they described so imaginatively. But to pinpoint precisely why they lied is more difficult. For one thing, standards about truth were not so high then as they are now. In fact, the ideal travel writer was one who had an inquiring mind—but bad eyes. Nor can we underestimate the importance of vanity. Someone who had ventured to a far place owed it to himself and his own self-esteem to return with marvelous stories, whether they were true or not. This sort of vanity was fed by two other motivations: prejudice and cupidity. One country or another had prejudices in favor of or against Jesuit missionaries, Germans, Frenchmen, Englishmen, pagan Indians and Africans—and they demanded books that bolstered these prejudices. An eager reading public and printers short of new travel books to publish offered writers an easy way to satisfy their cupidity. It all comes down to this: In the eighteenth century throughout Europe, from Peter the Great's Russia to

gold-seeking Portugal, from colonizing Britain to pros-
elytizing Spain, travelers lied simply because their
speech communities expected it of them, and paid them
and fed their vanity when they performed well.

No listener can, of course, ever be certain whether or
not a speaker is employing the strategy of lying. A
speaker may say *Everything I'm telling you is the God's
honest truth,* yet be uttering an antinomy. We might
naturally wonder why any weight at all is ever given to
words, but language does not stand as defenseless before the liar as might at first appear. In theory the only
human beings who could lie to me would have to be
members of my own speech community. Since I do not
speak Chinese, obviously I would not recognize the
difference between true and false utterances in that
language. But even among speakers of my native English, I would be less likely to put faith in an utterance
by someone who belongs to a speech community of
which I am not a member. If I found myself on the
Maine seacoast and asked a native's advice about a
good restaurant for a lobster dinner, I would not be
likely to take his reply at face value. I would ask one
or two other people, compare and contrast what they
said, note inconsistencies in their statements, and evaluate their suggestions against the objective recommen-
dations published by national travel organizations. I
would do all of these things with conscious awareness
as I protected myself against the self-interest of people
I asked, one of whose relatives or friends might own
the recommended restaurant, or against the Down
Easter's penchant for pulling the leg of an outsider.

Nor do members of my immediate speech community find it easy to lie to me with consistent success.
As a native speaker and a member of the same community, I unconsciously evaluate each utterance. If it
seems nonsensical or is of doubtful authenticity, I am
likely to ask that it be repeated or supported. And as a
member of the same speech community as the speaker,

I am alert to the full array of nonverbal and paralinguistic signals—eye movements, facial expressions, gestures, tone of voice, and so on—that accompany speech and indicate to me the degree of faith the speaker is placing in his own utterances. I will also assume that while I am assessing the speaker, he is assessing me. So in the same way that I will be careful about the credibility of what I say, I can assume that he will be equally concerned about what my assessment of him reveals—which provides an incentive for him not to lie. Further, in any verbal game, both I and the person I am speaking with hope to win something by our words, whether it be to convince, to profit financially, to obtain information, or to assert social status. Therefore, both of us have a continuing reason for not lying, since the detection of a lie by one of us will immediately negate the entire conversation.

Nevertheless, despite all these safeguards, speakers in my community occasionally will lie, just as in the game of poker some players will bluff. The poker player might utter misleading words, feign certain facial expressions, and place unusual bets—but when he does so he takes the risk that I will infer more about the cards he holds from his misdirections than if he played the game scrupulously. Similarly, in the language game, the liar would in effect be challenging me to a verbal duel. But as a member of the same speech community, I can hope to be approximately as skilled as he is in detecting lies. Like the dealing of cards in a poker game, utterances in the language game come one by one—and so my risk in either game is reduced because each fractioned play must withstand scrutiny. A poker player who takes a single risk in slipping one card from the bottom of the deck out of the hundreds dealt in the game has thereby jeopardized the entire game—and a speaker who distorts one of his utterances into a lie has similarly jeopardized whatever he hoped to obtain from his conversation with me.

This discussion has been based on the substantive lie and not on the trivial lies that all of us tell every day. If someone in my town greets me with *How you feelin' today, Mister Farb?* I am likely to reply *Fine, thanks, and yourself?*—even though I might at that moment be suffering from flu, be hurrying to the drugstore to get my prescriptions refilled, and not be the least interested in how the person who greeted me is. But my *Fine, thanks, and yourself?* should not really be considered a lie. It is simply one of the stereotyped gambits offered me in my speech community's greeting ritual. By selecting this gambit, I have not actually lied but rather have chosen a strategy whereby I can suppress further conversation about my health, with the result that I can continue on my way to the drugstore. If I had not chosen the gambit of the trivial lie but instead had replied truthfully *I have a fever and headache and cough and my legs feel like they're ready to collapse,* I would have chosen a very poor option from the array of those open to me in the greeting interaction. Rather than suppressing further conversation, this option demands that the person who greeted me reply by expressing words of sympathy, whether or not he feels such an emotion: *Gee, Mister Farb, I'm terribly sorry to hear that.* Because as a native member of my speech community I unconsciously knew that he would have to express sympathy—and that I, further, would have to respond to it by continuing the conversation—I suppressed further interaction simply by replying to his initial greeting with the trivial lie *Fine, thanks.*

Whatever I have just said about the defenses against lying applies to face-to-face interactions between speakers in the same speech community. I am much more vulnerable to lying from a different direction—from political figures, heads of corporations, leaders of social and economic movements, anyone who commands loyalties that extend beyond his own immediate domain. Such people can manipulate events, dictate to sources of information, control what will be said aloud and what will be hidden. Americans alive today can date the year and the occasion when they ceased to accept as the truth statements from the highest levels of the United States government. In 1964 citizens overwhelmingly elected a peace candidate, Lyndon Johnson, who almost immediately plunged the nation into the longest and most shameful war we have ever fought. Since then, Americans have been the victims of deception after deception regarding Vietnam, with the result that an entire generation has grown up to believe that lying is built into the American political system.

The Vietnam War—not a *war* according to the Pentagon but an *international armed conflict*—inspired lying at a national level rarely seen before in history. The predominant strategy was the ornate euphemism— an effort to divert attention from the true horrors of death and destruction by labeling something the opposite of what it truly was. An aggressive attack by an armada of airplanes, which most speakers of English call simply an *air raid,* was instead spoken of as a momentary defensive strategy, a *routine limited duration protective reaction.* Defoliation of an entire forest, with the result that it may not sprout another green leaf for decades or even hundreds of years, was labeled a *resources control program.* The thirty-four dollars given to families of South Vietnamese civilians killed by mistake were called *condolence awards,* and bombing errors against friendly villages were termed *navigation misdirections.* Starving and homeless Vietnamese, fleeing from the horrors of war, did not seek survival in a *refugee camp* but instead discovered freshening experiences in what the Pentagon dubbed a *new life hamlet* or an *Open Arms camp.* A further strategy was the creation of a whole new set of "before" and "after" terms which bestowed tremendous dignity upon minor military objectives, but only after they had been destroyed. What before had been simply a *straw-thatched hut* became, after its bombardment, a *structure*. A sunken one-man dugout was elevated to a *vessel,* and a splintered set of logs thrown across a stream became a *bridge;* a gimcrack bomb-shelter, once destroyed, was referred to as a *bunker* or a *network of tunnels*.

Lyndon Johnson's deceptive involvement in Southeast Asia eventually led to a "credibility gap," and his becoming a one-term president. Safeguards built into most verbal interactions in a speech community reduce to a minimum the possibilities of a successful lie—and make the risk of detection, with the resulting loss of credibility as a member of the speech community, tremendous. Lying, therefore, proves to be an inefficient and hazardous strategy to play with the conventions of language.

7

Linguistic Chauvinism

In 1492 Queen Isabella of Spain was formally presented with a copy of Antonio de Nebrija's *Gramática,* the first grammar written about any modern European language. When the queen bluntly asked, "What is the book for?" the Bishop of Avila replied: "Your Majesty, language is the perfect instrument of empire."

Language and the state, as the bishop wisely said, have been companions throughout history. The ancient Greeks and Romans spread their languages as far as their armies maintained outposts, and every other colonial power has attempted to do the same thing. In our time, millions of people fell before the Aryan myth of the Third Reich—a belief in a race of superior beings that was false to its very roots. The Aryans were not a race but rather a great variety of peoples who spoke the early Indo-European (also sometimes known as Indo-Aryan) languages. Rather than being primeval Germans, they were Asiatic invaders who settled the Iranian plateau and the Indian subcontinent, from which centers their language spread westward to the Near East and Europe. And in the Union of South Africa today, language is similarly being made the servant of a political philosophy by which the Afrikaners maintain their ethnic identity in the midst of speakers of both English and native languages. The Afrikaner has symbolized his culture in the form of his own language (a variety of Dutch with African and Malayan admixtures known as Afrikaans) as the national one to be taught in the schools and to transact all government business.

A nation usually demands that its citizens express their loyalty to the state by speaking the single approved language. A government is suspicious even of dialects of its own language, because these appeal to local loyalties rather than to a single national loyalty. And as soon as a new nation is formed, it often attempts to adopt a national language that is exclusively its own. That happened after the American Revolution when several patriots urged that the new nation switch from English to Latin or even to some newly invented language. Noah Webster, however, stated in his *Dissertation on the English Language* that he was willing to settle for an American form of English: "As a nation we have a very great interest in opposing the introduction of any plan of uniformity with the British language." Finland in the nineteenth century developed its own written language out of a rarely written dialect, and Israel in the twentieth century developed Modern Hebrew out of a rarely spoken ancient language that had survived principally in written form. Both Finnish and Modern Hebrew today are standard languages capable of conveying every subtlety of modern thought and of creating literature. The Finnish author Frans Eemil Sillanpää received the Nobel Prize for Literature in 1939 and S. Y. Agnon, who wrote in Modern Hebrew, was awarded it in 1966.

The successful revival and modernization of Hebrew is today encouraging speech communities elsewhere to save their mother tongues from oblivion: the Catalans of Spain, the Provençals of southern France, the Bretons of northern France, the Frisians of the North Sea islands now ruled by Denmark, Netherlands, and West Germany, and others. The new nations of Africa and Asia very much want their own national languages. But the multiplicity of languages found within the borders of these nations—more than a thousand tribal languages are spoken throughout Africa—presents them with a severe and nearly insoluble problem. Nigeria alone includes speakers of more than two hundred native tongues, with the result that none of them could be agreed upon as the official language of government and English has been chosen instead. In fact, the only languages in Africa that afford communication across tribal barriers are the colonial ones—usually English, French, and Arabic—which is why the Chinese trade and military missions there negotiate in these rather than in Chinese or in native languages. The African nations desire to uproot the foreign tongues that symbolize past oppression and convey an alien culture, but they have not been able to agree on which native language to substitute. As of 1973, forty-one of the forty-nine African nations have designated English, French, or Arabic as one of their official languages, and seven of the remaining eight use Spanish, Portuguese, or Italian (only Ethiopia, with a long history of independence, has designated a native language, Amharic). So pervasive is the influence of the colonial languages that in the sole linguistically homogeneous state in Africa—the Somali Republic, in which 96 per cent of the population speaks Somali—the native language does not have official status, although Italian, English, and Arabic do.

To achieve a national language, the state often scorns those in its midst who speak minority languages. The ancient Greeks demeaned the foreigners whom they fought as "barbarians" because, to superior Greek ears, foreign speech sounded like a stammering *bar-bar;* Genghis Khan's Mongolian hordes received their name "Tatars" from the Chinese, who thought their outlandish speech sounded like *ta-ta;* and "Hottentot" is a coinage by the South African Dutch to indicate their low opinion of native speech. The people of the Aztec

Empire of Mexico called their language *nahuatl*, which means "pleasant-sounding," but used the word *nonotli*, "stammering," to describe other languages. And so it has probably always been since the first speech communities arose, each one considering its own tongue superior to that of its neighbors or of the people it colonizes.

The strategy of oppression of minority tongues by the state has not been successful. In fact, no nation on earth has achieved complete linguistic uniformity, nor is any likely to. A recent attempt to make Sindhi the official language in the province around Karachi, Pakistan, resulted in fatal riots by demonstrators who wanted equivalent status for Urdu. And in recent years French-speaking students in the Canadian province of Quebec protested against the use of English in their schools and employed the strategy of speaking their own tongue to induce English-speaking shopkeepers to learn French; Flemings in Belgium demanded full equality for Dutch in the Brussels area; nationalists daubed out English signs along the highways in Wales; and Jews protested the Soviet government's forced closing of Yiddish schools, theaters, and publishing houses.

Closely related to the unequal treatment of a minority language by a majority language is the unequal treatment many languages give to the two sexes. The Bible regards Eve as merely an offshoot from Adam's rib —and English follows suit by the use of many Adam's-rib words. The scientific name for both sexes of our species is the word for only one of them, *Homo*, "man" in Latin; our species is also referred to as *human* (derived from *Homo*) or *mankind*, two other words which similarly serve to make women invisible. The average person is always masculine (as in *the man in the street*) and so is the hypothetical person in riddles and in examination questions (*If a man can walk ten miles in seven minutes, how many miles can he walk in twelve minutes?*). The word *he* is often used as a common-gender pronoun, even though it is possible that a female is being referred to (as in *When the vice-president of the company came to town, he . . .*). If the antecedent is a high-prestige occupational role— such as a vice-president, manager, doctor, director, and so forth—then the pronoun is very likely to be *he*, whereas if the antecedent is a secretary, nurse, or elementary-school teacher, the pronoun is apt to be *she*. In discussions among college faculty (usually a "he" word), students who cheat are often referred to as *he* and students who do not as *she*. The English language is riddled with other examples of conceptual categories which apply to one sex or the other. Males *roar, bellow,* and *growl;* females *squeal, shriek,* and *purr.* By the way, *female* originally was a non-sexist Middle English word, *femelle,* meaning "small woman," but popular speech changed it to *female* because of its apparent resemblance to the word *male.*

Clearly, English is a sexist language that expresses stereotyped attitudes toward one sex at the expense of the other. The same thing could be said about many other languages, such as French, although in the case of that language the sexism is a bit more complicated. Numerous French words use the same form for either male or female, such as *artiste* and *touriste,* apparently exempting the language from accusations that it makes distinctions based on sex. And, in fact, in the case of a few nouns—*la sentinelle* ("the sentry") and *la personne* ("the person")—the feminine form is the normal one for both sexes. But in all other cases the French language is as sexist as English in that it designates the masculine gender as the norm and the feminine as the deviation. Feminine nouns are formed by adding *e* to the masculine (as when *l'ami,* "the male friend," becomes *l'amie,* "the female friend") or by changing the masculine ending *-eur* in some cases to the feminine *-euse* (*le chanteur,* "the male singer," *la chanteuse,* "the female singer"). And words for high-prestige roles are almost always masculine, such as *le professeur, le docteur,* and *l'auteur*—which can sometimes result in bizarre statements like *Le professeur est enceinte,* "The professor is pregnant."

Even when the sexism is not built into the grammar and usage, as it is in French and English, the speech community often regards masculine values as the norm. Words like *master* and *father* have traditionally been those of leadership and power—as in *master of my fate* and *the father of modern science*—while feminine words are used to imply unpredictability or treachery, which is one reason why the U. S. Weather Bureau has given feminine names to hurricanes. *Heir, poet, laundry worker, singer,* and *Negro* are sexually neuter words in English and therefore they should apply equally to males and females. Yet, when referring to females, these words are often qualified to *heiress, poetess, laundress, songstress,* and *Negress,* as if males represented the standard and females a deviation from it.

Successive generations unconsciously absorb sexism in language because each speech community conveys to its children both a way to construct grammatical sentences and a value system for the use of its language. A young reader who sees in a school textbook *The courageous pioneer defended his land* forms a mental image of the pioneers that eliminates females—unless, of course, they are referred to elsewhere in the book by the qualified *women pioneers.* More often, though, history books refer to pioneer women as luggage, in such statements as *The pioneers crossed the Plains with their wives, children, and personal belongings.* The child learns about the history of our species—*man* or *mankind*—from the time of *Peking man* or *Neanderthal man,* even though a large number of the fossil skulls that have been unearthed are those of females.

The teacher is likely to further contrast for the student the primitive ways of the *ape-men* with modern *man-made* accomplishments. The child learns to recite such documents as the Gettysburg Address: "Fourscore and seven years ago our *fathers* brought forth upon this continent a new nation, conceived in liberty and dedicated to the proposition that all *men* are created equal."

The prevalence of sexism in the English language has been recognized in recent years, and so the question arises: What can be done about it? Some people have suggested abandoning the offensive forms *he, she, him, her, his,* and *hers* in favor of *it* and *its* to refer indiscriminately to both sexes. But a solution of this sort would drastically revise English grammar, which makes important distinctions between the human (*he, she*) and the nonhuman (*it*), and would result in unacceptable sentences like *It is the mother of my children.* Another suggestion has been to introduce into English a new third-person pronoun that refers to human beings only, regardless of sex; among those offered have been *shis, tey,* and *vis.*

But even if such changes were accepted by speakers of English, no evidence exists that they would necessarily improve the status of women. For example, the dialects spoken in the Ozark Mountains of Missouri and elsewhere have seemingly solved the grammatical problem of sexist pronouns by overriding the rule that the pronoun must agree in number with its antecedent. It is perfectly acceptable in these dialects to utter such a nonsexist statement as *The child fell out of the tree and hurt themself* in place of the grammatical *and hurt himself* or *and hurt herself.* Similarly, Turkish lacks much of the sexual chauvinism of English. It has a personal pronoun *o* that can mean either "he" or "she" and it uses a single word for siblings, *kardes,* regardless of sex. Yet the status of women both in the Ozark Mountains and in Turkey is certainly lower than that of women in most English-speaking communities that use sexist language. The fact is that language merely reflects social behavior and is not the cause of it. The problem of woman's status in English-speaking communities will not be solved by dismantling the language—but by changing the social structure. Even if it were in our power to legislate changes in the platitudes of words, the attitudes would nevertheless remain.

Language has traditionally been thought of as unyielding; political regimes come and go, but usually the language endures with only minor modifications. Ancient Egypt, for example, was conquered by the Hyksos, the Assyrians, the Persians, the Greeks, and the Romans, but the people persisted in speaking Egyptian. Only after the Arabs not only conquered Egypt but also brought about a religious upheaval did the language finally change, in that way achieving what four thousand years of conquest had been unable to do. Even so, Coptic, a dialect of ancient Egyptian, survives today. Similarly, Navaho, Nahuatl, Maya, and other aboriginal languages of the New World are still spoken by many millions of Indians—despite nearly five centuries of suppression, forced migrations, religious conversions, and various atrocities perpetrated by Europeans to extirpate the native cultures.

Yet language does sometimes yield to changes in social structure, as is seen in the most sweeping social, political, and economic revolution of modern times. The Russian Revolution was not so much a single upheaval as a cumulative change that began in 1861 with the emancipation of the serfs and continued through several minor revolutions, the eventual toppling of the czarist regime, and numerous purges. Russians today still speak Russian, but important changes have taken place, such as in their vocabulary of kinship words. Linguists and anthropologists often appear preoccupied with kinship, but such an interest is entirely justified. Kinship presents a clear picture of relationships within a community and the way in which the community itself views these relationships; and since the terms that describe these relationships are so elemental, they usually have great tenacity in a language.

Part of a foreigner's difficulty in reading classic Russian novels lies in the complex kinship relationships they describe. A reader of S. T. Aksakov's *A Family Chronicle,* for example, encounters 43 kinship classifications. Elaborate as that may seem, it represents only a small part of the some 300 Russian kinship terms used in the middle of the last century. The average Russian probably employed about 150 of them in everyday speech, and no doubt he understood most of the others. "Relatives" had a much broader meaning to nineteenth-century Russians than it does to English-speaking peoples. A Russian village used to contain several hundred people living in households which were small domains in themselves. An elder male ruled over his uncles and aunts, brothers and unmarried sisters, sons, daughters-in-law and their relatives, unmarried daughters, nephews and nieces, grandchildren, and cousins—in addition to a varied assemblage of unrelated people who had become attached to the household, such as widows, orphans, servants, adopted children and grandchildren, and friends. All members of the household were considered relatives, even though they might not have been so in terms of blood or marriage. They ate together, shared the work—and defined their relationships to one another by the use of very precise kinship terms.

The "great family" system of Russia de-emphasized the primary bonds between husband and wife and instead emphasized the ties between a large group of real and fictitious "relatives" in a household. Russians distinguished different kinds of nephews, such as the brother's sons in contrast to the sister's sons; in-laws were differentiated depending upon whether their link to the household was through a son-in-law or a daughter-in-law; one term was used for a daughter who remained in the household after marriage and another for a daughter who went to live with her husband's family. Extramarital liaisons created an additional set of relationships: the illegitimate children as well as their mother and siblings and other relatives, all of whose names were prefixed with a modifier that meant "on the side." Since adoption was commonplace to aid the village's bereaved and to distribute economic responsibility among the households, six additional terms were used for various kinds of adopted persons. The ceremony of baptism created relationships between the godparents and the godchild's other relatives. As if all this were not enough, other kinship terms identified people that most speech communities regard as too distant to name, such as the cousins of a grandparent.

This intricate social structure was shattered by the emancipation of the serfs, wars, revolutions, and Soviet socio-economic reforms. The tightly woven fabric of village life was unraveled as the "great family" system disintegrated; large families virtually disappeared and obligations to all but the closest relatives were ignored. Today the typical family in the Soviet Union is nuclear —a married couple and their children, plus one or two old people—and official government policy supports such a structure as a virtue.

Paralleling these changes has been a sweeping change in kinship terminology, probably never before equaled in a language. Terms for adopted relatives, for kin resulting from extramarital liaisons or godparenthood, and baptism-ceremony relatives have become extinct. Even terms for close relationships by blood or marriage —such as those for the brothers and sisters of one's spouse—have dropped out of the language or are used with much less precise meanings. *Svoyak,* which used to refer specifically to a man's wife's sister's husband, now refers to any male relative by marriage. Only with the greatest difficulty can Russians today verbalize the kinship relationships of their grandparents' generation—and most of the kinship categories, once in such common use, are as unknown as if they had never existed. Nor have any new terms arisen to take their places. In Russia today, the rich fabric of social relationships and the vocabulary that once described them has been reduced to remnant threads.

When groups of people who speak different languages come into contact, any one of a number of things may happen. If their contact is only brief or occasional, they may simply dispense with speech and communicate through gestures, as in the dumb-barter of the bazaar. Or the two groups may communicate by speaking a third language which they both know—as in India, where speakers of 14 different languages and numerous dialects find a common tongue in English. A third possibility is for members of one group to learn the language of the other, but such a solution is usually accomplished only by conquest or domination. The fourth alternative, the one that I will discuss in this chapter, is for them to speak pidgin—a language that belongs to no one.

Considerable dispute exists about what a pidgin language is, for the simple reason that so many mistaken notions have been held for so long. Pidgin is not the corrupted form of a standard language—like the "broken" English spoken by an Italian tourist guide or that classic example of pseudo-pidgin, *Me Tarzan, you Jane.* Nor is it a kind of baby talk spoken by a plantation owner to his slaves, a master to his servants, or a merchant to his customers. And, finally, it is not a language that patronizingly makes concessions to the limited intelligence of "natives." A pidgin can best be described as a language which has been stripped of certain grammatical features. It is a new language that is not the mother tongue of any of its users, and it usually survives only so long as members of diverse speech communities are in contact.

A pidgin is a "simple" language, but this is to the credit of the pidgin rather than a condemnation. Pidgins have eliminated many of the finicky characteristics of language that contribute little to understanding what is said. Someone who speaks a pidgin French does not have to contend with masculine and feminine endings, and a speaker of pidgin English does not have to worry about the large number of irregular verbs. When it comes to the important features of language—such as the grammatical formation of questions and commands or the patterns of subordinated sentences—pidgin has rules for them just like any other language has. Pidgin is not simply a random collection of ways of putting together sentences, but rather a system that allows its speakers to constantly create new sentences they have never heard before.

To understand the process of pidginization, imagine that speakers of various Chinese dialects (which are not mutually intelligible) come together in a foreign place to trade or to work. Since the speakers lack a common language, they are forced to develop a new kind of language that takes its vocabulary from whatever language is dominant in their new home. If these Chinese live in a place where English is the dominant colonial language, such as Hong Kong or Singapore, they will develop what has been called Chinese Pidgin English, but which should more properly be known as English-based Chinese Pidgin. The English on which the pidgin is based is a continuing presence while the new language is developing, and it remains available as a source from which words for the pidgin can be borrowed. If the hypothetical Chinese had instead come together in the Portuguese colony of Macao, their pidgin would then be based on Portuguese, as indeed happened when the Portuguese-based Chinese Pidgin known as Makista developed. In other words, the Chinese develop a pidgin to communicate among themselves—and only afterward will the pidgin be learned by some speakers of English, who use it to communicate with the Chinese.

Most pidgins are based on European languages for the simple reason that pidgins arise as by-products of colonialism, and the European powers have been notable colonizers. (Some pidgins, though, have been based on native languages. Swahili, now spoken by perhaps twenty-five million people throughout East Africa and as far west as the Republic of Congo, arose as a pidgin language based on a dialect of Zanzibar that was spread by Arab slave traders.) A pidgin language, therefore, is a strategic response to a social situation. It arises during a time of social ferment, whether the cause be military conquest, enslavement of one people by another, or trade imperialism (the very word *pidgin* is Chinese Pidgin for the English *business*). Without such ferment, no disruptions of population would have taken place to bring people from many different speech communities into contact, and to make it necessary for them to develop a pidgin language. Once a pidgin does develop, its future depends not on its intrinsic value for communication but rather on its role in the community that speaks it. Many pidgins simply die out when the need for them disappears, but some others expand when the social situation calls on the language to perform a role greater than minimal communication. It may evolve into what is known as a "creole," with an enlarged vocabulary and grammar. And it may then become the mother tongue of a speech community or even an official language of a country, as has been the case with French Creole in Haiti, Indonesian in Indonesia, and Swahili in Kenya and Tanzania.

A strange thing about the nearly one hundred European-based pidgin and creole languages spoken around the world is their similarity in grammar—even though no opportunity existed for many of them to come into contact and even though they are based on languages as different as English, French, Dutch, Spanish, and Portuguese. The descendants of H.M.S. *Bounty* mutineers who now live on Pitcairn Island in the South Pacific speak a creole language whose structure is not much different from the creole spoken by the descendants of African slaves in the Caribbean. The theory that seems to account best for the world-wide similarity of European-based pidgins is that they all can be traced back to a single pidgin language, a Portuguese-based one which in the fifteenth and sixteenth centuries replaced Arabic and Malay as the trade language of Africa and the Far East. During these centuries, Portugal was in the forefront of contacts with non-European peoples, and it apparently spread a pidginized version of its language to its colonies around the globe.

Support for this theory comes from the fact that words in many pidgin languages are derived from Portuguese even though the pidgin language as a whole may be based on English, French, or another language. The familiar *savvy,* which is so common that it immediately indicates a pidgin language almost anywhere in the world, has been traced back to Portuguese-based Chinese Pidgin; it apparently was derived from *sabe,* the third person singular of the Portuguese verb "to know." Similarly, words from English-based Chinese Pidgin like *joss,* "god," and *mandarin,* "official," are survivals of seventeenth-century Pidgin Portuguese—derived, respectively, from Portuguese *dios,* "god," and *mandarim,* "commander." *Pickaninny* originally meant "little" in English-based Chinese Pidgin (as in *Yu kari pikanini hola?* "Do you want a little whore?"), but it has been shown to derive ultimately from the Portuguese word *pequenino,* "little."

The history of the word "creole" itself dates back to

the slave trade. After slaves had been gathered from many parts of Africa, they were imprisoned in West African camps, euphemistically called "factories," for "processing" before being shipped out to "markets." The managers of the factories took great care to separate slaves who spoke the same tribal language, thereby lessening the danger of revolt because the slaves were prevented from communicating with one another. And further separation on the basis of language was made by the purchasers in the New World. As a result, the only tongue the slaves had in common was a pidgin that originated in West Africa and developed in the colonies to which they were sent. These pidgins became entrenched, and after a generation or two they began to expand to meet the needs of the slaves' way of life. The slaves' new language became known as *créole,* a French word meaning "native" which in turn was derived from Portuguese.

Nowadays "creole" refers to any language that developed from a pidgin by expansion of vocabulary and grammar and became the mother tongue for many speakers in a community. The largest center of creole languages today is undoubtedly the Caribbean area, with more than six million speakers. Several million additional people speak creoles in West Africa, South Africa, and Southeast Asia, and probably another three million people around the world use various pidgin languages. Clearly, pidgin and creole are not rare or isolated phenomena; they number more speakers today than do such languages as Dutch, Swedish, or Greek.

When a pidgin becomes a creole it escapes the extinction that would ordinarily result if the social conditions that brought it into being disappear. As its vocabulary and grammar expand by borrowing from the base language, the creole can become a full-fledged means of communication used in newspapers, on radio stations, even in poetry and novels. Nevertheless, if the

European colonial language on which the creole was based is still widely used in their community, creole speakers usually encounter a deep-rooted prejudice. The colonial language is looked up to as the prestige one, oriented toward the white world of power and wealth, while the creole is regarded as the language of the dark-skinned masses, a reminder of their former status as slaves or exploited laborers. Whenever a creole language exists side by side with one of the European tongues in a former colony, the result is likely to be linguistic schizophrenia—technically known as "diglossia," which means "two languages" in Greek.

In such a situation, speakers of the creole often deny their mother tongue. Children who learn the European language in school usually are ashamed of the creole still spoken by their relatives and friends. They migrate to the cities to use their new language skill by finding employment in government or trade—and there they claim that they never learned creole or that they have forgotten any they once knew. They join the vociferous ranks of those who condemn creole as a mongrel tongue, who claim that it is an ugly language which hurts the ears just to hear it. Yet, deep down, most speakers never completely lose trust in their mother creole as the language of warmth and sincerity in contrast to the European tongues of duplicity. In Haiti, for example, a speaker says "I'm talking creole to you" when he means "I'm telling you the truth," and the expression "to talk French" means "to bribe."

Diglossia exists not only in areas where a creole language is spoken but also in countries that use varieties of the same language—as in some Swiss cantons where both High German and Swiss German are spoken—and in those bilingual communities that speak two or more entirely different and unrelated languages. For example, a government worker in Brussels is likely to discuss the same topics in Standard French at his office, in Standard Dutch at his club, and in a local variant of Flemish in his home. In most such cases, though, one of the two languages is accorded high prestige, the other low. In New York City, Spanish-English bilinguals of Puerto Rican descent regard English as the language of social prestige and advancement but identify Spanish with the values of friendship and intimacy. And each language performs different functions within the society, with the result that speakers must learn, as part of their speech strategies, the occasions on which the use of each language is appropriate. Who speaks what language to whom is not based on spur-of-the-moment inclinations or whims. Proper usage demands that either the high-prestige or the low-prestige language be chosen in particular speech situations.

The strategies of switching back and forth between languages have been closely studied in Paraguay, where considerably more than half of the entire population is fluent in both Spanish, the official language, and Guarani, the indigenous American Indian language; in the cities of Paraguay almost everyone is bilingual. Spanish is the language used for all formal occasions; it is spoken in schools, in government, in conversation with well-dressed strangers, and in the transaction of most business. Guarani is spoken with friends, servants, poorly dressed strangers, when telling a joke, when making love, and in most casual situations. Spanish is much more likely to be used in the cities, and Guarani is almost always spoken by the lower classes in rural areas.

These are all clear-cut speech situations in which the strategy of speaking one language instead of the other is employed, but the choice can often be much more subtle. Some parents speak Spanish to their school-age children, in that way helping them with their studies, but then switch to Guarani when the children are out of earshot. Upper-class males who are close friends usually speak to each other in Guarani, but their upper-class wives tend much more to use Spanish in similar speech situations. Males usually speak Guarani when they have a drink or two with friends, but some in whom alcohol instills a feeling of power switch to Spanish when they become drunk. Courtship among young people begins in Spanish but changes to Guarani after a few meetings. The selection of Spanish or Guarani depends on a cluster of factors: whether the conversation takes place in the city or the country, the formality or informality of the occasion, the status of the person being addressed, the degree of intimacy between the speakers, the seriousness or levity of their conversation, and so on. All of this means that throughout the day the bilingual speaker must unerringly switch from one language to the other in response to changing speech situations.

Nevertheless, it is quite clear that Spanish is still the language of high prestige, and a Guarani speaker, coming to market in the city, quickly feels his inferiority. Probably all bilingual situations equally stigmatize those who use low-prestige languages. Pima Indian children in Arizona, for example, were interviewed about their beliefs regarding the English and Pima languages. Most of them had a low opinion of their own tongue. English was thought to be the best of all languages, but two other Indian languages—Navaho and Maricopa—and even Mexican and Japanese were regarded as superior to Pima by some children. The older the child, the more he considered English the superior language, presumably because he looked upon it as a passport into the affluent world of the majority culture. Nor were the Pima children impressed by their own bilingualism; the great majority of them doubted that it was a mark of intelligence.

Whether or not it has anything to do with intelligence, a bilingual speaker has accomplished something remarkable. By switching from one language to another, he has performed several distinct operations. He selected words from a completely different vocabulary; he used the words in different kinds of grammatical structures; and he changed the sound system to give the appropriate accent for each language. The bilingual speaker is able, in some way not yet clearly understood, to set aside one entire linguistic system and to function with a second, completely different one. Then, a moment later, he is able to switch the process and reactivate the previous system while setting aside the second language. Regardless of the lack of prestige for the minority language in most speech communities, we must admire the bilingual process. And we must also be in awe of the fact that well over half of the world's population achieves the bilingual switch from one language system to another scores of times each day.

Very few white Americans are aware of the extent to which the great majority of black Americans suffer from linguistic schizophrenia—of a unique sort. The diglossia problem of the lower-class black is unusual because he does not speak a colloquial or "incorrect" form of Standard English. Instead, he speaks a dialect that has a strikingly different grammar and sound system, even though to white ears the black appears to be trying to speak Standard English. Anyone who speaks Black English is likely to find himself stigmatized as a user of an inferior kind of Standard English, whereas actually he is speaking a radically different dialect that is as consistent and elegant as whites consider their Standard English to be. (I must emphasize that my discussion of the history of Black English is both hypothetical and controversial. At least three major points of view exist: that Black English is a completely different language despite its apparent similarity to Standard English, that it is a radically different dialect, and that it is no more different from Standard English than is any other dialect. The position taken in this book is the second one because I feel that linguistic research now being carried on will ultimately prove it correct.)

The whole subject of Black English is so tied up with both racism and good intentions that it rarely is discussed calmly, even by specialists in the field. At one extreme is the racist, conscious or unconscious, who attributes black speech to some physical characteristic like thick lips or a large tongue; he is certain that it is inferior speech and that it must be eradicated. At the other extreme is the well-intentioned liberal who denies that he detects much of a departure from white speech; he regards Black English as simply a southern United States dialect, and he is likely to attribute any departure from white speech to the black's educational deprivation. Both views, I feel, are wrong. Black English's radical departure from Standard English has nothing to do with the anatomy of race or with educational deprivation. The history of the English spoken by New World blacks shows that it has been different from the very beginning, and that it is more different the farther back in time one goes. Of course, some blacks speak exactly like whites, but these cases are exceptional; the overwhelming majority speak Black English some or all of the time.

By "Black English" I do not mean the spirited vocabulary whose adoption by some whites gives them the mistaken impression that they are talking real soul to their black brothers. These rich and metaphoric words are much less important than grammar for a description of Black English. They originated by the same processes that gave rise to the slang, jargon, and argot words of Standard English, and, like the Standard words, they have seeped out to become part of the general vocabulary. Many words that were once the exclusive property of speakers of Black English—*groovy, square, jive, rap, cool, chick, dig, rip off,* and so on—are now commonly used by speakers of the white Standard. When

I say that Black English is different from Standard English, I do not refer to the superficial vocabulary which changes from year to year, but to its largely different history, sound system, and basic structure.

What we hear today as Black English is probably the result of five major influences: African languages; West African pidgin; a Plantation Creole once spoken by slaves in the southern United States as well as by blacks as far north as Canada; Standard English; and, finally, urbanization in the northern ghettos. The influence of African languages on black speech was long denied, until in 1949 Lorenzo Dow Turner published the results of his fifteen-year study of Gullah, a black dialect spoken in the coastal region around Charleston, South Carolina, and Savannah, Georgia. Gullah is important in the history of Black English because this region continued to receive slaves direct from Africa as late as 1858—and so any influence from Africa would be expected to survive there longer. Turner accumulated compelling evidence of resemblances in pronunciation, vocabulary, and grammar between Gullah and various West African languages. He listed some 4,000 Gullah words for personal names, numbers, and objects that are derived directly from African languages. Some of these words—such as *tote, chigger, yam,* and *tater* ("potato")—eventually entered Standard English.

The second influence, pidginization, is more apparent because the languages spoken today by the descendants of slaves almost everywhere in the New World— regardless of whether these languages were based on English, French, Dutch, Spanish, or Portuguese—share similarities in sound patterns and in grammar. For example, the common Black English construction *He done close the door* has no direct equivalent in Standard English, but it is similar to structures found in Portuguese Pidgin, Weskos of West Africa, French Creole of Haiti, the Shanan Creole of Surinam, and so on.

An analysis of the speech of slaves—as recorded in eighteenth-century letters, histories, and books of travel —indicates that the great majority of them in the continental United States spoke pidgin English, as much in the North as in the South. This was to be expected since blacks speaking many languages were thrown together in the West African slave factories and they had to develop some means of communication. No matter what their mother tongues were, they had been forced to learn a second language, an African Pidgin English that at least as early as 1719 had been spread around the world by the slave trade. We can be certain of that year because it marked the publication of Daniel Defoe's *Robinson Crusoe,* which contains numerous examples of this pidgin and also uses, in the character Friday, the West African and slave tradition of bestowing personal names based on the days of the week.

Therefore most slaves must have arrived in the New World speaking a pidgin that enabled them to communicate with each other and eventually also with their overseers. In the succeeding generations a small number of blacks were taught Standard English. But the great majority apparently expanded their pidgin into a creole language—called Plantation Creole by some linguists even though it was also spoken in the North —by grafting an English vocabulary onto the structures of their native languages and pidgins. This creole probably began to develop as soon as the first generation of slaves was born in the New World. Cotton Mather and other writers record its use in Massachusetts; the writings of T. C. Haliburton (creator of the humorous Yankee character Sam Slick) show that it reached as far north as Halifax, Nova Scotia; Harriet Beecher Stowe attests to its use in New York and Benjamin Franklin to its presence in Philadelphia. Emancipation did not do away with Plantation Creole. In fact, it spread its use to the offspring of the former house slaves who had been taught Standard English. That is because segregated schools and racial isolation after the Civil War caused the great number of speakers of Plantation Creole to linguistically overwhelm the small number of black speakers of Standard English. Nevertheless, the fourth step—a process known as decreolization—has been constantly at work as blacks tend to move closer in speech to the Standard English they hear all around them. The final step in the creation of the Black English heard today was the surge of blacks into northern ghettos. The ghetto experience placed the final stamp on Black English by mixing various kinds of Plantation Creole, filtering out some features and emphasizing others. Variations are apparent in the Black English spoken locally in such cities as Baltimore, New York, Detroit, Chicago, and Los Angeles, but these variations are minor in comparison to the major differences between Black English in general and Standard English.

I would need an entire volume to discuss these differences adequately, but let me at least point out a few of them. Black English does not sound like Standard English because it often uses different sounds. In the case of vowels, groups of words like *find–found–fond* and *pen–pin* are pronounced almost exactly alike. The distinctive sounds of Black English, though, result more from the pronunciation of the consonants. *Th* at the beginning of a word is often pronounced either *d,* as in *dey,* or *t,* as in *tink;* in the middle of a word or at the end, *th* often becomes *v* or *f,* with the result that *father* is pronounced *faver* and *mouth* is pronounced *mouf.* Black English dispenses with *r* to an even greater extent than the Standard speech heard along the eastern coast of North America. It not only loses the *r* after vowels and at the end of words, as do some Standard dialects which pronounce *sore* and *saw* in the same way, but in addition it dispenses with *r* between vowels, thus making *Paris* and *pass* sound alike. *L* also is almost completely lost except when it begins a word, with the result that no distinction is made between such pairs of words as *help–hep* and *toll–toe*. Final clusters of consonants are nearly always simplified by the loss of one of the consonants, usually *t* or *d* but often *s* or *z* as well, with the result that *meant–men–men, start–started,* and *give–gives* are pronounced in the same way.

Some linguists have stated that Black English grammar resulted simply from the loss of the consonant sounds that carry much of the burden of forming suffixes in Standard English. The absence of verb tenses, for example, was attributed to the loss of *d* (as when *burned* becomes *burn'*) or *l* (as when *I'll go* becomes *I go*). The statement in Black English *He workin'* was long thought to be the same as the Standard *He's working,* except that black pronunciation dropped the *s* in the contraction of the verb *is.* But it now appears that the structure of Black English is much more complicated than the mere loss of suffixes due to a failure to pronounce them.

The black speaker is apparently using a different grammar, which disregards *is* in the Standard *He's working* and instead chooses to emphasize the auxiliary verb *be. He be workin'* means that the person referred to has been working continuously for a long time; but *He workin',* without the *be,* means that the person is working now, at this very moment. A speaker of Black English would no more say *He be workin' right now* (that is, use the habitual *be* to tell about something happening only at this moment) than a speaker of Standard English would say *He is sleeping tomorrow* (that is, ignore the tense of the verb). The use and non-use of the auxiliary *be* is clearly seen in the Black English sentence *You makin' sense, but you don't be makin' sense*—which in Standard English means "You just said something smart, but you don't habitually say anything smart." The speaker of Black

English, therefore, is obliged by his language to mark certain kinds of verbs as describing either momentary action or habitual action. In contrast, the speaker of Standard English is not obliged to make this distinction—although he must make others which speakers of Black English ignore, such as the tense of the verb.

Black English also differs considerably from Standard English in the various ways in which negative statements are structured. The Black English *He ain't go* is not simply the equivalent of the Standard *He didn't go*. The speaker of Black English is not using *ain't* as a past tense, but rather to express the negative for the momentary act of going, whether it happened in the past or is happening right now. If the Black English speaker, on the other hand, wants to speak of someone who is habitually the kind of person who does not go, he would say *He ain't goin'*. *Ain't* also serves several other functions in Black English. *Dey ain't like dat* might be thought by speakers of Standard to mean "They aren't like that"—but it actually means "They didn't like that," because in this usage *ain't* is the negative of the auxiliary verb *to do*. *Ain't* can also emphasize a negation by doubling it, as in *He ain't no rich*. And in what would be a negative *if*-clause in Standard English, the rules of Black English eliminate the *if* and invert the verb—with the result that the equivalent of the Standard *He doesn't know if she can go* is the Black English *He don't know can she go*.

I have touched on merely a few of the obvious differences between the rules of Black English and the rules of Standard English in regard to verbs. Numerous other aspects of Black English verbs could be discussed—such as *I done go, I done gone, I been done gone,* and *I done been gone.* Or I could mention other constructions, such as the possessive case, in which I could demonstrate that *John book* in Black English is a different kind of possessive than *John's book* is in Standard English. But by now it should be apparent that important differences exist between the two dialects.

The wonder is that it took people so long to realize that Black English is neither a mispronunciation of Standard English nor an accumulation of random errors made in the grammar of Standard. Utterances in Black English are grammatically consistent and they are generated by rules in the same way that utterances in Standard English are generated by rules. Miss Fidditch may not regard utterances in Black English to be "good English"—but that is beside the point, because Black English is using a different set of rules than those of Standard English.

In addition to pronunciation and grammatical distinctions, Black English differs from Standard in the way language is used in the speech community. Black speakers generally place much more emphasis on effective talking than do white speakers, and they are immersed in verbal stimulation throughout the day to a considerably greater extent than middle-class whites. Playing the dozens is only one of the numerous speech events which depend upon the competitive exhibition of verbal skills in the ghetto. Rapping, jiving, rifting, louding, and toasting are other verbal ways in which the black achieves status in his community. Whereas a white is apt to feel embarrassed when he repeats himself, a black feels he has the license to repeat whatever he is saying, sometimes from the very beginning. And he expects to evoke a feedback from his audience that not only permits him to continue talking but also urges him to do so by such expressions of audience approval as *right on* or *amen*. Status within the black community is sometimes determined by one's material or spiritual attributes, but it is almost always determined by a speaker's ability to demonstrate his command over the different uses of language. Speech is, in fact, regarded as a performance in which the speaker is continually on stage. His verbal behavior is appraised by the standards of performance as being either *cool* or *lame*—and not by the white standards of tactful conversation.

The sharing of much the same vocabulary camouflages basic differences between Black and Standard English. And that is why most schoolsystems are unaware that lower-class black children enter the first grade speaking a mother dialect that is not Standard English. The exasperated white teacher, who knows little about Black English, usually concludes that the black child is unteachable because he refuses to learn to read the simple English of his mother tongue. The teacher reprimands the black child for saying *they toys* and *He work* when he clearly sees printed in his reader *their toys* and *He's working*. Actually, the black child should be commended for his quickness in translating Standard English symbols on the printed page into his own dialect, Black English.

The black child's ability to read Black English, even though he may fail in reading Standard, is supported by an incident that happened to William A. Stewart, at the time with the Center for Applied Linguistics in Washington, D.C. He was in the process of translating "The Night Before Christmas" into Black English, ignoring Black English pronunciation but otherwise using Black English grammar:

It's the night before Christmas, and all through the
  house
Ain't nobody moving, not even a mouse.
There go them stocking, hanging up on the wall.
So Santa Claus can full them up, if he pay our house
  a call.

While he was working on the translation, a ten-year-old black girl, who was regarded in her school as having a reading problem, glanced over his shoulder. With speed and accuracy, she read aloud what Stewart had written.

But when he asked her to read the same lines in the original Standard English form, she failed miserably. Clearly, the girl could read perfectly well—not Standard English, but the language of her mother dialect, Black English.

Experiences such as this one have led some linguists to advocate teaching ghetto children the rules of Standard English as if they were learning a foreign language. But Stewart would go even further. He wants black children to be taught to read Black English first, so that the words and structures they see on the printed page would correspond directly to the daily speech they hear in their community. He argues that once the child has mastered the principle of reading the tongue in which he is fluent, he will find it comparatively easy to make the transition to the Standard. To that end he has produced several readers in parallel Black and Standard versions, one of which, *Ollie,* contains such sentences as:

> Ollie big sister, she name La Verne. La Verne grown up now, and she ain't scared of nobody. But that don't mean she don't never be scared. The other day when she in the house, La Verne she start to screaming and hollering. Didn't nobody know what was the matter.

If the black child survives the trauma of school—and most black children do not, because of the problem in the early years of learning to read that strange dialect, Standard English—he will have become, in effect, bilingual in two dialects that use English words. And, like most bilinguals, he will have to employ the strategy of language-switching. But whereas someone in Paraguay has to know only when to speak either Spanish or Guarani, the black must know the two extremes of Black English and Standard English, as well as the many gradations in between. The expert dialect-switcher can quickly place his speech somewhere along the spectrum ranging from Black English to Standard English, depending upon whom he is talking to: upper-class white, lower-class white, educated black, lower-class black, recent black migrant from the South, family and close friends, and so on. It is a formidable linguistic accomplishment.

The problems faced by the bilingual black speaker are the same as those faced by American-born children of immigrant parents who enter school knowing Spanish, Italian, Greek, Yiddish, Polish, Hungarian, or other foreign languages—with one important difference. Teachers feel that the white children speak real languages, languages with their own dictionaries and literature, and therefore the teachers are likely to be patient in starting at the beginning when teaching these children English. But few teachers display the same sympathy toward the black child who speaks a language that they believe is the same as their own, the only difference being that the black child speaks it carelessly and stubbornly refuses to be grammatical. Often black teachers themselves are the worst offenders in stigmatizing Black English. They struggled for an education and put tremendous effort into learning to speak Standard English. Obviously, they view as inferior that speech which they worked so hard to unlearn in themselves.

The native languages of Africa were suppressed long ago, in the slave factories and on the plantations, but pressure against the numerous foreign languages spoken by immigrants to the United States did not begin until after the First World War. That was when many native-born Americans considered "Americanization" and "the melting-pot philosophy" to be the alchemy that would transmute the "baser" languages of immigrants into the golden American tongue. Americanization placed a special emphasis on extirpating the languages of the immigrants, for the obvious reason that language carries the culture of its speakers. Get rid of the language—and the nation has also rid itself of the alien's instrument of perception, his means of expressing foreign values, his maintenance of a culture transported from another continent. Theodore Roosevelt's statement in 1919 is typical of the Americanization position:

> We have room for but one language here and that is the English language, for we intend to see that the crucible turns our people out as Americans and not as dwellers in a polyglot boarding house.

The Americanization movement reached its height in the 1930s, but its effects continue to be felt. Every census since then has revealed that fewer Americans claim a non-English mother tongue. And even those who acknowledge their bilingualism do so with a feeling that they have traitorously maintained an alien way of life. The crime of Americanization is that it convinced those whose tongues were stigmatized that they were deserving of the stigma.

Other people, though, regard the maintenance of a diversity of languages as a source of strength for the nation. They recall that English is not an indigenous language of America, that it was merely one of the languages exported to the New World by colonial powers. Opponents of Americanization also point out that no nation in the world speaks only one language. Even France, which comes closest to the uniformity of a single national language, has German speakers in Alsace-Lorraine, Breton speakers in Brittany, Basque speakers in the Pyrenees, and Provençal speakers in the south.

The simple truth is that a culturally diversified society is a vital one and affords maximum freedom for creativity and achievement. But if a practical benefit of linguistic diversity is needed, then it can be found in the fact that non-English speakers in America provide a natural resource that both in war and in peace has met national needs. Millions of Americans were shamed into losing their foreign-language competence at the very time that the federal and local governments spent vast amounts of money to increase the teaching of foreign languages in schools.

It is as dispiriting to hear a language die as it is to stand idly by and watch the bald eagle, the whooping crane, or any other form of life disappear from the face of the earth. The supporters of linguistic diversity do not propose a return to the curse of Babel; they do not urge a world fragmented into groups that are unable to communicate. Instead, linguistic sciences can possibly achieve the best of two worlds. As the last chapter of this book will show, some linguists are searching for language universals, the common denominators of all languages, in the hope that the damage done at Babel can be repaired. And some applied linguists, who find great value in the diversity of the thousands of tongues spoken on the planet today, seek to preserve minority languages from being swamped by dominant languages. Since more than half of the world's speakers have shown that the strategy of bilingualism is workable, common sense dictates that the search for universals and the maintenance of a rich diversity of languages go hand in hand.

III

IS THE GAME RIGGED?

8

Man at the Mercy of Language

Every human being is creative both in putting together novel statements and in employing them in various speech situations. Yet no one is free to employ his innate capacity in any way he wishes. Indeed, freedom of speech does not exist anywhere, for every community on earth forbids the use of certain sounds, words, and sentences in various speech situations. In the American speech community, for example, the habitual liar faces social sanctions—and criminal punishment should he lie under oath. Speakers are not allowed to misrepresent what they are selling, to defame other people in public, to maliciously shout "Fire!" in a crowded movie theater, or to utter obscenities on the telephone. In addition, less obvious constraints upon freedom of speech may exist. They may be the structures of languages themselves—and they may restrict the speaker as rigidly as do the community's social sanctions.

Every moment of the day the world bombards the human speaker with information and experiences. It clamors for his attention, claws at his senses, intrudes into his thoughts. Only a very small portion of this total experience is language—yet the speaker must use this small portion to report on all the experiences that exist or ever existed in the totality of the world since time began. Try to think about the stars, a grasshopper, love or hate, pain, anything at all—and it must be done in terms of language. There is no other way; thinking is language spoken to oneself. Until language has made sense of experience, that experience is meaningless.

This inseparableness of everything in the world from language has intrigued modern thinkers, most notably Ludwig Wittgenstein, of Cambridge University, who was possibly this century's most influential philosopher. He stated the problem very directly: "The limits of my language mean the limits of my world." Wittgenstein offered pessimistic answers to questions about the ability of language to reveal the world. He claimed that language limited his capacity to express certain ideas and opinions; nevertheless, he did manage to say a great deal about topics he felt were inexpressible. By the time of his death in 1951, Wittgenstein had arrived at a more positive view of language. If its limits—that is, the precise point at which sense becomes non-sense—could somehow be defined, then speakers would not attempt to express the inexpressible. There-fore, said Wittgenstein, do not put too great a burden upon language. Learn its limitations and try to accom-modate yourself to them, for language offers all the reality you can ever hope to know.

For tens, and perhaps hundreds, of thousands of years, people regarded language as a holy instrument that let them look out upon the world in wonder and fear and joy. "In the beginning was the Word" is the reassuring first line of the Gospel According to St. John. Only in the last few decades have people suspected that their window on the world has a glass that gives a dis-torted view. Language no longer is certain to open up new sights to the imagination; rather, it is thought by some to obscure the vision of reality. The French philos-opher Jean-Paul Sartre, who has often written about what he calls today's "crisis of language," has stated: "Things are divorced from their names. They are there, grotesque, headstrong, gigantic, and it seems ridiculous to . . . say anything at all about them: I am in the midst of things, nameless things." Indeed, in this century many of the foundation "things" of civilization—God, truth, fact, humanity, freedom, good and evil—have become nameless and have lost their traditional reference points. An entire generation has grown up that distrusts language's ability to express a true picture of reality and that relies upon the empty intercalations of *like, you know, I mean*. The world has grown inarticulate at the very time that an unprecedented number of words flood the media. The output has burgeoned, but speakers have retreated into the worn paths of stock phrases. A statistical study of telephone speech showed that a vocabulary of only 737 words was used in 96 per cent of such conversations. Apparently people speak more, yet say less.

Exaggerated anxieties about language's ability to express reality result in the pathology of "logophobia" (literally, "fear of words"). Logophobia has found popular expression in recent decades in the movement known as General Semantics. Two books with this point of view have had a wide readership—Stuart Chase's *Tyranny of Words* and S. I. Hayakawa's *Language in Action*—and both derive their ideas largely from the writings of a Polish count. Alfred Korzybski (1879–1950) was an engineer, an officer in the Russian army, an official at the League of Nations, and a researcher into mental illness after he migrated to the United States. The key element in his theory about language was: "The map does not represent all of the territory." That is, no matter how much detail a cartographer puts into a drawing of a map, it can never represent all of the ridges, slopes, valleys, and hillocks in a territory. Korzybski similarly believed that language can no more say everything about an event than the map can show everything in a territory. *The grass is green* cannot be a true utterance because it is incomplete. What kind of grass? Where is it growing? What shade of green is meant?

Korzybski felt that speakers could nevertheless emancipate themselves from the tyranny of language by changing their orientation. They must imitate mathematics as a way to state precise relationships between things; they must avoid abstractions; they must be wary of the troublesome word *is* because it often implies an identification that does not exist in reality. Freedom from language's distortions would be achieved by rigorously rating all statements to determine whether speakers could back them up. And no longer would general words that expressed categories be acceptable. A *cow* would not be just a cow, but a particular kind of animal, with certain characteristics, named "Elsie" or "Bossie."

Almost all linguists reject Korzybski's theories on the basis of their logophobia and their inadequate solutions. Nevertheless, he did isolate a logical contradiction: Language is supposed to communicate experience, yet by its very nature it is incapable of doing so. A moment's thought reveals how ill-equipped language is to render a true account of an experience. Picture an autumn scene with a single leaf close up: its color scarlet and edged with burnished gold, the spaces between the veins eaten out by insects in a filigree pattern, the edges gracefully curled, the different textures of the upper and lower surfaces, the intense light of Indian summer falling on the leaf. And this leaf which I have scarcely begun to describe is only one out of the countless millions that surround a stroller in the autumn woods, each unique in its color and shape, the way it catches the light and flutters in the breeze.

How can language possibly render such an experience? The obvious fact is that it cannot—and few people would want it to, for such detail would bog down language in a morass of trivial observations. People do not demand that language describe an entire experience, even if it could. No one confuses speech about a leaf with a real leaf any more than people confuse a painting of a leaf with a leaf. The function of language is not to duplicate reality, but to recall it, comment upon it, and make predictions about it. A much more significant limitation upon language is that each language can comment upon experience only in its own way. Some languages of interior New Guinea, for example, are severely hampered in conveying even leaf color because they lack a convenient terminology to describe colors other than black and white.

Since human beings are born with the same senses and approximately the same degree of intelligence, they should be able to report equally well whatever they experience. But different languages make such equality difficult to achieve. Imagine two forest rangers, one a white speaker of Standard English and the other an Indian speaker of Navaho, riding together on inspection in Arizona. They notice a broken wire fence. When they return to their station, the English-speaking ranger reports *A fence is broken*. He is satisfied that he has perceived the situation well and has reported it conscientiously. The Navaho, though, would consider such a report vague and perhaps even meaningless. His report of the same experience would be much different in Navaho—simply because his language demands it of him.

First of all, a Navaho speaker must clarify whether the "fence" is animate or inanimate; after all, the "fence" might refer to the slang for a receiver of stolen goods or to a fence lizard. The verb the Navaho speaker selects from several alternatives will indicate that the fence was long, thin, and constructed of many strands, thereby presumably wire (the English-speaking ranger's report failed to mention whether the fence was wood, wire, or chain link). The Navaho language then demands that a speaker report with precision upon the act of breaking; the Indian ranger must choose between two different verbs that tell whether the fence was broken by a human act or by some nonhuman agency such as a windstorm. Finally, the verb must indicate the present status of the fence, whether it is stationary or is, perhaps, being whipped by the wind. The Navaho's report would translate something like this: "A fence (which belongs to a particular category of inanimate things, constructed of long and thin material composed of many strands) is (moved to a position, after which it is now at rest) broken (by nonhumans, in a certain way)." The Navaho's report takes about as long to utter as the English-speaking ranger's, but it makes numerous distinctions that it never occurred to the white ranger to make, simply because the English language does not oblige him to make them.

Each language encourages its speakers to tell certain things and to ignore other things. *The women bake a cake* is an acceptable English sentence. Speakers of many other languages, though, would regard it as inadequate and would demand more specific information, such as whether exactly two women or more than two women did the baking, and whether the women are nearby or distant. Some languages would force their speakers to select a word for "cake" that tells whether the cake is round or rectangular and whether or not the cake is visible to the listener at the time of speaking. Many languages are not as concerned as English that the tense of the verb tell whether the cake was baked in the past, is being baked now, or will be baked in the future—although some languages make even finer distinctions of tense than English does. Several American Indian languages of the Pacific Northwest divide the English past tense into recent past, remote past, and mythological past.

The way people talk about the color spectrum, and even perceive it, varies from one speech community to another, although all human eyes see the same colors because colors have their own reality in the physical world. Color consists of visible wavelengths which blend imperceptibly into one another. No sharp breaks in the spectrum separate one color from another, such as orange from red. But when speakers in most European communities look at a rainbow, they imagine they see six sharp bands of color: red, orange, yellow, green, blue, and purple. Chopping the continuous spectrum of the rainbow into color categories in this way is an arbitrary division made by European speech communities. People elsewhere in the world, who speak languages unrelated to European ones, have their own ways of partitioning the color spectrum. The Shona of Rhodesia and the Bassa of Liberia, for example, have fewer color categories than speakers of European languages, and they also break up the spectrum at different points, as the diagrams show:

ENGLISH

red	orange	yellow	green	blue	purple

SHONA

cipsuka	cicena	citema	cipsuka

BASSA

ziza	hui

The Shona speaker divides the spectrum into three portions, which he pronounces approximately as *cipsuka, cicena,* and *citema* (*cipsuka* appears twice because it refers to colors at both the red end and the purple end of the spectrum). Of course, the Shona speaker is able to perceive and to describe other colors —in the same way that a speaker of English knows that *light orangish yellow* is a variant of yellow—but the Shona's basic divisions represent the portions of the spectrum for which his language has convenient labels.

Charts obtainable at paint stores provide samples of hundreds of colors to help homeowners select the exact ones they want. An English speaker who glances quickly at one of these charts recognizes certain colors and can name them immediately as *yellow, green,* and so forth. Other colors require a moment of hesitation before the speaker finally decides that a particular hue falls into the category of, let us say, *green* rather than *yellow.* Still other colors demand not only considerable thought but also a hyphenated compromise, such as *greenish-yellow.* Finally, the English speaker finds himself totally unable to name many colors by any of the categories available to him; he is forced to make up his own term or to use a comparison, such as *It looks like the color of swamp water.* The case with which verbal labels can be attached to colors is known as "codability." The color that a speaker of English unhesitatingly describes as *green* has high codability for him, and it also evokes a quick response from speakers of his language, who immediately know what hues fall into that category. Similarly, when a Shona says *citema,* a high-codability color, other members of his speech community immediately know that he refers to "greenish-blue." In contrast, the color that a speaker describes as *like swamp water* has low codability, which means that other speakers cannot be certain exactly what color is intended.

Some linguists have found in color codability a fruitful way to experiment with the relationships between thought and language. In one such experiment, people who served as test subjects were shown a large selection of plastic squares, each colored differently. Usually, when someone sees a color, his mind stores it for a mere few moments and he can identify the color again only if he sees it almost immediately. If a delay occurs, the stored image is no longer a reliable guide because it has become faint and distorted. Yet when the squares were hidden from sight even for several minutes, the test subjects could pick out again certain colors—the high-codability ones for which the English language has convenient labels like *red, blue, yellow,* and so on. Subjects were able to remember the high-codability colors because they had simply attached common English-language words to them. In other words, they stored colors in their minds not as colors but as verbal labels for them. Even though the images had completely faded from their memories after a few moments, the subjects still remembered the verbal labels they had given the colors—and they were therefore able to identify the plastic squares again. The human being's ability to encode experience in this way is not limited to color. Similar experiments have been performed with other experiences, such as the recognition of facial expressions, and the results have been the same.

Experiments like these have shown that at least one aspect of human thought—memory—is strongly influenced by language. That is not the same thing, however, as proving that man is at the mercy of his language. The convenient labels that a speech community gives to certain colors are a great aid in remembering them, but the absence of such labels does not prohibit a community from talking about the low-codability colors. When people develop a need for an expanded color vocabulary—as have artists, decorators, and fashion designers—they simple invent one. Witness the recent plethora of colors for decorating the home: *riviera blue, alpine green, lime frost, birch gray,* and so forth.

Nevertheless, the colors that a speaker "sees" often depend very much upon the language he speaks, because each language offers its own high-codability color terms. Recently, two anthropologists at the University of California, Brent Berlin and Paul Kay, have attempted to show that speech communities follow an evolutionary path in the basic color terms they offer their speakers. For example, several New Guinea tribes have in their vocabularies only two basic color words, which translate roughly as "black" (or "dark") and "white" (or "light"). A greater number of languages in widely separated areas of the world possess three color terms—and the startling fact is that they usually retain words for "black" and "white" and add the same third color, "red." The languages that have four color terms retain "black," "white," and "red"— and almost always add either "green" or "yellow." Languages with five color terms add the "green" or the "yellow" that was missed at the fourth level, with the result that nearly all such languages have words for "black" (or "dark"), "white" (or "light"), "red," "green," and "yellow," and for no other colors. Languages with six terms add a word for "blue," and those with seven terms add a word for "brown."

The completely unanticipated inference of this study is that the languages of the world, regardless of their grammars, follow an evolutionary sequence, at least so far as color terms go. A language usually does not have a word that means "brown" unless it already has the six earlier color words. A language rarely has "blue" in its vocabulary unless it already has words for both "green" and "yellow." (English, and most western European languages, Russian, Japanese, and several others add four additional color terms—"gray," "pink," "orange," and "purple"—but these languages do not do so until they already offer the seven previous color terms.) Berlin and Kay believe that a language, at any given point in time, can be assigned to only one stage of basic color terms and apparently must have passed through the prior stages in the appropriate sequence. Such regularity on the part of unrelated languages in adding color terms is astonishing, and no one has as yet offered a suitable explanation for it.

Berlin and Kay have also correlated this sequence with the general complexity of the cultures in which the languages are spoken. Languages with only the two color terms "black" and "white" are spoken in cultures at a very simple level of technology—and the only languages known to have all eleven terms are spoken in cultures with a long history of complexity. Between these two extremes are the languages of such peoples as the Tiv of Africa with three terms, the Homeric Greeks and Ibo of Africa with four terms, the Bushmen of Africa and the Eskimos of North America with five, and the Mandarin Chinese as well as the Hausa and Nupe of Africa with six. Of course, it is understandable that cultures have more need to talk about different colors as they grow more complex. Small bands of New Guinea hunters need to evaluate the darkness of shadows which might conceal enemies or animal prey; complex European cultures need additional terms to talk about color-coded electrical circuits. Ever since Berlin and Kay put forth in 1969 their startling analysis of the basic color terms in ninety-eight languages, their findings have been under attack, primarily on the basis of questioned methodology and ethnocentric bias. But their general conclusions have also been defended by other researchers. Apparently Berlin and Kay have isolated some general truths about how people around the world talk about color and the possible evolutionary implications of language—even though neither they nor anyone else has been able to offer a suitable explanation for why languages seem to add words for colors to their vocabularies in such an orderly sequence.

Nor is the way in which a speech community rounds off its numbers haphazard; rather it is explainable as an interplay between language and culture. Americans and Englishmen have traditionally expressed excellence in sports by certain round numbers—the 4-minute mile, the 7-foot high jump, the 70-foot shot put, the .300 baseball batting average. Once a speech community has established a general range of goals of excellence that are within the realm of possibility, the exact number chosen has little to do with the objective reality of measurable goals. Instead, the community chooses an exact goal that makes sense to it linguistically in terms of the measures it uses and the way it rounds off numbers. That is why Americans and Englishmen never talk about the 3⅞-minute mile or the 69-foot shot put.

The American-British target for the 100-yard dash is 9 seconds, but the French speech community, which uses the metric system, expresses the target as 100 meters in 10 seconds. Simple arithmetic shows that the two goals do not refer to equal distances covered in comparable amounts of time. Allowing for 10 seconds of running time, the metric race would mean covering 109.36 yards and the American-British race would mean covering 111.1 yards. Obviously, the French goal for excellence speaks about a different real distance than the American or English—simply because a Frenchman rounds off his numbers for distances and for time in a different way than English-speaking peoples do. When speakers thus round off numbers to make them manageable, they give preference to those numbers that their speech community regards as significant. Americans see nothing wrong with rounding off numbers to 4 because they are familiar with that number for measurement, as in 4 ounces in a quarter pound or 4 quarts in a gallon. A Frenchman, however, would not regard such a number as round at all; because of his familiarity with the decimal system, he would round off to 5.

A speech community's method of rounding off its numbers often bears no relation to the real situation, and it may actually work against the best interests of the community. Fishing laws in some states specify, for example, that half a dozen trout larger than 10 inches may be caught in a day. Research by fish-management specialists might instead indicate that trout would thrive better if fishermen took 7 (not half a dozen) trout larger than 10½ (not 10) inches—but Americans round off to 6 and 10, not to 7 and 10½. The ideal speed for a stretch of highway, as scientifically determined by engineers, might be 57 miles per hour—but that number will be rounded off to a too-slow 55 or a too-fast 60 because it is customary for highway speeds to be based on the decimal system. Only one justification exists for the use of imprecise rounded numbers: The speech community has decreed that the linguistic ease of inexact combinations is preferable to the linguistic complexity of precise numbers.

That the way speakers round off numbers is often a linguistic convenience is clearly seen by comparing English with other languages. The ancient Greeks rounded off to 60 and 360 for their high numbers; and the old Germanic languages of northern Europe used 120 to mean "many." Most of the Indian tribes in primeval California based their numbers on multiples of 5 and 10. However, at least half a dozen tribes found great significance in the number 4, no doubt because it expressed the cardinal directions. Others emphasized the number 6, which probably represented the four directions plus the above-ground and below-ground worlds. The Yuki of northern California were unique in counting in multiples of 8 and in rounding off high numbers at 64.

A misunderstanding about the way Chinese speakers round off their numbers has led many Europeans to state glibly that "in China you're a year old when you're born." That is because most European systems of stating one's age are different from the Chinese. In English, a speaker usually states his age as his most recent birthday followed by the measure *years old*. Exceptions are young children who often place their age between birthdays, as in *I'm three and a half years old,* and parents who usually express the age of infants in months and weeks. Chinese also use a round number followed by the measure *swei* in place of the English measure *years old*. Confusion has resulted because *swei* is not exactly equivalent to the English measure but rather is closer in meaning to "the number of years during all or part of which one has been alive." In the case of newborn infants, they have, according to the *swei* measure, already lived for "part" of a year— and therefore their age is *yi swei*, which English translators usually render erroneously as "one year old" instead of as "part of one year."

Each language also encourages certain kinds of place names and makes difficult the formation of others. *Golden Gate* is a typical English place name, a noun (*Gate*) modified by an adjective (*Golden*)—but *Gately Gold* is an improbable construction in English and no place is likely to bear such a name. The importance of a language's structure in determining place names was pointed out by the anthropologist Franz Boas when he compared terms used by the Kwakiutl Indians and the Eskimos. The Kwakiutl are a seafaring people of British Columbia, Canada, whose survival is based almost solely on what they can wrest from the Pacific Ocean and the nearby rivers. So it is no wonder that their place names rarely celebrate history or myth but instead are descriptive in order to give practical benefits in navigation and in food-gathering, such as Island at the Foot of the Mountains, Mouth of the River, Having Wind, Place for Stopping, and so on. The Kwakiutl language makes it easy to form descriptive names because suffixes can be conveniently added to stem words. For example, a Kwakiutl speaker can discriminate among a great number of different kinds of islands—Island at the Point, Island in the Middle, and so on—simply by adding the suffixes for "at the point" and "in the middle" to the stem word for "island."

The nearby Eskimos also base their culture on the sea, and so they might be expected to name places in a similar way. But they do not—because the structure of their language makes it very difficult to do so. What are suffixes in Kwakiutl are in Eskimo the very words to which suffixes are added. Eskimos cannot create the name Island at the Point because in their language "at the point" is not a suffix but a stem word to which other words are added. To describe a place as Island at the Point, the Eskimo speaker would have to put together a circumlocution much too complicated for everyday use. Furthermore, the Eskimo language offers its speakers only a limited number of suffixes to attach to stem words, whereas Kwakiutl offers a great many. The result is that Kwakiutl possesses an extraordinarily rich and poetic catalogue of place names—such as Birch Trees at the Mouth of the River and Receptacle of the North Wind, names that make one's heart yearn to visit the places they identify—whereas the Eskimo list is considerably shorter and much less metaphorical.

Eskimos do not differ significantly from Kwakiutls in intelligence, imagination, the ability to abstract, or other mental capacities. Solely because of the structure of his language, the Eskimo fisherman is unable to talk easily about a place the Kwakiutl names Birch Trees at the Mouth of the River. If an Eskimo has no easy way to talk about a clump of birches at the mouth of a river, will he therefore be less alert to perceive that kind of a place? And is it possible that language, instead of clarifying reality, forces the Eskimo to think about the world in ways different from speakers of Kwakiutl or other languages?

Such a connection between language and thought is rooted in common-sense beliefs, but no one gave much attention to the matter before Wilhelm von Humboldt, the nineteenth-century German philologist and diplomat. He stated that the structure of a language expresses the inner life of its speakers: "Man lives with the world about him, principally, indeed exclusively, as language presents it." In this century, the case for a close relationship between language and reality was stated by Edward Sapir:

> Human beings do not live in the objective world alone, nor alone in the world of social activity as ordinarily understood, but are very much at the mercy of the particular language which has become the medium for their society. . . . The fact of the matter is that the "real world" is to a large extent built up on the language habits of the group. No two languages are ever sufficiently similar to be considered as representing the same social reality. The worlds in which different societies live are distinct worlds, not merely the same world with different labels attached.

About 1932 one of Sapir's students at Yale, Benjamin Lee Whorf, drew on Sapir's ideas and began an intensive study of the language of the Hopi Indians of Arizona. Whorf's brilliant analysis of Hopi placed common-sense beliefs about language and thought on a scientific basis—and it also seemed to support the view that man is a prisoner of his language. Whorf concluded that language "is not merely a reproducing instrument for voicing ideas but rather is itself the shaper of ideas. . . . We dissect nature along lines laid down by our native languages."

Whorf emphasized grammar—rather than vocabulary, which had previously intrigued scholars—as an indicator of the way a language can direct a speaker into certain habits of thought. The Eskimo speaker, for example, possesses a large and precise vocabulary to make exacting distinctions between the kinds and conditions of seals, such as "young spotted seal," "swimming male ribbon seal," and so on. But such an extensive vocabulary has less to do with the structure of the Eskimo language than with the fact that seals are important for the survival of its speakers. The Eskimo would find equally strange the distinctions that the English vocabulary makes about horses—*mare, stallion, pony, bay, paint, appaloosa,* and so forth. And both Eskimos and Americans would be bewildered by the seventeen terms for cattle among the Masai of Africa, the twenty terms for rice among the Ifugeo of the Philippines, or the thousands of Arabic words associated with camels.

Instead of vocabulary, Whorf concentrated on the differences in structure between Hopi and the European languages—and also on what he believed were associated differences in the ways speakers of these languages viewed the world. In his analysis of plurality, for example, he noted that English uses a plural form for both *five men* and *five days. Men* and *days* are both nouns, but they are otherwise quite different. A speaker can see with his own eyes a group of five men, but he cannot perceive five days through any of his senses. To visualize what a day looks like, the speaker of English has to conjure up some sort of abstract picture, such as a circle, and then imagine a group of five such circles. The Hopi has no such problem. He does not rely on his imagination to provide him with plurals that cannot be detected by his senses. He would never use a cyclic noun—one that refers to "days," years," or other units of time—in the same way that he would use an aggregate noun ("men"). His language is more precise, and he has a separate category altogether for cycles. For him, cycles do not have plurals but rather duration, and so the Hopi equivalent for the English *He stayed five days* is "He stayed until the sixth day."

Nor does the Hopi language possess tenses, which in most European languages stand time in a row as distinct units of past, present, and future. A speaker of English expresses an event that is happening in the present as *He runs* or *He is running,* but the speaker of Hopi can select from a much wider choice of present tenses, depending upon his knowledge, or lack of it, about the validity of the statement he is making: "I know that he is running at this very moment." "I know that he is running at this moment even though I cannot see him." "I remember that I saw him running and I presume he is still running." "I am told that he is running."

A further contrast between the two languages concerns duration and intensity. English employs such words as *long, short,* and *slow* for duration and *much, large,* and *high* for intensity. Speakers of English, accustomed to this usage, overlook the fact that these words refer to size, shape, number, or motion—that is, they are really metaphors for space. Such a situation is quite ridiculous because duration and intensity are not spatial. Yet speakers of English unconsciously use these metaphors for space in even the simplest utterances—such as *He* SLOWLY *grasped the* POINT *of the* LONG *story* or *The* LEVEL *of the assignment was* TOO HIGH *and so the student considered it a* LOT OF *nonsense.* The Hopi language is equally striking in its avoidance of metaphors of imaginary space for qualities that are non-spatial.

After his painstaking analysis of such differences between Hopi and European languages, Whorf asked the question that was central to his research. Do the Hopi and European cultures confirm the fact that their languages conceptualize reality in different ways? And his answer was that they do. Whereas European cultures are organized in terms of space and time, the Hopi culture, Whorf believed, emphasizes events. To speakers of European languages, time is a commodity that occurs between fixed points and can be measured. Time is said to be *wasted* or *saved;* an army fighting a rear-guard action tries to *buy* time; a television station *sells* time to an advertiser. People in the European tradition keep diaries, records, accounts, and histories; their economic systems emphasize wages paid for the amount of time worked, rent for the time a dwelling is occupied, interest for the time money is loaned.

Hopi culture has none of these beliefs about time, but instead thinks of it in terms of events. Plant a seed —and it will grow. The span of time the growing takes is not the important thing, but rather the way in which the event of growth follows the event of planting. The Hopi is concerned that the sequence of events in the construction of a building be in the correct order, not that it takes a certain amount of time to complete the job. That is why the building of a Hopi house, adobe brick by adobe brick, may go on for years. Whorf's comparison of Hopi and European languages and cultures—considerably more involved than the summary I have presented—convinced him that the contrasting world views of their speakers resulted from contrasts in their languages. He concluded that, linguistically speaking, no human being is born free; his mind was made up for him from the day he was born by the language of his speech community. Whorf questioned people's ability to be objective, and he threw into doubt the rationality of everyday utterances. He suggested that all their lives English speakers have been tricked by their language into thinking along certain channels —and it is small consolation to know that the Hopi has also been tricked, but in a different way.

Whorf's theories about the relationship between culture and language have been greeted enthusiastically by some scholars and attacked or treated warily by others. The weakness of the Sapir-Whorf Hypothesis, as it has come to be known, is the impossibility of generalizing about entire cultures and then attributing these generalizations to the languages spoken. The absence of clocks, calendars, and written histories obviously gave the Hopis a different view of time than that found among speakers of European languages. But such an observation is not the same thing as proving that these cultural differences were caused by the differences between Hopi and European grammars. In fact, an interest in time-reckoning is not characteristic solely of European cultures but can be found among speakers of languages as different as Egyptian, Chinese, and Maya. And, on the other hand, thousands of unrelated speech communities share with the Hopis a lack of concern about keeping track of time. To attempt to explain cultural differences and similarities as a significant result of the languages spoken is to leave numerous facts about culture unexplained. The great religions of the world—Judaism, Christianity, Hinduism, and Mohammedanism—have flourished among diverse peoples who speak languages with sharply different grammars. Mohammedanism, for example, has been accepted by speakers of languages with grammars as completely different as those of the Hamito-Semitic, Turkish, Indo-Iranian, Tibeto-Burman, and Malayo-Polynesian families. And the reverse is true as well. Cultures as diverse as the Aztec Empire of Mexico and the Ute hunting bands of the Great Basin spoke very closely related tongues.

Nevertheless, attempts have been made to prove the Sapir-Whorf Hypothesis, such as one experiment which used as test subjects bilingual Japanese women, living in San Francisco, who had married American servicemen. The women spoke English to their husbands, children, and neighbors, and in most everyday speech situations; they spoke Japanese whenever they came together to gossip, reminisce, and discuss the news from home. Each Japanese woman thus inhabited two language worlds—and according to the predictions of the hypothesis, the women should think differently in each of these worlds. The experiment consisted of two visits to each woman by a bilingual Japanese interviewer. During the first interview he chatted with them only in Japanese; during the second he carried on the same discussion and asked the same questions in English. The results were quite remarkable; they showed that the attitudes of each woman differed markedly, depending upon whether she spoke Japanese or English. Here, for example, is the way the same woman completed the same sentences at the two interviews:

"When my wishes conflict with my family's . . .
. . . it is a time of great unhappiness." (Japanese)
. . . I do what I want." (English)

"Real friends should . . .
. . . help each other." (Japanese)
. . . be very frank." (English)

Clearly, major variables in the experiment had been eliminated—since the women were interviewed twice by the same person in the same location of their homes, and they discussed the same topics—with but one exception. And that sole exception was language. The drastic differences in attitudes of the women could be accounted for only by the language world each inhabited when she spoke.

The Sapir-Whorf Hypothesis also predicts that language makes its speakers intellectually lazy. They will categorize new experiences in the well-worn channels they have been used to since birth, even though these channels might appear foolish to an outsider. The language spoken by the Western Apaches of Arizona, for example, has long had its own channels for classifying the parts of the human body, a system which ignores certain distinctions made in other languages and which makes different ones of its own. Then, about 1930, a new cultural item, the automobile, was introduced into the Apache reservation. An automobile, surely, is different from a human body, yet the Apaches simply applied their existing classification for the human body to the automobile. The chart on the next page lists approximate pronunciations of the Apache words for the parts of the human body, the way they are categorized

—and the way their meanings were extended to classify that new cultural item, the automobile.

APACHE WORDS
FOR PARTS OF THE HUMAN BODY
AND THE AUTOMOBILE

HUMAN ANATOMICAL TERMS		EXTENDED AUTO MEANINGS
EXTERNAL ANATOMY:		
daw	"chin and jaw"	"front bumper"
wos	"shoulder"	"front fender"
gun	"hand and arm"	"front wheel"
kai	"thigh and buttocks"	"rear fender"
ze	"mouth"	"gas-pipe opening"
ke	"foot"	"rear wheel"
chun	"back"	"chassis"
jnda	"eye"	"headlight"
FACE:		
chee	"nose"	"hood"
ta	"forehead"	"auto top"
ENTRAILS:		
tsaws	"vein"	"electrical wiring"
zik	"liver"	"battery"
pit	"stomach"	"gas tank"
chih	"intestine"	"radiator hose"
jih	"heart"	"distributor"
jisoleh	"lung"	"radiator"

Many linguists nowadays are wary of the Sapir-Whorf Hypothesis. Attempts to confirm the hypothesis, such as the experiment with the Japanese women or the study of Apache terms for the automobile, are usually regarded as fascinating examples rather than as universal truths about the way speech communities view the world. Neither Whorf nor any of his followers has proven to everyone's satisfaction that differences between two speech communities in their capacity to understand external reality are based entirely or even overwhelmingly on differences in their languages. Whorf overemphasized one point (that languages differ in what *can* be said in them) at the expense of a greater truth (that they differ as to what is *relatively easy* to express in them). Languages, rather than causing cultural differences between speech communities, seem instead to reflect the different cultural concerns of their speakers. The history of language is not so much the story of people misled by their languages as it is the story of a successful struggle against the limitations built into all language systems. The Western Apache system for classifying the human body did not lock them into certain habitual patterns of thought that prevented them from understanding the automobile. In fact, the existence of these patterns may have aided the Apaches in making sense out of that new cultural item.

The true value of Whorf's theories is not the one he worked so painstakingly to demonstrate—that language tyrannizes speakers by forcing them to think in certain ways. Rather, his work emphasized something of even greater importance: the close alliance between language and the total culture of the speech community. No linguist today doubts that language and culture interpenetrate one another; nor does any linguist fail to pay due respect to Whorf for emphasizing this fact.

9

How to Talk about the World

If human beings paid attention to all the sights, sounds, and smells that besiege them, their ability to codify and recall information would be swamped. Instead, they simplify the information by grouping it into broad verbal categories. For example, human eyes have the extraordinary power to discriminate some ten million colors, but the English language reduces these to no more than four thousand color words, of which only eleven basic terms are commonly used. That is why a driver stops at all traffic lights whose color he categorizes as *red,* even though the lights vary slightly from one to another in their hues of redness. Categorization allows people to respond to their environment in a way that has great survival value. If they hear a high-pitched sound, they do not enumerate the long list of possible causes of such sounds: a human cry of fear, a scream for help, a policeman's whistle, and so on. Instead they become alert because they have categorized high-pitched sounds as indicators of possible danger.

Words, therefore, are more than simply labels for specific objects; they are also parts of sets of related principles. To a very young child, the word *chair* may at first refer only to his highchair. Soon afterward, he learns that the four-legged object on which his parents sit at mealtimes is also called a *chair.* So is the thing with only three legs, referred to by his parents as a *broken chair*, and so is the upholstered piece of furniture in the living room. These objects form a category, *chair*, which is set apart from all other categories by a unique combination of features. A *chair* must possess a seat, legs, and back; it may also, but not necessarily, have arms; it must accommodate only one person. An object that possesses these features with but a single exception—it accomodates three people—does not belong to the category *chair* but rather to the category *couch*, and that category in turn is described by a set of unique features.

Furthermore, Americans think of *chairs* and *couches* as being related to each other because they both belong to a category known in English as *household furniture*. But such a relationship between the category *chair* and the category *couch* is entirely arbitrary on the part of English and some other speech communities. Nothing in the external world decrees that a language must place these two categories together. In some African speech communities, for example, the category *chair* would most likely be thought of in relation to the category *spear*, since both are emblems of a ruler's authority.

The analysis of words by their categories for the purpose of determining what they mean to speakers of a particular language—that is, what the native speaker, and not some visiting linguist, feels are the distinguishing features or components of that word—is known as "componential analysis" or "formal semantic analysis." The aim, in brief, is to determine the components or features that native speakers use to distinguish similar terms from one another so that more exact meanings can be achieved.

Anyone who visits an exotic culture quickly learns that the people are linguistically deaf to categories he considers obvious, yet they are extraordinarily perceptive in talking about things he has no easy way to describe. An English-speaking anthropologist studying the Koyas of India, for example, soon discovers that their language does not distinguish between dew, fog, and snow. When questioned about these natural phenomena, the Koyas can find a way to describe them, but normally their language attaches no significance to making such distinctions and provides no highly codable words for the purpose. On the other hand, a Koya has the linguistic resources to speak easily about seven different kinds of bamboo—resources that the visiting anthropologist utterly lacks in his own language. More important than the significance, or the lack of it, that a language places on objects and ideas is the way that language categorizes the information it does find significant. A *pig,* for example, can be categorized in several ways: a mammal with cloven hoofs and bristly hairs and adapted for digging with its snout; a mold in which metal is cast; a British sixpence coin. The Koyas categorize the pig in none of these ways; they simply place it in the category of animals that are edible. Their neighbors, Muslims, think of it in a different way by placing it in the category of defiled animals.

Everyone, whether he realizes it or not, classifies the items he finds in his environment. Most speakers of English recognize a category that they call *livestock,* which is made up of other categories known as *cattle, horses, sheep,* and *swine* of different ages and sexes. An English speaker who is knowledgeable about farm life categorizes a barnyardful of these animals in a way that establishes relationships based on distinguishing features. For example, he feels that a *cow* and a *mare,* even though they belong to different species, are somehow in a relationship to each other. And of course they are, because they both belong to the category of Female Animal under the general category of Livestock. The speaker of English unconsciously groups certain animals into various sub-categories that exclude other animals:

LIVESTOCK

	CATTLE	HORSES	SHEEP	SWINE
Female	cow	mare	ewe	sow
Intact Male	bull	stallion	ram	boar
Castrated Male	steer	gelding	wether	barrow
Immature	heifer	colt/filly	lamb	shoat/gilt
Newborn	calf	foal	yeanling	piglet

A table such as this shows that speakers of English are intuitively aware of certain contrasts. They regard a *bull* and a *steer* as different—which they are, because one belongs to a category of Intact Males and the other to a category of Castrated Males. In addition to discriminations made on the basis of livestock's sex, speakers of English also contrast mature and immature animals. A *foal* is a newborn horse and a *stallion* is a mature male horse.

The conceptual labels by which English-speaking peoples talk about barnyard animals can now be understood. The animal is defined by the point at which two distinctive features intersect: sex (male, female, or castrated) and maturity (mature, immature, or newborn). A *stallion* belongs to a category of horse that is both intact male and mature; a *filly* belongs to a category of horse that is both female and immature. Nothing in external reality dictates that barnyard animals should be talked about in this way; it is strictly a convention of English and some other languages.

In contrast, imagine that an Amazonian Indian is brought to the United States so that linguists can intensively study his language. When the Indian returns to his native forests, his friends and relatives listen in disbelief as he tells about all the fantastic things he saw. He summarizes his impressions of America in terms of the familiar categories his language has accustomed him to. He relates that at first he was bewildered by the strange animals he saw on an American farm because each animal not only looked different but also seemed to represent a unique concept to the natives of the North American tribe. But after considerable observation of the curious folkways of these peculiar people, at last he understood American barnyard animals. He figured out that some animals are good for work and that some are good for food. Using these two components—rather than the Americans' features of sex and maturity—his classification of livestock is considerably different. He categorized *stallion, mare,* and *gelding* as belonging to both the Inedible and Work (Riding) categories. The *bull* also belonged to the Inedible category but it was used for a different kind of Work as a draught animal. He further placed a large number of animals—*cow, ewe, lamb, sow,* and so on—in the category of Edible but Useless for Work. Since his method of categorizing the barnyard failed to take into account the breeding process, which depends upon the categories of sex and maturity, he no doubt found it inexplicable that some animals—*ram, colt, boar,* and so on—were raised even though they could not be eaten or used for work.

To an American, the Amazonian Indian's classification of barnyard animals appears quite foolish, yet it is no more foolish than the American's system of classification by the features of sex and maturity. Speakers of each language have the right to recognize whatever features they care to. And they have a similar right to then organize these features according to the rules of their own speech communities. No one system is better than another in making sense out of the world in terms that can be talked about; the systems are simply different. A speaker of English who defines a *stallion* as a mature, male horse is no wiser than the Amazonian who claims it is inedible and used for riding. Both the speaker of English and the speaker of the Amazonian language have brought order out of the multitudes of things in the environment—and, in the process, both have shown something about how their languages and their minds work.

All speech communities similarly recognize categories of kinship by which they give verbal labels to their relatives. And the simpler the culture, the more apt it is to emphasize kinship categories—because people in simple cultures must rely upon their kinsmen for protection and cooperation in the absence of the political and economic institutions typical of more complex societies. Americans unconsciously assume that their way of categorizing relatives is standard because it has been familiar to them since birth. But the American system no doubt furnished endless amusement to the hypothetical Amazonian visitor to the United States. He must have thought that Americans were joking, or possibly were simpleminded, when he heard them use the word *uncle* to refer both to their father's brother and to their mother's brother.

Most people think that all kinship systems are approximately the same because they deal with obvious differences between males and females, between siblings, and between generations. That may be true of most European languages, but kinship categories in other parts of the world usually are more complicated. Even the categories used by most Americans are not quite so simple as they might appear. The American system possesses, first of all, a category of basic kinship terms—*father, mother, brother, sister, son,* and *daughter*—that refers to the people usually regarded as the "closest" relatives. These labels can be used with the modifiers *-in-law* and *step-* to produce such combinations as *mother-in-law* and *stepdaughter*.

A second category consists of *grandfather, grandmother, grandson, granddaughter, uncle, aunt, nephew,* and *niece,* all of which can be used with the modifiers *grand-* or *great-*. The kin belonging to this second category are felt to be slightly more remote than those in the first category. And such a feeling is indeed true in fact: A *niece* is one degree more remote than a *daughter* in genealogical distance; *grandparents* are one generation more remote than *parents*. And the use of a modifying *great-* or *grand-* removes these kin an additional degree.

All kinsmen who are more distant are described in the English language by the basic term *cousin*. It is the only kin term that can be used with such modifiers as *first, second, third* (and, in some American dialects, *once removed, twice removed, three times removed*) to refer to the most remote relatives. No precise boundary exists in English at which people consider relatives too distant to be given labels, but in most cases the division takes place at about *second* or *third cousin*. (The Famous Relative Exception, though, allows the relationship to a distinguished person to be traced no matter how distant he or she may be. Witness the several million people in the United States who are said to be F.F.V.s—First Families of Virginia—who claim descent from Pocahontas and John Rolfe.)

In addition to these categories, English distinguishes between consanguineal kinsmen (blood relatives) and affinal kinsmen (in-laws), although this distinction is weaker than it is in many other languages. *Uncle,* for example, usually refers to a blood relative, the brother of one's father or mother, and often to the man who marries one's blood aunt. But a man who becomes an uncle because of one's marriage to his niece is usually referred to as *my wife's uncle*. No such ambiguity exists, though, in regard to the affinal relations of the basic kin: *father, mother, brother, sister, son, daughter*. If these relatives are kin by marriage, then they are all obligatory *-in-law*.

A peculiarity of the English categories for relatives is that they are permanent. Once kin, always kin; divorce, remarriage, or death does not dissolve the bond.

A man still refers to his divorced wife as *my ex-wife* and to her mother as *my former mother-in-law*. After the death of one's blood uncle, his wife is usually still called *aunt*—even though she never was a consanguineal relative, her bond of affinal relationship was dissolved at the death of the blood uncle, and she may even have remarried into another family altogether.

Clearly, the English-speaking system of naming kin is more complex than it appears at first thought. English makes three basic contrasts: sex (*brother/sister*), generation (*father/grandfather*), and genealogical distance (*uncle/nephew*). Then it makes two additional distinctions in regard to consanguinity (that is, blood relative vs. in-law) and the precise generational location of someone who becomes kin by marriage (such as *daughter-in-law* or *father-in-law*).

People who speak non-European languages usually talk about their relatives in quite different fashion. For one thing, they often place much farther out the boundary at which kinship ends. Some American Indian speakers, for example, know the precise kinship label for every person in their community, no matter how distant the relationship and whether the relationship is real or imagined. Secondly, some languages lump several American categories into a single category—as in Hawaiian, which uses the same word to refer to both "father" and "father's brother." Thirdly, many languages split a single American category into several categories, such as making a distinction between the kinds of cousins that are known as the "mother's brother's child" and the "mother's sister's child."

Speakers of Jinghpaw, a language of northern Burma, are interested in making much different distinctions about relatives than speakers of English make. The Jinghpaw language offers eighteen basic terms for kin, not one of which can be translated into an equivalent English word. For example, the Jinghpaw word *nu* refers not only to the person called *mother* in English but also to any female relative, such as a maternal aunt, who belongs to the mother's family and is in her approximate age group. *Hpu* can be one's older brother and also the older son of the father's brother; *nau* might be a younger brother, a sister, or even a child of the father's brother. English often seems preoccupied with giving labels to differences between the sexes and to generational-genealogical relationships, but Jinghpaw kinship is concerned with the social order. Jinghpaw's vocabulary emphasizes who belongs to a family unit, who has an obligation to help whom, who can marry. The Jinghpaw system seems very strange to speakers of English, but of course to the Jinghpaws it functions very well in their kind of culture. They would no doubt consider it trivial that an aged American male bothers to make a distinction between his *grandson* and his *grandnephew,* since both of them would be equally obliged to help the old man.

Categorization is related to the problem of what is generally called the "meaning" of words and sentences —a problem that has proved so troublesome that many linguists, until very recently, have chosen to ignore it altogether. One difficulty is that linguists have been unable to agree on the "meaning" of "meaning," and another is that they have been suspicious of an elusive concept that often resists analysis. Not only linguists but philosophers and logicians (like Lewis Carroll) have been plagued by the problem of meaning, as is seen in this exchange from *Through the Looking-Glass:*

"When *I* use a word," Humpty Dumpty said, in rather a scornful tone, "it means just what I choose it to mean—neither more nor less."

"The question is," said Alice, "whether you *can* make words mean so many different things."

"The question is," said Humpty Dumpty, "which is to be master—that's all."

Despite what most people believe, dictionaries do not give the "meanings" of words, nor do they define words in terms of components or features recognized by the speech community, in the way that this chapter has dealt with livestock and relatives. Rather, dictionaries present "meanings" by offering a selection of synonymous words and phrases—which are themselves listed in the dictionary. The dictionary thus is a closed system in which someone interested in the meaning of a word can go around and around and end up exactly where he started, simply because words are defined in terms of other words, and these, in turn, are defined in terms of still other words. Most dictionaries, for example, define *beauty* in terms of *pleasing quality; pleasing* is then defined in terms of *agreeable;* consult *agreeable* and it is found to "mean" *pleasing.* A person can energetically explore a dictionary and still be left with other words, not with "meanings."

The scholarly dictionaries do a somewhat better job of supplying meaning when they present the full derivational roots of a word—the tracing of its lineage, for example, back through Middle English, Old French, and Latin—for words, like human beings, are sometimes better understood when the reader knows the company they keep. That is why some dictionaries, like the *Oxford English Dictionary,* also give numerous examples of usage to breathe life into words. *Unplumbed,* standing isolated in the dictionary columns, sounds like a rather unpleasant word evocative of plumbing or of an architect's plumb. But the word comes alive in the context of Matthew Arnold's haunting line from his poem "Isolation"—"The unplumb'd, salt, estranging sea." The "meaning" of a word in the dictionary, therefore, is not the meaning at all. It serves merely as a reminder to a speaker who already knows his language, has grown up in a speech community that uses the word, and who employs the hints in the dictionary to make a guess at the meaning.

The dictionary emphasizes the trivial matters of language at the expense of what is truly important. The precise spelling of a word is relatively trivial because, no matter how the word is spelled, it nevertheless remains only an approximation of the spoken word. A *machine chose the chords* is a correctly spelled English sentence, but what is written as *ch* is spoken with the three different sounds heard in the words *sheen, catch,* and *kiss*. A further flaw in all dictionaries is that they give a distorted view of a language because they are organized alphabetically. This kind of organization emphasizes the prefixes, which come at the beginning of words, rather than the suffixes, which come at the end. Yet, in English and in many other languages, suffixes as a whole have more effect on words than do prefixes. Finally, an adequate dictionary usually takes at least a decade to prepare (the *Oxford English Dictionary* required about fifty years), and by the time it has been completed it is the dictionary of a changed language, simply because the meanings of words do not stay the same from year to year.

Most people assume that a text in one language can be accurately translated into another language, so long as the translator uses a good bilingual dictionary. But that is not so, because words that are familiar in one language may have no equivalent usage in another. The word *home,* for example, has special meaning for English speakers, particularly those who live in the British Isles. To an Englishman, a *home* is more than the physical structure in which he resides; it is his castle, no matter how humble, the place of his origins, fondly remembered, as well as his present environment of happy family relationships. *This is my home* says the Englishman, and he thereby points not only to a structure but also to a way of life. The same feeling, though, cannot be expressed even in a language whose history is as closely intertwined with English as is French. The closest a Frenchman can come is *Voilà ma maison or Voilà mon logis*—words equivalent to the English *house* but certainly not to the English *home*.

Mark Twain humorously demonstrated the problems of translation when he published the results of his experiment with French. He printed the original version of his well-known story "The Celebrated Jumping Frog of Calaveras County," followed by a Frenchman's translation of it, and then a literal translation from the French back into English. Here are a few sentences from each version:

Twain's Original Version: "Well, there was a feller here once by the name of Jim Smiley, in the winter of '49—or maybe it was the spring of '50—I don't recollect exactly, somehow though what makes me think it was one or the other is because I remember the big flume wasn't finished when he first come to the camp."

French Version: "—Il y avait une fois ici un individu connu sous le nomme de Jim Smiley: c'était dans l'hiver de 49, peut-être bien au printemps de 50, je ne me rappelle pas exactement. Ce qui me fait croire que c'était l'un ou l'autre, c'est que je me souviens que le grand bief n'était pas achevé lorsqu'il arriva au camp pour le première fois."

Literal Retranslation into English: "It there was one time here an individual known under the name of Jim Smiley; it was in the winter of '49, possibly well at the spring of '50, I no me recollect exactly. That which makes me to believe that it was one or the other, it is that I shall remember that the grand flume was no achieved when he arrives at the camp for the first time."

Such anecdotes about failures in translation do not get at the heart of the problem, because they concern only isolated words and not the resistance of an entire language system to translation. For example, all languages have obligatory categories of grammar that may be lacking in other languages. Russian—like many languages but not like English—has an obligatory category for gender which demands that a noun, and often a pronoun, specify whether it is masculine, feminine, or neuter. Another obligatory category, similarly lacking in English, makes a verb state whether or not an action has been completed. Therefore, a Russian finds it impossible to translate accurately the English sentence *I hired a worker* without having much more information. He would have to know whether the *I* who was speaking was a man or a woman, whether the action of *hired* had a completive or noncompletive aspect ("already hired" as opposed to "was in the process of hiring"), and whether the *worker* was a man or a woman.

Or imagine the difficulty of translating into English a Chinese story in which a character identified as a *piao-mei* appears. The obligatory categories to which this word belongs require that it tell whether it refers to a male or a female, whether the character is older or younger than the speaker, and whether the character belongs to the family of the speaker's father or mother. *Piaomei* therefore can be translated into English only by the unwieldy statement "a female cousin on my mother's side and younger than myself." Of course, the translator might simply establish these facts about the character the first time she appears and thereafter render the word as "cousin," but that would ignore the significance in Chinese culture of the repetition of these obligatory categories.

The Russian and Chinese examples illustrate the basic problem in any translation. No matter how skilled the translator is, he cannot rip language out of the speech community that uses it. Translation obviously is not a simple two-way street between two languages.

Rather, it is a busy intersection at which at least five thoroughfares meet—the two languages with all their eccentricities, the cultures of the two speech communities, and the speech situation in which the statement was uttered.

Many linguists who have worked with completely unrelated tongues bear testimony to just how intractable language can be. Each language represents a system of conceptual patterns that have evolved over a long period of time, and each language has developed its own categories with its own style of expressing them. Therefore, an inner resistance often makes translation impossible, even for an anthropological linguist who is not only fluent in the exotic language but also knowledgeable about the total culture.

Portions of the Bible have been translated into some two thousand languages around the world—and in every case the process of translation involved the loss of information originally in the Bible, the addition of new information, or the distortion of information. Eugene A. Nida, who has made a study of attempts to translate the Bible, states the problem directly: "The basic principles of translation mean that no translation in a receptor language can be the exact equivalent of the model in the source language." As an example of loss, see what sometimes happens to the rhetorical device often used in the Bible of repeating words for emphasis, as in "Truly, truly, I say to you." This device cannot be used in a number of languages of the Philippines. In these languages, repetition is a device of de-emphasis, so that "truly, truly" would really mean something like "perhaps."

More commonly, additions must be made to the original Bible text because of obligatory categories in the language it is being translated into. Very early in the Gospel According to St. Matthew we are told that Jesus visited Capernaum, but we are not told whether this was his first trip or whether he had visited the place previously. In many languages, though, a speaker is forced to distinguish between actions which occur for the first time and those which have occurred previously. The translator is offered no other choice, and so he must guess at information which is not given in the Gospel. Another example: Considerable ambiguity exists in the New Testament as to Jesus' status as a rabbi; his followers recognized his role as a teacher, others in Palestine were skeptical, and still others actively disputed that role. We cannot always be certain about the exact opinion of each person in the New Testament who addresses Jesus—yet some languages, such as Javanese and others in eastern Asia, oblige the translator to be certain, because these languages demand the use of different levels of speech and honorifics.

And in case after case, statements in the Bible must be distorted, occasionally beyond recognition. (The penalty for failing to distort can sometimes be severe. When the Biblical expression "heap coals of fire on one's head"—which, of course, means making a person feel very ashamed by being good to him—was literally translated into some languages of the Congo, the speakers there interpreted the statement as an excellent new method of torture.) It is impossible to translate without distortion Jesus' statement "Get thee behind me, Satan" into the Quechua language of Peru, for the simple reason that this language conceptualizes the orientation of experience differently than most other languages. A Quechua speaker thinks of the future as being "behind oneself" and the past as being "ahead of one." He very logically states that past events can be seen in the mind since they already happened, and therefore they must be in front of his eyes. But since he cannot "see" into the future, these events must therefore be out of sight or "behind" him.

Even though Quechua and English speakers orient themselves differently in regard to what is behind and what is in front, the thoughts of one language can still be expressed in the other language—if we are willing to admit a certain number of distortions, circumlocutions, and awkward grammatical constructions. But no way whatever exists to capture an unrelated language's style, as is demonstrated by a comparison between English and Yokuts, an American Indian language spoken in California. English, like other languages, occasionally makes changes in words for no apparent grammatical reason and for no advantages in improved meaning; an example is the consonant change from *invade* to *invasion*. But Yokuts is unremitting in its attention to such formalities, and it does so without bestowing any other benefit upon its speakers than the esthetic pleasure that such changes in style entail. The Yokuts language does many other things that are strange to speakers of English. It does them not to convey subtle meanings but to achieve what Yokuts speakers regard as elegant speech—and these stylistic features are completely untranslatable into English.

Yokuts style emphasizes symmetry and consistency at the expense of variety and richness of metaphor, two characteristics of English. A speaker of English has many ways of expressing *walk*, for example; he can say *stroll, saunter, tread, plod, amble, peregrinate, trudge, shuffle, step along, stamp, lurch, waddle,* and so on. English style regards variety in its verbs as a virtue, and Miss Fidditch works laboriously to extirpate repetition of the same words in a sentence. A Yokuts speaker is confused by the variety of English, and he lacks in his own verbs any equivalent way to express the delicate nuances characteristic of each of the English synonyms for *walk*. To a Yokuts, the verb stem that means "walk" is sufficient, and he will repeat it in sentence after sentence. He is also likely to deplore the reckless way in which English separates words from their literal meanings and uses them figuratively, as in *a "sharp" tongue, "foot" of the mountain,* or *a family "tree."* Yokuts is stubbornly literal; a "tree" is a woody plant that grows out of the ground, not a family lineage. The Yokuts language makes it extremely difficult for its speakers to use the vivid imagery, poetic metaphors, and word play so characteristic of English. Yokuts not only fails to cut any capers; it could not even express this cliché.

Yokuts and English clearly exist in different domains of style. To a speaker of English, Yokuts appears monotonous, drab, colorless, lacking in vitality. In contrast to English's spirited and varied structures, Yokuts sentences are brief, almost cryptic, and they progress from one thought to another with what seems like the sterility of a telegram. On his part, a Yokuts speaker would undoubtedly have a low estimation of English because it lacks the restraint and consistency that he is proud to have attained in his own language. His sentences are all consistently of about the same length, and he finds English erratic and arbitrary as it makes some sentences so short that they are abrupt and other sentences so long that they are tedious. He would undoubtedly consider the most beautiful sentences in the English language to be freaks because of their feverish piling up of subordinate clauses, their qualifiers, their tricks of using words that mean one thing to express a metaphor about something completely different. Inevitably, he must conclude that English lacks the quiet dignity, balance, and restraint of Yokuts. And no doubt he must also conclude that he could never translate English into Yokuts.

10

In Other Words

"There was speech in their dumbness, language in their very gesture," wrote Shakespeare in *The Winter's Tale*. Gestures and facial expressions do indeed communicate, as anyone can prove by turning off the sound on a television set and asking watchers to characterize the speakers from the picture alone. The evaluations made about the people on the screen need not be correct. The significant fact is that watchers are willing to state an opinion without hearing what is said—thereby acknowledging that they feel confident they have enough evidence to react to other communication channels besides audible speech. The point of such a simple home experiment is that both speakers and listeners will play the language game in the absence of spoken words, although they are usually quite unaware they are doing so. Therefore, it is reasonable to assume that people continue to pay attention to nonverbal signals even when words also are heard. Clearly, the entirety of the language game cannot be understood by examining spoken words in the absence of nonverbal strategies that emphasize or deny what is said.

The human face can be twisted and turned into tens of thousands of different expressions; the hands, torso, legs, and even the posture of the body express probably tens of thousands of additional signals. Out of this vast repertory, each speech community selects a limited number—in the same way that each spoken language is composed of only a limited number of sounds out of the vast repertory of sounds the human vocal organs are capable of making. The slump of a speaker's shoulder, the tilt of his head, or the movement of his eyes can deeply affect the message being communicated. An employee may sit in his boss's office and verbally acknowledge—in words of apparent deference and respect—that he is content with his subordinate status. But the way he holds himself in his chair while speaking, crosses his legs, flicks his eyelids, or moves his fingers may subtly deny his words and instead indicate that he has designs on his boss's job. Says Erving Goffman, the influential sociologist at the University of Pennsylvania who has specialized in observing nonverbal communication:

> Although an individual can stop talking, he cannot stop communicating through body idiom; he must say either the right thing or the wrong thing. He cannot say nothing. It should be noted that while no one in a society is likely to be in a position to employ the whole expressive idiom, or even a major part of it, nevertheless everyone will possess some knowledge of the same vocabulary of body symbols. Indeed, the understanding of a common body idiom is one reason for calling an aggregate of individuals a society.

Although a few nonverbal signals are universal, such as laughter or crying, most gestures and facial expressions belong to specific speech communities in the same way that the spoken utterances themselves do. Ray L. Birdwhistell, of the University of Pennsylvania, who has pioneered in the study of gestures as an exact science states: "We have found no gesture or body motion which has the same social meaning in all societies." Human beings everywhere rotate their heads upon their necks, blink and open wide their eyes, move their arms and hands—but the significance of these nonverbal signals varies from society to society. What speakers of English interpret as a smile in their community may denote acute embarrassment in a different community and a threat in still another. Speakers of most European languages nod the head up and down to emphasize their verbal "yes" and shake it from side to side when they are saying "no." The Eskimo gestural system also includes head-nodding and head-shaking motions like those used in European communities —but among the Eskimos the two varieties of head movement have exactly the opposite meanings.

The notion that nodding of the head is a sign of affirmation universal to humankind goes back to Charles Darwin who, in *The Expression of the Emotions in Man and Animals* (1872), ascribed it to the search by the child for the mother's breast. But actually, nodding of the head to emphasize "yes" is not very widespread in other than European speech communities— even though infants in those communities also are breast-fed. Asia alone offers a tremendous number of examples of ways in which body motions accompany the stating of an affirmation. Among the Ainu of Japan, "yes" is expressed by bringing the arms to the chest and waving them. The pygmy Negritos of interior Malaya thrust the head sharply forward, but someone from the Punjab of India throws his head sharply backward. A Ceylonese curves his chin gracefully downward in an arc to the left shoulder whereas a Bengali rocks his head rapidly from one shoulder to the other. Clearly, the construction of the human body offers people everywhere equal opportunities to use the tens of thousands of gestures and facial expressions of which they are innately capable—but the individual speech community determines exactly which motions will be used, just as the community determines the language that will be spoken.

When someone learns a language, he also unconsciously learns an accompanying gestural system. That was demonstrated by the examination one specialist in nonverbal communication made of newsreel footage showing Fiorello La Guardia, the long-time mayor of New York City. La Guardia was the son of an Italian father and a Jewish mother and he spent most of his life in New York City, with the result that he spoke Italian, Yiddish, and the New York English dialect fluently. When the newreels were viewed without the sound, anyone familiar with these three speech communities could immediately detect from La Guardia's nonverbal signals which language he was speaking. The Yiddish quip "I talked my hands off" and the Italian ethnic joke "I held his arms to shut him up" are both true statements about the use of the hands or arms among Jewish and Italian immigrants. The Jewish immigrant rarely gestures with the upper arm but rather makes choppy gestures with the hands in the immediate area of the chest and face. In contrast, the Italian sweeps broadly with the entire arm, even while making finger gestures at the same time.

Speakers of every language accompany their words with nonverbal signals that serve to mark the structure of their utterances. In some speech communities, such as Arabic, these signals are quite free, whereas in others, such as Hopi, they are extremely subtle. A speaker of English usually raises his head very slightly at the end of a question, as if looking around for a reply. His listener would be confused if the speaker asked a question but signaled a contradictory interest by lowering his chin somewhat and averting his gaze. The listener would then be entitled to assume that the person who asked the question was really not interested in knowing the answer. Imagine that a speaker of English interrupts another speaker to make a statement, which he immediately follows with a question, such as *Just a minute! I'm going home first. What are you planning to do?* The speaker's head will jut forward slightly during his interruption. Then, at the end of the statement about going home, his head will bow a trifle, in much the same way that his voice falls at the end of a sentence. Finally, the question about the listener's plans will be accompanied by a nearly imperceptible raising of the head, much as the pitch of the spoken words rises at the end of a question. Careful observation of this speaker would probably reveal that his entire body was in motion as well—the hands rising and falling slightly in company with the rise or fall of the head and the pitch of voice, the eyelids drooping at the end of phrases and opening wide at questions.

Just as people avoid bumping into one another on the street by using subtle body signals that determine who has the right of way, speakers use various turn-taking cues to avoid verbally bumping into one another. Speakers who have grown up in the American community unconsciously know its rules about taking turns in conversations—in the same way that they know the rules of grammar and the rules about appropriate speech in various situations. A listener usually does not take his turn to speak until the previous speaker has given him a turn-yielding cue. The cue could, of course, be a direct question, but it is more likely to be a drawl on the final syllable of an utterance or a change in the pitch of voice, either rising to indicate wonderment or falling to signal finality. Many cues, though, consist of subtle body motions—as when the speaker halts the hand gestures he has been using or, if he has not been gesturing, relaxes a tensed hand into a rest position on the arm of a chair or on a desk. The speaker can also signal by gesturing with the hands that he does not wish to yield his turn. For his part, the listener unconsciously pays attention to such cues and responds to them, thereby keeping a two-way conversation going.

Of course, the interaction between two speakers in a conversation usually is much more complex than this because both can employ various strategies, particularly when conversations are emotionally charged. The speaker may signal turn-yielding cues, but then immediately follow with a turn-suppressing cue. The listener, too, might employ the strategy of refusing to take his turn, even though he is being flashed turn-taking signals by the speaker. A listener often can avoid taking his turn by nodding his head or by uttering such approving sounds as *mm . . . hmm . . . yes . . . I see*. Of course, any signaling system is subject to misinterpretations which might result in a breakdown. That is why sometimes both participants in a conversation speak at the same time, although almost always the fault lies with the speaker who has not properly yielded his turn after he had signaled his intention to do so.

Most people assume that the expressive sounds of paralanguage and the silent signals of body language are primitive, animal-like traits that are gradually being replaced by speech in human evolution. But the truth is that nonverbal communication has blossomed side by side with the evolution of speech. Modern humans have elaborated both paralanguage and gestures beyond anything known in the animal world. Nonverbal communication enriches everyday life by adding another dimension to speech, and it also enriches the arts by combining with speech to create poetry, song, and drama. The independent growth of gestural systems alongside speech indicates that they can perform tasks which speech is unable to perform alone—and rather than being animal-like are very human indeed.

Nonverbal communication is a wide-ranging subject, but this chapter will limit itself to two aspects because of their importance in understanding the language game —the conscious sign languages developed by some speech communities and the unconscious, usually unnoticed, gestures that accompany speech. One of the most extensive known sign languages flourished during the nineteenth century when the North American Plains between the Mississippi River and the Rocky Mountains teemed with Indians from many different tribes. Their languages belonged to six quite different and unrelated families, and even speakers of tongues that were of the same language family often could not understand one another. All of these tribes, though, were in easy communication because of the elegant sign-language system they developed.

Many people, perhaps as Boy Scouts or Girl Scouts, have learned a few of these signs at one time or another. *Cold* was gestured by clenching both fists, then crossing the arms in front of the chest and holding them there for a moment with a trembling motion. To gesture *rain* or *snow,* the palms were held at the level of the shoulders with the suspended fingers making downward motions. Such knowledge of a smattering of signs has given people the mistaken impression that Indians could communicate only a few ideas by signs, and even these are often considered mere approximations of spoken sentences. Although the sign language of the Plains was makeshift, it nevertheless had a grammar of its own that allowed communication in great detail. The early explorers of the Plains told about Indian warriors who recounted their exploits—by the use of signs alone—at great length to members of other tribes incapable of understanding a word of the narrators' spoken language. As recently as several decades ago, a Shoshone Indian related to the anthropologist Robert Lowie his tribe's folk tale of a giant bird that snatched up and devoured people; the myth was explained in all its detail by signs, without the utterance of a single word.

Such complex discourse could be carried on by gestures because sign language, like any true language, had its own consistent modes of expression. In English the qualifying adjective precedes the noun—as when a speaker describes a coyote as a *small wolf*—but in the Plains sign language a message could be understood much more easily if the concrete word (*wolf*) were gestured first, followed by the specifier or qualifier (*small*) which commented upon it. If, on the other hand, the first sign were *small,* the receiver of the signals would be no wiser, because signs for any number of small objects or ideas might follow.

The Plains sign language lacked true nouns, verbs, or adjectives in the way that speakers of English know them, yet it contained elements which could function like those parts of speech. In the example just given, *small wolf* in sign language was somewhat equivalent to a noun and an adjective in English. Various signs that indicated action functioned like verbs, with tense being indicated by the addition of such time gestures as *now, soon,* or *long ago.* The passive tense could be signaled by reversing the motions of a gesture. The pronouns *I* and *you* were dealt with simply by pointing; if the *he* being gestured about was present, that person could also be pointed out, but sign language had no pronouns for people who were out of sight. The possessive case, as in *father's horse,* was simply enough indicated by adding the gesture for possession to the sign for *father.* The grammatical sign for a question—a slight twisting of the upraised open hand— always preceded the question so as to alert the receiver about the form the statement would take.

All known sign languages developed as a way for people who spoke different languages to communicate with each other—with the exception of the gestural system developed by some five hundred Urubu Indians who inhabit an isolated jungle in the Amazon Basin. Their sign language developed for the purpose of communication within their own speech community, not for communication with outsiders. This system apparently arose because of the proportionately large number of deaf people among the Urubu in comparison with other speech communities. During 1962–1965, Jim Kakumasu, of the Wycliffe Bible Translators, made several trips to the Urubu and estimated that about one person in every seventy-five was deaf, a condition which he guessed might be due to such diseases as scarlet fever. However, on a trip Kakumasu and I made to the Urubu in 1969, I calculated the incidence of deafness, with or without muteness, to be about twice as high. I also suggested that the high incidence must be due to genetic inheritance rather than to disease. That is because deaf people would have to be consistently present, generation after generation, for a sign language to arise and to be maintained. If the cause were disease, on the other hand, any long period of decreased rate of disease would result in the extinction of the sign system through disuse.

Whatever the explanation, one must admire a society in which everyone learns a complete system of gestural communication simply to accommodate the handicap of a small minority. An equivalent case would be if everyone in the United States learned to read and write Braille for the benefit of the small percentage of the American population that is blind. And the sign language that the Urubu have developed is not merely dumb show; it represents a complete linguistic system which can fully communicate the utterances of the spoken language. I have sat with four or five Urubu men and listened to one of them tell a story. But as soon as we were joined by a deaf person, the speaker immediately switched to the sign language, apparently without omitting a thought.

No contact could possibly have existed between the Urubu of the Amazon Basin and the Indians of the North American Plains—yet both languages share many points of resemblance. Like the Plains Indians, the Urubu point their fingers to indicate the personal pronouns *I, you, he,* and *she.* But the Urubu can also gesture about people who are not in sight because everyone is known to everyone else in their small community. They do this by signaling some distinctive feature of the person who is absent, a sign which is equivalent to a personal name in the spoken language. I saw one man being named by the sign for *mustache*—the rubbing of the index finger across the upper lip—because everyone knew that was his distinctive feature. His wife was referred to by the same gesture plus the sign for *woman*. Like the Plains Indians, the Urubu also can signal questions and indicate tenses. And they can also make an imperative statement by tensing the facial muscles and enlarging the eyes while their hands tell in gestures what they want done. An order such as *Put away the knife* in the spoken language can also be signaled by converting it into a conditional threat: *If you don't put away your knife, I will throw it into the river*.

In contrast to the many anthropologists and linguists who have studied the Plains Indians' sign language, so far only Kakumasu has been interested in the Urubu system. Yet he has already recorded a large number of gestures, and he has gone far toward understanding the grammatical rules by which signs are combined to make complex statements. But his most important discovery is that generation after generation some five hundred Urubu speakers learn from birth a system of nonverbal communication to accommodate the dozen or so deaf people in their speech community.

Early in this century, a horse named Hans amazed the people of Berlin by his extraordinary ability to perform rapid calculations in mathematics. After a problem was written on a blackboard placed in front of him, he promptly counted out the answer by tapping the low numbers with his right forefoot and multiples of ten with his left. Trickery was ruled out because Hans's owner, unlike owners of other performing animals, did not profit financially—and Hans even performed his feats whether or not the owner was present. The psychologist O. Pfungst witnessed one of these performances and became convinced that there had to be a more logical explanation than the uncanny intelligence of a horse.

Because Hans performed only in the presence of an audience that could see the blackboard and therefore knew the correct answer, Pfungst reasoned that the secret lay in observation of the audience rather than of the horse. He finally discovered that as soon as the problem was written on the blackboard, the audience bent forward very slightly in anticipation to watch Hans's forefeet. As slight as that movement was, Hans perceived it and took it as his signal to begin tapping. As his taps approached the correct number, the audience became tense with excitement and made almost imperceptible movements of the head—which signaled Hans to stop counting. The audience, simply by expecting Hans to stop when the correct number was reached, had actually told the animal when to stop. Pfungst clearly demonstrated that Hans's intelligence was nothing but a mechanical response to his audience, which unwittingly communicated the answer by its body language.

The "Clever Hans Phenomenon," as it has come to be known, raises an interesting question. If a mere horse can detect unintentional and extraordinarily subtle body signals, might they not also be detected by human beings? Professional gamblers and con men have long been known for their skill in observing the body-language cues of their victims, but only recently has it been shown scientifically that all speakers constantly detect and interpret such cues also, even though they do not realize it.

An examination of television word games several years ago revealed that contestants inadvertently gave their partners body-language signals that led to correct answers. In one such game, contestants had to elicit certain words from their partners, but they were permitted to give only brief verbal clues as to what the words might be. It turned out that sometimes the contestants also gave body signals that were much more informative than the verbal clues. In one case, a contestant was supposed to answer *sad* in response to his partner's verbal clue of *happy*—that is, the correct answer was a word opposite to the verbal clue. The partner giving the *happy* clue unconsciously used his body to indicate to his fellow contestant that an opposite word was needed. He did that by shifting his body and head very slightly to one side as he said *happy,* then to the other side in expectation of an opposite word.

Contestants on a television program are usually unsophisticated about psychology and linguistics, but trained psychological experimenters also unintentionally flash body signals which are sometimes detected by the test subjects—and which may distort the results of experiments. Hidden cameras have revealed that the sex of the experimenter, for example, can influence the responses of subjects. Even though the films showed that both male and female experimenters carried out the experiments in the same way and asked the same questions, the experimenters were very much aware of their own sex in relation to the sex of the subjects. Male experiments spent 16 per cent more time carrying out experiments with female subjects than they did with male subjects; similarly, female experimenters took 13 per cent longer to go through experiments with male subjects than they did with female subjects. The cameras also revealed that chivalry is not dead in the psychological experiment; male experimenters smiled about six times as often with female subjects as they did with male subjects.

The important question, of course, is whether or not such nonverbal communication influences the results of experiments. The answer is that it often does. Psychologists who have watched films made without the knowledge of either the experimenters or the subjects could predict almost immediately which experimenters would obtain results from their subjects that were in the direction of the experimenters' own biases. Those experimenters who seemed more dominant, personal, and relaxed during the first moments of conversation with their subjects usually obtained the results that they secretly hoped the experiments would yield. And they somehow communicated their secret hopes in a completely visual way, regardless of what they said or their paralanguage when they spoke. That was made clear when these films were shown to two groups, one of which saw the films without hearing the sound track while the other heard only the sound track without seeing the films. The group that heard only the voices could not accurately predict the experimenters' biases —but those who saw the films without hearing the words immediately sensed whether or not the experimenters were communicating their biases.

A person who signals his expectations about a certain kind of behavior is not aware that he is doing so—and usually he is indignant when told that his experiment was biased—but the subjects themselves confirm his bias by their performances. Such bias in experiments has been shown to represent self-fulfilling prophecies. In other words, the experimenters' expectations about the results of the experiment actually result in those expectations coming true. That was demonstrated when each of twelve experimenters was given five rats bred from an identical strain of laboratory animals. Half of the experimenters were told that their rats could be expected to perform brilliantly because they had been bred especially for high intelligence and quickness in running through a maze. The others were told that their rats could be expected to perform very poorly because they had been bred for low intelligence. All the experimenters were then asked to teach their rats to run a maze.

Almost as soon as the rats were put into the maze it became clear that those for which the experimenters had high expectations would prove to be the better performers. And the rats which were expected to perform badly did in fact perform very badly, even though they were bred from the identical strain as the excellent performers. Some of these poor performers did not even budge from their starting positions in the maze. The misleading prophecy about the behavior of the two groups of rats was fulfilled—simply because the two groups of experimenters unconsciously communicated their expectations to the animals. Those experimenters who anticipated high performance were friendlier to their animals than those who expected low performance; they handled their animals more, and they did so more gently. Clearly, the predictions of the experimenters were communicated to the rats in subtle and unintended ways—and the rats behaved accordingly.

Since animals such as laboratory rats and Clever Hans can detect body-language cues, it is not surprising that human beings are just as perceptive in detecting visual signals about expectations for performance. It is a psychological truth that we are likely to speak to a person whom we expect to be unpleasant in such a way that we force him to act unpleasantly. But it has only recently become apparent that poor children— often black or Spanish-speaking—perform badly in school because that is what their teachers expect of them, and because the teachers manage to convey that expectation by both verbal and nonverbal channels. True to the teachers' prediction, the black and brown children probably will do poorly—not necessarily because children from minority groups are capable only of poor performance, but because poor performance has been expected of them. The first grade may be the place where teachers anticipate poor performances by children of certain racial, economic, and cultural backgrounds—and where the teachers actually teach these children how to fail.

Evidence of the way the "Clever Hans Phenomenon" works in many schools comes from a careful series of experiments by psychologist Robert Rosenthal and his co-workers at Harvard University. They received permission from a school south of San Francisco to give a series of tests to the children in the lower grades. The teachers were blatantly lied to. They were told that the test was a newly developed tool that could predict which children would be "spurters" and achieve high performance in the coming year. Actually, the experimenters administered a new kind of IQ test that the teachers were unlikely to have seen previously. After IQ scores were obtained, the experimenters selected the names of 20 per cent of the children completely at random. Some of the selected children scored very high on the IQ test and others scored low, some were from middle-class families and others from lower-class. Then the teachers were lied to again. The experimenters said that the tests singled out this 20 per cent as the children who could be expected to make unusual intellectual gains in the coming year. The teachers were also cautioned not to discuss the test results with the pupils or their parents. Since the names of these children had been selected completely at random, any difference between them and the 80 per cent not designated as "spurters" was completely in the minds of the teachers.

All the children were given IQ tests again during that school year and once more the following year. The 20 per cent who had been called to the attention of their teachers did indeed turn in the high performances expected of them—in some cases dramatic increases of 25 points in IQ. The teachers' comments about these children also were revealing. The teachers considered them more happy, curious, and interesting than the other 80 per cent—and they predicted that they would be successes in life, a prophecy they had already started to fulfill. The experiment plainly showed that children who are expected to gain intellectually do gain and that their behavior improves as well.

The results of the experiment are clear—but the explanation for the results is not. It might be imagined that the teachers simply devoted more time to the children singled out for high expectations, but the study showed that was not so. Instead, the influence of the teachers upon these children apparently was much more subtle. What the teachers said to them, how and when it was said, the facial expressions, gestures, posture, perhaps even touch that accompanied their speech —some or all of these things must have communicated that the teachers expected improved performance from them. And when these children responded correctly, the teachers were quicker to praise them and also more lavish in their praise. Whatever the exact mechanism was, the effect upon the children who had been singled out was dramatic. They changed their ideas about themselves, their behavior, their motivation, and their learning capacities.

The lesson of the California experiment is that pupil performance does not depend so much upon a school's audio-visual equipment or new textbooks or enriching trips to museums as it does upon teachers whose body language communicates high expectations for the pupils—even if the teacher thinks she "knows" that a black, a Puerto Rican, a Mexican-American, or any other disadvantaged child is fated to do poorly in school. Apparently, remedial instruction in our schools is misdirected. It is needed more by the middle-class teachers than by the disadvantaged children.

The last three chapters have granted that at times language can be confusing, illogical, and infuriating; that it can play tricks on both speaker and listener; that though all human beings belong to the same species, they do not categorize their experience in any mutually intelligible way; that a mere flicker of the eyelids can sometimes belie the most carefully structured and grammatical utterance. In view of all this, can we regard the language game as an honest one? Yes, we can —despite the flaws. The flaws and limitations in language are a reflection of the flaws and limitations in our species, and an understanding of these will allow us to function within the boundaries of language with greater freedom and understanding than heretofore. The next group of chapters will seek to show that differences between speakers are less significant than the fact that human beings everywhere are born to speak a language that is more like other languages than it is different.

IV

BORN TO SPEAK

Man the Talker

Some twenty-five hundred years ago, Psamtik, an Egyptian pharaoh, desired to discover man's primordial tongue. He entrusted two infants to an isolated shepherd and ordered that they should never hear a word spoken in any language. When the children were returned to the pharaoh several years later, he thought he heard them utter *bekos,* which means "bread" in Phrygian, a language of Asia Minor. And so he honored Phrygian as man's "natural" language. Linguists today know that the story of the pharaoh's experiment must be apocryphal. No child is capable of speech until he has heard other human beings speak, and even two infants reared together cannot develop a language from scratch. Nor does any single "natural" language exist. A child growing up anywhere on earth will speak the tongue he hears in his speech community, regardless of the race, nationality, or language of his parents.

Every native speaker is amazingly creative in the various strategies of speech interaction, in word play and verbal dueling, in exploiting a language's total resources to create poetry and literature. Even a monosyllabic *yes*—spoken in a particular speech situation, with a certain tone of voice, and accompanied by an appropriate gesture—might constitute an original use of English. This sort of linguistic creativity is the birthright of every human being on earth, no matter what language he speaks, the kind of community he lives in, or his degree of intelligence. As Edward Sapir pointed out, when it comes to language "Plato walks with the Macedonian swineherd, Confucius with the head-hunting savage of Assam."

And at a strictly grammatical level also, native speakers are unbelievably creative in language. Not every human being can play the violin, do calculus or jump high hurdles, no matter how excellent his teachers or how arduous his training—but every person constantly creates utterances never before spoken on earth. Incredible as it may seem at first thought, the sentence you just read possibly appeared in exactly this form for the first time in the history of the English language—and the same thing might be said about the sentence you are reading now. In fact, if conventional remarks —such as greetings, farewells, stock phrases like *thank you,* proverbs, clichés, and so forth—are disregarded, in theory all of a person's speech consists of sentences never before uttered.

A moment's reflection reveals why that may be so. Every language groups its vocabulary into a number of different classes such as nouns, verbs, adjectives, and so on. If English possessed a mere 1,000 nouns (such as *trees, children, horses*) and only 1,000 verbs (*grow, die, change*), the number of possible two-word sentences therefore would be $1,000 \times 1,000$, or one million. Of course, most of these sentences will be meaningless to a speaker today—yet at one time people thought *atoms split* was a meaningless utterance. The nouns, however, might also serve as the objects of these same verbs in three-word sentences. So with the same meager repertory of 1,000 nouns and 1,000 verbs capable of taking an object, the number of possible three-word sentences increases to $1,000 \times 1,000 \times 1,000$, or one billion. These calculations, of course, are just for minimal sentences and an impoverished vocabulary. Most languages offer their speakers many times a thousand nouns and a thousand verbs, and in addition they possess other classes of words that function as adverbs, adjectives, articles, prepositions, and so on. Think, too, in terms of four-word, ten-word, even fifty-word sentences—and the number of possible grammatical combinations becomes astronomical. One linguist calculated that it would take 10,000,000,000,-000 years (two thousand times the estimated age of the earth) to utter all the possible English sentences that use exactly twenty words. Therefore, it is improbable that any twenty-word sentence a person speaks was ever spoken previously—and the same thing would hold true, of course, for sentences of greater length, and for most shorter ones as well.

For a demonstration of just why the number of sentences that can be constructed in a language is, at least in theory, infinite, show twenty-five speakers of English a cartoon and ask them to describe in a single sentence what they see. Each of the twenty-five speakers will come up with a different sentence, perhaps examples similar to these:

> I see a little boy entering a magic and practical-joke shop to buy something and not noticing that the owner, a practical joker himself, has laid a booby trap for him.

> The cartoon shows an innocent little kid, who I guess is entering a magic shop because he wants to buy something, about to be captured in a trap by the owner of the shop, who has a diabolical expression on his face.

It has been calculated that the vocabulary and the grammatical structures used in only twenty-five such sentences about this cartoon might provide the raw material for nearly twenty *billion* grammatical sentences —a number so great that about forty human life spans would be needed to speak them, even at high speed.

Obviously, no one could ever speak, read, or hear in his lifetime more than the tiniest fraction of the possible sentences in his language. That is why almost every sentence in this book—as well as in all the books ever written or to be written—is possibly expressed in its exact form for the first time.

This view of creativity in the grammatical aspects of language is a very recent one. It is part of the revolution in ideas about the structure of language that has taken place since 1957, when Noam Chomsky, of the Massachusetts Institute of Technology, published his *Syntactic Structures*. Since then Chomsky and others have put forth a theory of language that bears little resemblance to the grammar most people learned in "grammar" school. Not all linguists accept Chomsky's theories. But his position, whether it is ultimately shown to be right or wrong, represents an influential school in theoretical linguistics today, one that other schools often measure themselves against.

Chomsky believes that all human beings possess at birth an innate capacity to acquire language. Such a capacity is biologically determined—that is, it belongs to what is usually termed "human nature"—and it is passed from parents to children as part of the offspring's biological inheritance. The innate capacity endows speakers with the general shape of human language, but it is not detailed enough to dictate the precise tongue each child will speak—which accounts for why different languages are spoken in the world. Chomsky states that no one learns a language by learning all of its possible sentences, since obviously that would require countless lifetimes. For example, it is unlikely that any of the speakers who saw the cartoon of the child entering the magic store ever encountered such a bizarre situation before—yet none of the speakers had any difficulty in constructing sentences about it. Nor would a linguist who wrote down these twenty-five sentences ever have heard them previously—yet he had no difficulty understanding them. So, instead of learning billions of sentences, a person unconsciously acquires a grammar that can generate an infinite number of new sentences in his language.

Such a grammar is innately within the competence of any native speaker of a language. However, no speaker —not even Shakespeare, Dante, Plato, or the David of the Psalms—lives up to his theoretical competence. His actual performance in speaking a language is considerably different, and it consists of numerous errors, hesitations, repetitions, and so forth. Despite these very uneven performances that a child hears all around him, in only a few years—and before he even receives instruction in reading and writing in "grammar" school —he puts together for himself the theoretical rules for the language spoken in his community. Since most sentences that a child hears are not only unique but also filled with errors, how can he ever learn the grammar of his language? Chomsky's answer is that children are born with the capacity to learn only grammars that accord with the innate human blueprint. Children disregard performance errors because such errors result in sentences that could not be described by such a grammar. Strong evidence exists that native speakers of a language know intuitively whether a sentence is grammatical or not. They usually cannot specify exactly what is wrong, and very possibly they make the same mistakes in their own speech, but they know—unconsciously, not as a set of rules they learned in school— when a sentence is incorrect.

The human speaker—born with a capacity for language, infinitely creative in its use, capable of constructing novel utterances in unfamiliar speech situations— shares the globe with a variety of animals that whistle, shriek, squeak, bleat, hoot, coo, call, and howl. And so it has been assumed, ever since Aristotle first speculated about the matter, that human speech is only some superior kind of animal language. Alexander Graham Bell saw nothing odd about his attempts to teach a dog to speak by training it to growl at a steady rate while he manipulated its throat and jaws. The dog finally managed to produce a sequence of syllables which sounded somewhat like *ow ah oo gwah mah*—the closest it could come to "How are you, Grandma?" And Samuel Pepys, in his *Diary* entry for August 24, 1661, noted:

> by and by we are called to Sir W. Batten's to see the strange creature that Captain Holmes hath brought with him from Guiny; it is a great baboon [apparently not a baboon at all but rather a chimpanzee], but so much like a man in most things, that though they say there is a species of them, yet I cannot believe but that it is a monster got of a man and a she-baboon. I do believe that it already understands much English, and I am of the mind it might be taught to speak or make signs.

Other experimenters concluded that animals could not be taught human languages, but they saw no reason why they themselves should not learn to speak the way animals do. A few enthusiasts have even published dictionaries for various bird and animal languages—among them E. I. Du Pont de Nemours, the French-born founder of the American chemical firm, who in 1807 compiled dictionaries for the languages of such birds as crows and nightingales. These efforts are ludicrous because human speech is quite different from most animal communication. Between the bird's call to its mate and the human utterance *I love you* lie a few hundred million years of evolution, at least one whole day of Biblical Creation. St. Francis of Assisi, talking to the birds, may have had much to say to them, but they had nothing to discuss with him.

Human speech seemingly resembles animal calls in that it employs a small number of sounds, often no more than the number emitted by many species of birds and mammals. But, unlike animal calls, human sounds are combined to form a vast vocabulary, which in turn is structured into an infinite number of utterances. The number of different units of sound in each human language, such as the *m* in *man* or the *ou* in *house,* varies between about a dozen and a little more than five dozen. English recognizes about 45 units, Italian 27, Hawaiian 13. This range is not notably different from the separate units of sound emitted by many kinds of animals: prairie dog, 10; various species of monkeys, about 20; domestic chicken, 25; chimpanzee, 25; bottle-nosed dolphin, 28; fox, 36.

Chimpanzees, with their 25 units of sound, are incapable of speech, while Hawaiians, with only 13 units, possess a very expressive language. That is because the chimpanzee employs one unit of sound in social play, another when a juvenile is lost, a third when attacked, and so on—but two or more calls cannot be combined to generate additional messages. In contrast, the 13 sounds of Hawaiian can be combined to form 2,197 potential three-sound words, nearly five million six-sound words—and an astronomical number if the full repertory of 13 sounds is used to form longer words. In the same way, a speaker of English can select three units of sound out of his store of 45—such as the sounds represented in writing by *e, n,* and *d*—and then combine them into such meaningful words as *end, den,* and *Ned.* But the chimpanzee cannot combine the three units of sound that mean play, lost juvenile, and threat of attack to form some other message. Nor can the chimpanzee's call that means "Here is food" ever be changed to talk about the delicacies it consumed yesterday or its expectations about finding certain fruits tomorrow. Generation after generation, as far into the future as the chimpanzee survives as a species, it will use that call solely to indicate the immediate presence of food.

Certain animals—most notably parrots, mynahs, and other mimicking birds—can emit a wide repertory of sounds, and they also have an uncanny ability to combine them into longer utterances. Nevertheless, they do not exploit their abilities the way human beings do. A trained mynah bird can so unerringly repeat an English sentence that it is scarcely distinguishable on a tape recording from the same sentence spoken by a human being. Parrots also can duplicate human speech with awesome fidelity, and they have been taught vocabularies of more than a hundred words. A parrot can easily enough be trained to mimic the utterance *a pail of water* and also to mimic a variety of nouns such as *sand* and *milk*. But, for all its skill, the parrot will never substitute nouns for each other and on its own say *a pail of sand* or *a pail of milk*.

Even the most vocal animals are utterly monotonous in what they say in a given situation. The well-known nursery rhyme does not reveal what Jack said to Jill when they went up the hill to fetch a pail of water, and in fact no way exists to predict which of the tremendous number of strategies two people will select in such a speech situation. But everyone knows what a male songbird will say when another male enters its territory during the breeding season. It will emit a distinctive series of sounds that signify "Go away!" It cannot negotiate with the intruder, nor can it say "I'm sorry that I must ask you to depart now, but I will be happy to make your acquaintance after the breeding season is concluded." The male defender of the territory is simply responding to the stimulus of an intruder at a certain time of the year by uttering a general statement about the existence of such a stimulus.

Specialists in animal behavior infer the "meaning" of animal sounds from the behavior of the animals at the time they emit the sounds, but it is safe to conclude that the sounds express only indefinable emotions. Individuals belonging to the same animal species emit approximately the same sounds to convey the same emotions. All expressions of pain uttered by any individuals of a monkey species are very much the same, but in the human species the sounds that a speaker uses to communicate his pain are quite arbitrary. A speaker of English says *ouch,* but a Spaniard says *ay* and a Nootka Indian *ishkatakh.* Jill might have emitted an animal-like cry of pain as she came tumbling down the hill—but, as a speaker of English, she also had the choice of saying *I hurt my head* or *Please take me to a doctor.* Even if Jill merely uttered the conventional word, *ouch,* which signifies pain in English, this sound is nevertheless considerably different from an animal's cry of pain. An animal's cry cannot be removed from its immediate context, but Jill's *ouch* can. She could, for example, tell someone the next day about her accident by saying *When I fell down the hill, I cried "ouch."* Or she could utter *ouch* in a completely different context, as when someone makes a feeble pun and she wishes to convey that her sensibilities, not her bones, have been wounded.

An animal, though, has no such choices. As Bertrand Russell remarked about a dog's ability to communicate, "No matter how eloquently a dog may bark, he cannot tell you that his parents were poor but honest." Despite the variety of sounds in the babel of the animal world, nonhuman calls are emotional responses to a very limited number of immediate stimuli. Every other kind of sound made by living things on the planet belongs to human speech alone.

The search for the genesis of speech in the lower animals has not uncovered a single species that can communicate with all the same features found in human speech. The most promising candidates in whom to search for the roots of human language would appear to be our closest relatives, the apes and monkeys. Many species possess extensive repertories of calls concerned with emotional states, with interpersonal relationships inside the troop or with animals outside of it. The chimpanzee, in particular, has important attributes for learning: intelligence, sociability, and a strong attachment to human beings. The potential for language in chimpanzees seems so great that several attempts have been made to teach them to speak. All such experiments failed, even when the chimpanzees were reared in households on an equal basis with human children. The most successful of these attempts, which involved six years of painstaking attention by a psychologist and his family, resulted in a chimpanzee's learning to speak merely approximations of four English words.

It is now known to be fruitless to teach chimpanzees a spoken language because their vocal apparatus is considerably different from that of human beings. But about 1966 two psychologists at the University of Nevada, Allen and Beatrice Gardner, had the novel idea that chimpanzees might possess a capacity for language even though they lack an apparatus to speak it, a situation similar to that of deaf-mute human children. They decided to attempt to separate the chimpanzee's possible capacity for language from its proven inability to utter the sounds of the language. Since use of the hands is a prominent feature of chimpanzee behavior, the Gardners employed visual rather than vocal signals by teaching a chimpanzee the American Sign Language system that is used with deaf children in North America. The Gardners theorized that their infant female chimpanzee, Washoe, should see as much sign language as possible, since they knew that merely exposing a human child to speech triggered its language-learning capacity. They took great care to keep her isolated from all other chimpanzees and from most human beings as well. The Gardners always communicated with each other in sign language whenever Washoe was present, and they demanded that anyone in contact with her remain silent and use hand signals.

Their efforts were rewarded almost immediately. Washoe began to repeat the gestures she was taught and also those she noticed the Gardners using between themselves. She built up a vocabulary of thirty-four words in less than two years. Much more important, when she learned a new word she enlarged its application from the specific thing it labeled to an entire class of similar objects. For example, she first learned the sign for *hurt* in reference to scratches and bruises, but later she used the same sign to indicate stains, a decal on the back of a person's hand, and a human navel. And she was able to communicate about things that were not present, as when she heard a distant bark and immediately made the sign for *dog*.

Her proficiency soon went beyond the mere naming of things. She learned verbs and pronouns, and she invented combinations of signs which she used correctly in appropriate speech situations. She combined the signs for *open, food,* and *drink* when she wanted something from the refrigerator and the signs for *go* and *sweet* when she wanted to be taken to a raspberry bush. Before she had reached the age of six, she had a vocabulary of 150 signs which she could combine to describe situations entirely new to her. At this writing in early 1974, Washoe is living at the University of Oklahoma with a colony of chimpanzees who are also being trained in sign language. As yet, no sign-language communication has taken place between them. Whether or not Washoe will transmit the signs she has learned to her progeny will not be known until at least 1975, when she becomes old enough to reproduce. She has, however, already demonstrated that she can spontaneously communicate with human children who know sign language—even though her status still remains that of an ape. One poignant illustration of that occurred when a mute girl and her parents came to visit the Gardners. Washoe spotted the child and eagerly rushed across the yard to play with her, excitedly giving the sign for *child*. But the child, seeing a chimpanzee come bounding toward her, responded by tickling her ribs— the sign for *ape*.

Washoe has successfully bridged the barrier between human and nonhuman communication, although she required human help to do so. She progressed from uttering a small number of automatic cries, which referred only to immediate emotions or situations, to learning a language system in which elements could be combined to make further statements. Beyond any doubt, she has learned more of a language, although in visual terms, than any other nonhuman before her. Nevertheless, Washoe's achievement falls far short of the human child's. The fact that a human child at an equivalent stage of development has a vocabulary of thousands of words instead of only 150 is the least significant difference. More important, Washoe apparently does not understand the principles of grammar, as human children do by age three when they construct sentences according to the patterns offered by their languages. An English-speaking child, for example, knows the difference between the subject-predicate-object pattern of *Baby going home* and the question pattern of *Is baby going home?*—but Washoe does not. When Washoe wants to be tickled, she signals any one of several combinations that have no reference at all to sentence structure: *you tickle, tickle you,* or *me tickle*.

The major deficiency in Washoe's accomplishment, though, concerns the relationship of language to human thought. Human beings conceive of their environment as interlocked objects, properties, and actions. A chair is not simply a kind of object, but rather it belongs to a particular category of inanimate objects. That is why *chair* can take a verb that refers to inanimate things, *break,* but not a verb that refers to animate ones such as *drink.* A child who unravels a simple statement like *The chair broke* thus must do more than decode a grammatical utterance. He must first master the subtle category of things that *break,* like *chairs* and also *machines* and *windowpanes.* Then he must distinguish the category of things that *break* from things that *tear,* like *paper* and *bedsheets,* or things that *smash,* like *vases* and *cars.* The child must next interpret the influence on the chair of the verb *broke* out of all the possibilities that verb implies, such as that the breaking of a chair is conceptually different from breaking the bank at Monte Carlo or from waves breaking on a beach. To achieve all this, the child unconsciously unravels the sentence into parts that can be analyzed, and then puts the elements together again in a meaningful fashion. Nothing in Washoe's behavior indicates that she uses language in this metaphorical way, which is, after all, the very hallmark of the human mind.

About the time that the Gardners began their experiments with Washoe, David Premack, a psychologist at the University of California, started to teach a chimpanzee named Sarah to read and write by means of a code of variously shaped and colored pieces of plastic, each of which represented a "word." Within six years she had mastered a vocabulary of more than 130 different pieces of plastic; amazingly, she seemed able to understand the grammatical relationships between words which Washoe did not understand. She often makes correct choices between questions, between the concepts of "same" and "different," between the ideas of color and size. She has even shown that she can understand the complex grammatical structure of a compound sentence. When her trainers arranged plastic pieces to mean *Sarah, put the apple in the pail and the banana in the dish,* she responded by the appropriate actions. To do so, she needed to understand that *apple* and *pail* belonged together, but not *apple* and *dish.*

Moreover, she had to know the grammatical function of *put,* that it referred to both the *apple* and the *banana*—and she had to interpret the sentence to mean that she was the one who was supposed to do all these things.

Despite Sarah's remarkable responses, serious doubts exist about her achievement. Since she performs correctly only about 75 to 80 per cent of the time, the question arises whether or not she has truly internalized the rules of her language. She appears to handle language in somewhat the same way that trained pigeons are able to "play" Ping-Pong. The pigeons, of course, are not truly playing the game of Ping-Pong. They do not unconsciously know the rules of the game even though they go through the motions of it; they lack the desire to win, the satisfaction of a successful play, individual styles, the selection of one strategy in place of another at various stages of the game. Evidence for a lack of internalization is Sarah's failure to generate sentences on her own; she merely accepts those offered by her trainers. A further question that must be raised is whether or not the "Clever Hans Phenomenon" is operative with Sarah. Since she performs better with some experimenters than with others, it is possible that she is detecting nonverbal cues.

Both Sarah and Washoe had to be taught language by human beings, but the honeybee has on its own evolved a communication system that possesses most of the features of human language—although it does so in a trivial way. When a foraging honeybee locates a source of pollen or nectar, she brings a sample of her find to the hive and thereby informs the other workers about the kind of flowers to look for. She also tells them the exact distance to the source by the tempo of a dance she performs in the form of a figure eight. And the exact direction in which to fly (after, unbelievably, the dancer compensates for wind direction) is indicated by the angle of the dance path. The dance thus conveys two kinds of information: the distance from the hive to the food source and the direction based on the angle of the sun. The other workers use this information to fly unerringly to a source that is sometimes as far away as eight miles.

Strictly speaking, the bee dance meets most of the criteria for a language. It uses arbitrary symbols (the various movements of the dance); it combines them in apparently infinite ways to communicate about something remote in space and time (the food source which the forager recently discovered but can no longer see); and it constantly communicates about situations which the bees have never before experienced (each food source is a unique occurrence at a particular time and place). The bee dance, though, is severely limited as to what it can communicate. It always contains two, and exactly two, components: distance and direction. Some English sentences also contain only two components—such as *Birds fly*—but speakers of English are not forced to construct all their sentences out of a single noun and a single verb. If the other bees in the hive refuse to respond to the communication by the forager, she cannot express the message in any other way. She cannot ask the question *Why don't you fly to the food?* Nor can she issue the imperative *Fly out and forage!* She can only repeat her dance over and over again.

The topics that bees can communicate about—pollen and new locations for hives—are undoubtedly of endless fascination to them but of limited interest to almost all other living things. Bees cannot use their language to explain English grammar, but human beings can talk about the way bees communicate. Human language is unique in that it can be used as what linguists call a "metalanguage": It can state the rules of any communication system, including its own. In other words, only human language can talk about language. A speaker can discuss the dance of the bees or anything else that he cares to, even when it is foolish or a lie. Because human beings alone possess language, they can hurdle the barriers of time and space, have a history, speculate about the future, and create in myths beings that never existed.

The study of animal communication reveals that human language is not simply a more complex example of a capacity that exists elsewhere in the living world. One animal or another may share a few features with human language, but it is clear that language is based on different principles altogether. So far as is known, people can speak because of their particular kind of vocal apparatus and their specific type of mental organization, not simply because of their higher degree of intelligence. No prototype for language has been found in the apes and monkeys, and no parrot or mynah bird has ever recombined the words it learned into novel utterances. In contrast, every human community in the world possesses a complete language system. Obviously, something happened in evolution to create Man the Talker. But what was it?

Since sentences do not leave anything equivalent to the fossils and pottery shards that allow anthropologists to trace the prehistory of human beings, linguists can only speculate about the origins of language. Theories have been advanced, have won adherents for a while, then later were shown to be fanciful—and given derisive baby-talk names. Because some of these theories occasionally reappear today in new guises, let me mention several of them as a guide to the wary.

The Bow-Wow Theory states that language arose when humans imitated the sounds of nature by the use of onomatopoeic words like *cock-a-doodle-doo, cuckoo, sneeze, splash,* and *mumble.* This theory has been thoroughly discredited. It is now known that many onomatopoeic words are of recent, not ancient, origin and that some of them were not derived from natural sounds at all. But the most telling argument against the Bow-Wow Theory is that onomatopoeic words vary from language to language. If the human species had truly based its words on the sounds of nature, these words should be the same in all languages because of the obvious fact that a dog's bark is the same throughout the world. Yet the *bow-wow* heard by speakers of English sounds like *gua-gua* to Spaniards, *af-af* to Russians, and *wan-wan* to Japanese.

The Ding-Dong Theory dates back to Pythagoras and Plato and was long honored, but nowadays it has no support whatsoever. This theory claims a relationship between a word and its sense because everything in nature is supposed to give off a harmonic "ring," which humans supposedly detected when they named objects. But the Ding-Dong Theory cannot explain what resonance a small four-footed animal gave off to make Englishmen call it a *dog* rather than any other arbitrary collection of vowels and consonants—and what different resonance it communicated to Frenchmen to make them call it a *chien* or to Japanese to make them call it an *inu*.

Still other explanations for the origin of language are the Pooh-Pooh Theory, which holds that speech originated with spontaneous ejaculations of derision, fear, and other emotions; the Yo-Heave-Ho Theory, which claims that language evolved from the grunts and groans evoked by heavy physical labor; the Sing-Song Theory, which placed the origin of speech in the love songs and the rhythmic chants of early humans; and the Ha-Ha Theory, which states that language evolved out of laughter. All these speculations have serious flaws, and none can withstand the close scrutiny of present knowledge about the structure of language and about the evolution of our species.

Lately, some anthropologists and linguists have speculated that language originated as a much more recent event than previously believed. Their evidence is largely circumstantial, but it is intriguing. It is based upon the slowness with which human culture evolved over millions of years until its sudden acceleration during the last Ice Age, between about 80,000 and 35,000 years ago. The forerunners of our species arose some five million years ago. Not until about three million years ago did they begin to make crude stone tools—and they continued to make them in almost the same way, with only relatively slight improvements, until the last Ice Age. Then a sudden burst in creativity occurred. This flowering of technology included the increasing diversity of design and materials—and, more important, the use of tools to make other tools by a variety of methods such as boring, scraping, cutting, and polishing. Of all the possible ways to account for this florescence of culture after millions of years of barely perceptible change, the most apparent is the rise of speech as we know it today (but no doubt building upon some earlier system of communication). One vital property of speech is that it can talk about the future; it can plan forward. The flowering of tool manufacture during the last Ice Age demanded just such forward planning, because the succession of different operations, one following the other in precise order, could be achieved only by involved discussions.

Every new discovery in animal behavior, human evolution, or human physiology provides the impetus for scholars to construct new theories about the origins of speech. We can expect that some linguists will continue to search back into the unrecorded past to discover the well-springs of speech, even though most of them today despair of ever finding it. In fact, since 1866 the Linguistic Society of Paris has had a rule that the origin of language is one topic it would not discuss at its meetings. Speculations may be provocative, well reasoned, and based on available evidence—but they never can be demonstrated to be anything more than possibilities. Evidence about language goes back only as far as the earliest written documents, a mere five thousand years or so ago. But by that time languages were already fully developed and not significantly different in kind from those spoken today. Since no hope exists of discovering a record of the earlier stages in development, a much more fruitful pursuit is discussed in the next chapter—the study of how living human beings acquire their languages.

12

The Language of Children

Carolus Linnaeus, the eighteenth-century inventor of the system of classification of living things still in use, listed *Homo ferus*, Latin for "wild man," as a subdivision of our species, *Homo sapiens*. The characteristics of the feral form of human life, he declared, were hairiness, walking on all fours—and lack of speech. When Linnaeus made his classification, he knew of ten cases of "wolf children" abandoned by their parents to fend for themselves and purportedly nurtured by wild animals. Since then upward of thirty more cases have been thoroughly documented, although it has never been demonstrated that these children were reared by wolves or by any other animals. Scientists and philosophers early recognized the importance of "wolf children," because such wild creatures provide natural experiments in the way human beings develop their behavior when isolated from society. In fact, the capture of "Wild Peter" in Hanover, Germany, in 1724 led a scientist to proclaim that he was more important than the discovery of thirty thousand new stars. When the twelve-year-old "Wild Boy of Aveyron" was captured in 1797 in France, contemporary readers of Rousseau anticipated that he would display the virtues of the "noble savage" uncontaminated by civilization. Scholars anxiously awaited his first words, which they conjectured would be man's "natural" language, most probably Hebrew. They were disappointed. The Wild Boy was not particularly hairy, as Linnaeus claimed, but he did trot along on all fours—and he was inarticulate.

A young French physician, J. M. G. Itard, expressed the belief that the speechless Wild Boy of Aveyron was not an "incurable idiot," as a leading scientist of the time had concluded. Itard set out to instruct the boy, whom he named Victor, in language. After five years of extraordinary patience, Itard showed that Victor possessed a capacity to learn many things—but not language. Victor did manage to understand a few simple words and phrases and to read written commands, but he never did learn how to speak. In contrast, a six-year-old abandoned girl, discovered in Ohio in the 1930s, was also instructed in language; in only two years she progressed through six years of language learning. By the time she was eight and a half, she had so accelerated her acquisition of language that her speech was little different from that of other girls her age. Although a few doubts remain to this day whether or not Victor was mentally deficient, he apparently failed to learn speech because he had missed the opportunity at a critical age. By the time he was captured as a twelve-year-old, his ability to speak could never again be recovered.

A complete contrast to wolf children, abandoned to fend for themselves in the wild, are normal children reared by doting parents. But the notion that children learn to speak merely by imitating their parents, somewhat like intelligent parrots, is sheer folklore. Unlike parrots, children are linguistically creative at a very early age. They say all kinds of things they have never heard previously from adults, and they often put together combinations of words which they use in speech situations novel to those utterances. For example, one linguist tape-recorded the following sequence of prattles by a three-year-old child before sleep:

pig (repeated many times)
big
sleep
big pig sleep now

The linguist was certain that the child had never encountered the final utterance in a storybook or heard it in conversation. For that child, it was a totally new creation.

Parents usually do not realize that they unconsciously speak differently to children, even those six or seven years old, than they do to adults. They exaggerate changes in pitch and sometimes they speak almost in singsong; they utter their words more slowly; they use simple sentence structures. And the sounds of their speech are much more precise, as seen, for example, in the pronunciation of *butter*. Most English-speaking adults talking to other adults pronounce it almost as if it were spelled *budder*, but in speaking to a child they usually use the strong *t* sound of *table*. Such careful attention to speech when talking to children is, however, different from the baby-talk words like *choo-choo* and *itsy-bitsy*. Baby talk, rather than representing a "natural" vocabulary that a child instinctively uses, actually is taught to children by adults—who, after a few years, then force the children to stop using it. Baby talk is simply a variation of the adult language, invented by adults for the sole purpose of talking to very young children. Once baby talk becomes part of the language system of speech communities, it persists for long periods. Some Latin baby-talk words are still being used in Romance languages after two thousand years, like today's Spanish *papa,* "food," which derives from the Latin word *pappa*.

The Comanche Indians of the North American Plains began to teach their children a rich vocabulary of special baby-talk words when they reached about one year of age. But shortly after the children learned baby talk, they were discouraged from using it. By the age of five they were supposed to switch to normal, adult language, but if they failed to make the transition at the appropriate time, they were ridiculed for their childish ways. Comanche baby talk used a limited number of the more simple sounds in the language, such as *p, b, m, t, d, k,* and a few basic vowels. The words were almost always reduplicated—that is, a single syllable was repeated. For example, Comanches transformed their adult word *pia,* meaning "mother," to *pipia* when speaking to children, much as English-speaking children are taught to say *nighty-night.*

Comanche baby-talk vocabulary reveals not so much what the children were interested in saying as what the attitudes of the adult culture were. Most of the baby-talk vocabulary seems preoccupied with words for snakes, fire, wounds, darkness, and mythological bogeymen—all obviously intended to frighten the child—and with words that admonish the child to control his actions and to be obedient. The same baby word, *asi,* could be used by the child to say that he had a bowel movement, to point out feces or anything else that Comanche society deemed filthy, to complain about a bad smell, or to talk about his penis. The equating of disgust with feces, dirt, and the genitals in baby talk says nothing about Comanche children but rather indicates adult attitudes toward the human body.

Baby-talk vocabulary has been compared in six quite different languages from around the world: two major European languages (English and Spanish), two major languages of Asia with strong literary traditions (Arabic and Marathi), one language of a small non-literate community in Siberia (Gilyak), and one language of a small nonliterate community in North America (Comanche). The actual baby-talk words in the six languages were, of course, different; nevertheless, the vocabularies revealed surprising similarities in linguistic characteristics. All the languages simplified clusters of consonants (as English speakers do when they substitute *tummy* for *stomach*); they replaced *r* with some other consonant (such as *wabbit* for *rabbit*); they reduplicated syllables (choo-choo, wee-wee); and most of the languages dropped unstressed syllables (as when *goodbye* becomes *bye*). The six languages altered words to form diminutives (such as the English *y* in *doggy, horsey,* and *dolly*) and substituted words to eliminate pronouns (*Daddy wants* instead of *I want*). We might expect that people from six widely separated cultures would want to talk about different things with their children—but the items in the baby-talk vocabularies were very much the same. Almost all the words referred to bodily functions, good or bad behavior, sensations like hot and cold, names of common animals, and kinship terms for close relatives.

Since children are not born to speak baby talk, what could possibly be the explanation for its prevalence around the world? Most adults in the six cultures claimed that baby talk made it easier for children to learn to speak. It is indeed true that in most cases baby-talk words have simpler consonant arrangements and fewer vowels than adult language. On the other hand, some baby-talk systems, such as that of Arabic, employ difficult sounds which children do not ordinarily master until they have considerable experience in speaking the adult language. And is it really easier for an English-speaking child to say *itsy-bitsy* than *tiny?* Despite such exceptions, folk wisdom about baby talk apparently is correct; it does give children practice in speaking. Baby talk presents the child with a stock of simple utterances, and reduplication increases practice in their use. These utterances can gradually be discarded when adult words begin to be used, by which time they have served their purpose.

Reduplication does, however, persist into adult speech, to a much greater extent in some languages than in English, which has comparatively few examples like *helter-skelter, fiddle-faddle, hocus-pocus, mish-mash,* and *teeny-weeny.* Other languages sometimes make reduplication serve functional uses, as when Indonesians say *igi-igi-igi-igi* to emphasize the idea of "multitudes," and when the Ewe of Africa form the reduplicated *gadagadagada* to express intensity, in this case the heat of a fire. Chinese in particular has found uses for reduplication with various parts of speech. A reduplicated noun adds the meaning "every," as when *tian,* "day," becomes *tiantian,* "every day." Reduplication applied to verbs adds a transitory meaning to the action: *zou* means "to walk," but *zouzou* signifies "to take a walk." Adjectives are converted to adverbs by reduplication plus the addition of the suffix *-de*—as when *kuai,* "quick," becomes *kuaikuaide,* "quickly."

The most common sounds in baby talk—the consonants made with the lips, such as *p, b,* and *m*—are the first ones the child can make, probably because the lips are used early for nursing. The next three consonants a child learns are formed with the teeth and gums—*t, d,* and *n*—and they are almost as important in the early stages of speech as the first three. So it is not surprising that the earliest words infants speak are those like *papa, dada, baba, mama,* and *nana.* At first children simply utter these sounds without reference to any particular people—and that is why most parents are incorrect when they believe the sounds refer to a recognition of father, brother, mother, and nursemaid. A sampling of "mother" and "father" words from a variety of languages shows the importance of the six consonants which are learned first:

	"MOTHER" WORDS	"FATHER" WORDS
French	*mère*	*père*
Welsh	*mam*	*tad*
Turkish	*ana*	*baba*

Hebrew	*ima*	*aba*
Russian	*mat*	*otyets*
Mongolian	*eme*	*echige*
Crow Indian	*masake*	*birupxe*

The cause for the similarities in "mother" and "father" consonants is in dispute, but the explanation is more apt to lie in the universal way that children learn to speak than in some common origin of these languages in the very distant past.

Child-development specialists occasionally argue over whether or not adults should speak baby talk to their children. Some believe that it retards the child in developing normal language; others feel that baby talk affords good practice in producing sounds. Apparently, speaking baby talk does no harm, and it may even be a valuable aid in the early stages of acquiring a language. On the other hand, if a child continues to speak it beyond the first several years of life, it may retard his speech at a babyish level.

Neither the grunts of wolf children nor the adult-imposed system of baby talk reveals anything about the way in which almost all children, healthy and reared within a social framework, acquire their language. Most communities have long believed that the human infant comes into the world inarticulate—and in fact the very word *infant* is derived from a Latin word that means "speechless." In an obvious way this belief is correct. The cry of an infant at birth, the pain cry when being vaccinated, the hunger cry several hours after a feeding, and the pleasure cry when being held—these expressions of emotions certainly are not language. They are like ape calls in that they are uttered only in immediate contexts and they are never combined.

Yet the infant emits a cry—and soon the hospital nurse, later the mother, responds in a way that is pleasurable. The infant has learned that language is a social instrument that evokes a response from other human beings. In the first days of life the child is already responsive to a sound and tries to move his head toward its source. Only a few weeks later he responds to the high-pitched female voice more readily than to any other sound. Soon the infant coos and babbles and makes other noises, and he notes that his mother reacts to each in a different way. The child has learned the appropriate use of speech in various situations.

Children normally begin to speak as early as eighteen months, occasionally as late as twenty-eight months; in the exceptional case of Albert Einstein, the onset of speech did not occur until he was nearly three years old. Certainly all mothers have not mutually agreed that it is time to teach infants to talk when they are approximately two years old. But the effort to learn what triggers a child's speech is somewhat like a problem presented to engineering students. They are shown the outside of a black box, with input wires leading to it and other wires leading out that produce an electrical result. The students must then try to infer the internal wiring of the box solely on the basis of the input-output relationships. The child's mind presents a similar sort of problem. It is a black box (or "language-acquisition device," as it has been called) that cannot be looked into in the living child. The linguist knows only that the language-acquisition device receives input in the form of relatively few utterances ,which emerge as utterances in accordance with the grammar of the child's native tongue. Furthermore, the mysterious device in the child's mind works wherever he happens to spend the first several years of life, with the result that the language he learns is that of his native community.

Noam Chomsky has given fresh insights to psychologists and linguists who are attempting to discover how the language-acquisition device works. In an earlier period of psycholinguistic research, many psychologists were influenced by behaviorists such as B. F. Skinner and Ivan P. Lalov. The behaviorists visualize the child's mind at birth as a blank slate which lacks any inborn capacity to acquire language. The fact that the child does eventually speak is attributed solely to training, in much the same way that an animal can be conditioned to learn by offering it rewards and other reinforcements. The behaviorists think in terms of the child as building up his language piece by piece in accordance with the orders given by the adult generation, which rewards him when he speaks correctly and ridicules him when he speaks incorrectly. This view looks upon learning language as little different from learning correct table manners. Chomsky instead regards language as a creative instrument that is the birthright of all healthy human children, who acquire it as a by-product of growing up, simply by exposure to it. They are born with a blueprint for language which they use to analyze the utterances heard in their speech community and then to produce their own sentences. To Chomsky, the influence of training is minimal—a view which is the direct opposite of behaviorist theories that a child learns the grammar of his language as a result of social pressures, conditioning, or simply the trial-and-error imitation of adults.

Chomsky feels that his theory can account for a basic and mystifying fact about language acquisition. The child hears a relatively small number of utterances, most of which are grammatically incorrect or misunderstood—yet, on the basis of this scanty and flawed information, in his pre-school years and with no special instruction, he discovers for himself the complex grammatical rules of his speech community. This fact can be explained only by assuming that the child is born with competence in the structure of language, in the same way that a child is genetically endowed at birth with numerous other abilities that make him human.

The situation is somewhat like learning to walk. The child possesses at birth the blueprint for the muscular coordination that he will develop later in order to walk. No one tells him how to lift his legs, bend his ankles or knees, or place his feet on the ground. He does not consciously arrive at the skill of balancing himself on his legs, any more than a three-year-old consciously figures out the rules for grammatical transformations. The child walks and the child talks—and in neither case does he know exactly how he did it.

A simple example of the way in which a child can be seen putting together the rules for his language's grammar is the English word *hisself*, an "erroneous" form of *himself* which most children use until about the age of four, despite attempts by parents to correct them. So persistent is this "error" that it has been known since the time of Chaucer and it survives in several dialects of English. What is the explanation for its persistence? And why is it constructed by children who usually have never heard it before? The answer is that *hisself* strictly follows the rules of English grammar that the child is acquiring. *Hisself* is a reflexive pronoun like *myself, yourself,* and *herself*—each of which is formed by combining the possessive pronoun *my, your,* or *her* with *self*. The masculine possessive in this set is *his* and therefore, when combined with *self,* should rightly produce the reflexive *hisself*. But English is inconsistent in this instance, as all languages are in one instance or another, and the preferred form is *himself*. So children, by insisting upon *hisself* until the age when they acquire knowledge about the irregularities of English, show that they have internalized a basic rule of their grammar and follow it for a long time, despite adult attempts to correct them.

Strong evidence supports Chomsky's view. Only human children learn to speak, thus indicating that some sort of blueprint for language must be transmitted from generation to generation in our species. And human children everywhere develop a language without instruction, unless they are isolated as "wolf children" during the critical acquisition years or unless they suffer from extreme mental deficiency. Bright children and stupid children, trained children and untrained children, all learn approximately the same linguistic system. Some street urchins do not have parents to instruct them, but they learn to speak nevertheless—and, as can be seen in international cities like Tangiers and Singapore, the homeless child may speak several languages fluently. (Imperfections in pronunciation or vocabulary are insignificant when compared with the tremendous accomplishment of acquiring the complex rules of a language.) But the same thing cannot be said about developing other skills, such as arithmetic or playing a musical instrument, both of which require long years of training. Even though two violin students take lessons from the same teacher and devote equal time to practice, one may become merely a good player while the other becomes a virtuoso. Natural endowments for the skill of violin-playing vary, but all children show equal aptitude for language in their early years.

At the same time that the child is acquiring grammatical rules, he is also learning rules for the correct use of his language in the various speech situations of his community. By the age of two or so, children already use speech to get what they want, to talk about things they know will interest the listener, and to influence the social behavior of others. They know some of the occasions on which it is proper to shout or to whisper; they know that it is permissible to say *gimme* to certain people but that they should use *please* in other speech situations; they have some idea of differences in age and rank of listeners and the kinds of speech appropriate with a child or an adult, with a stranger or a neighbor. Only a little later children begin to play word games and to make up nonsense rhymes—clear evidence that they have already internalized the rules and can exploit the alternative possibilities of their language. Although most children acquire their grammar at a steady rate, largely insulated from major influences in the social environment, learning the appropriate use of language depends upon the speech community in which the child grows up and the social group to which he belongs. Children from various social classes differ considerably in their abilities to talk about certain things, and to do so in the appropriate situations. Middle-class white children in the United States usually place a high value on the ability to read at an early age; lower-class black children, on the other hand, may consider such a skill irrelevant and are likely to emphasize nimbleness in verbal encounters.

The age at which a child is considered capable of understanding speech varies greatly from culture to culture. Most Europeans feel that children cannot comprehend what is said to them until they are a year or so old. In contrast, the Ashanti of Ghana believe that a fetus possesses the ability to understand speech and they sometimes address questions to it in the womb. Psycholinguists now know that infants are aware of speech at a very early age, although not so early as the Ashanti believe. Before the age of one month, the child associates the sound of the human voice with pleasurable sensations, such as feeding, fondling, and the changing of diapers. Very soon afterward the child detects different emotional attitudes in the speaker's tone of voice and responds by smiling or crying. A two-month-old infant in an English-speaking community can often discriminate between the sounds *p* and *b,* which is a very exact discrimination indeed. A child's language gradually unfolds in a sequence of stages of development during the first few years of life. A parent can say to a child *Speak only when spoken to,* and the child may obey—but the language-acquisition device in the child's brain will not obey. Biology does the work, and fond parents can add little except simply to talk within earshot of the child. The course of language for most normal children, regardless of the speech communities they are born into, is thought to be keyed to motor development—as seen below in one possible correlation—although some researchers believe it is keyed to a child's general cognitive development.

When supports head while lying on stomach (age about three months): The infant responds to speech by smiling and by making the gurgling sound known as "cooing," which is vowel-like and has pitch.

When plays with a rattle placed in hands (about four months): The infant turns his head and eyes to seek the source of a speaker's voice. He adds chuckling noises to cooing.

When sits propped up (about five months): The vowel-like cooing sounds now become interspersed with consonant-like sounds.

When can bear weight if held in a standing position (about six months): Cooing changes to babbling of one-syllable utterances like *ma, mu, da, di,* and so on.

When picks up objects with thumb and forefinger (about eight months): Reduplication, such as *mama,* or *dada,* becomes frequent. Strings of sounds are expressed with emphasis and seem to signal emotion. Intonation, as heard in adult questions and exclamations, becomes noticeable.

When pulls self to standing position (about ten months): Bubble-blowing and other sound play is now added to vocalizations. The infant apparently tries to imitate sounds but is rarely successful. He begins to discriminate between words by reacting differently to various utterances.

When walks held by one hand (about one year): The infant definitely understands some words and attempts to carry out simple commands. He can also speak a few words.

When creeps down stairs backward (about one and a half years): The child is now on the threshold of speech and displays a much greater understanding of what is said to him. His vocabulary consists of between three and fifty words, although little attempt to communicate information is made as yet. He can utter brief stock phrases, such as *thank you,* but he does not attempt to join these into more complicated statements.

When walks up or down stairs (about two years): The typical child now has a vocabulary of more than fifty words and can name almost everything he has daily contact with in the home or on walks. Rather than repeating stock phrases, he often utters two-word phrases which are his own creation. Language acquisition gains momentum and a definite interest in words is displayed.

When jumps with both feet (about two and a half years): Vocabulary increases very rapidly and new words are added daily. Babbling ceases. Utterances are intended to have communication value, and the child is frustrated when he is not understood. He seems to understand almost everything said to him, and he responds with statements up to five words in length.

When rides tricycle (about three years): This stage marks the end of the naming explosion, at which time the child has a vocabulary of about a thousand words. He probably understands an additional two or three thousand words he has not yet learned to use. The grammatical complexity of the utterance is about equal to that of colloquial adult speech, although numerous errors occur.

When catches ball in arms (about four years): The child has now mastered the essentials of his native tongue.

A child of four has performed an awesome intellectual feat. He has not merely learned the names of things; he has acquired an entire linguistic system that enables him to create sentences for the rest of his life. If among the words a child knows are *hill, water, Jill, fetch, Jack, pail,* and *go,* he may eventually put them together into a sentence like *Jack and Jill went up the hill to fetch a pail of water.* Think for a moment how remarkable this sentence is. The child has taken a random assortment of words and given them order. *Jack* and *Jill* do not appear just anyplace in the sentence, but at the beginning of it, where they are made to serve as the subjects of the verb *go.* Equally important, the child added what are known as "markers" in the form of functor words (*and, up, the, to, a, of*). Functors identify the different classes of words (as when *the* or *a* indicates that a noun follows); they specify relationships between words (*and,* for example, ties together *Jack* and *Jill*); and they signify meanings by the tense of the verbs. If the child had arranged the same words differently—such as *Jack fetched Jill's pail of water and went up the hill*—he would have used other marks (*-ed* and *-'s*) and a different word order. The child knows unconsciously that he should not use the markers in the second sentence to construct the first kind of sentence, since his grammar tells him that a sentence like *Jack and Jill's went up the hill to fetched a pail of water* is an impossible creation in English.

Considerable dispute exists as to exactly how a child of four or five attains such remarkable proficiency in these, and even more difficult, grammatical tasks. One explanation is that the child codes the words he learns into grammatical classes, thereby eliminating the necessity of knowing the grammar of each word in his vocabulary. For example, if a child possesses a category that he codes as "nouns," then he recognizes words belonging to this class whenever they occur. He knows that they can be used only in certain ways in sentences and that they are associated with certain markers (such as *the* and *a*). He also realizes that not all words in English are equal. Some content words (such as *Jack, Jill, went,* and *hill* in the nursery rhyme quoted in the previous paragraph) carry important burdens of meaning, while other, functor words (*and, up, the* and so on) can be eliminated with a high probability that the message will still be understood. Adults employ the distinction between content and functor words when they send a telegram and eliminate "unnecessary" words. The telegram ARRIVING KENNEDY SEVEN TONIGHT AMERICAN easily enough translates as *I will be arriving at Kennedy Airport at seven o'clock tonight on American Airlines.* "Telegraphic" English communicates very well because it retains the content words like *arriving* and *Kennedy* that one would have difficulty in guessing and eliminates those that can easily be guessed (*I, at, on*). Content words alone are usually sufficient to tell the story, but functor words alone are gibberish.

Where and *want* are among the most common "operator" words of children at certain ages, although most children go through fads in their preferences for particular operators. They fasten on a favorite operator and then use it with a variety of other words belonging to a single class, in that way learning the entire class. For example, a child who for a time regards *want* as a favorite operator will employ it with most of the nouns he knows to create two-word sentences like *want outside, want doggy,* and *want milk.* Children are also very exact in discriminating between the noun class, which refers to things, and the verb class, which refers to actions. In a typical experiment, preschool children were given a selection of pictures and then asked to associate them with nonsense words. When they heard *a sib,* they immediately reached for pictures that showed a single object, thereby indicating that they had put *a sib* into the class of singular nouns. When asked to show *some sibs,* they reached for pictures of confetti-like material (the class of plural nouns). And when asked to find something *sibbing,* they selected pictures showing action (the class of verbs). Since the words themselves were meaningless, the children obviously made correct choices because grammatical clues helped them to recognize that the words belonged to certain classes.

By the age of four, the child is well on the way to knowing these and other aspects of grammar. During the next several years, this knowledge is consolidated, becomes automatic, and is extended to include words with irregular patterns (*men* and not *mans* as the plural of *man*). A six-year-old child may use *he bought* and *he buyed* interchangeably, but he usually corrects himself, showing that he knows the proper form even though he does not yet employ it automatically. Surprisingly, some features of language that appear to be simple are not learned until quite late. One such is the "tag question"—as in *The doggy can come in the house, can't he?*—which is very complex because the tag (*can't he?*) is determined completely by the structure of the declarative sentence to which it is attached and for which it requests confirmation. If the declarative sentence had instead been *The doggy will come home,* then a different kind of tag question would be needed: *won't he?* (The problem does not arise in French and German where the tag questions—*n'est-ce pas?* and *nicht wahr?* respectively—do not vary; English also has several invariant forms, among them *right?* and *huh?*) Think of the complex grammatical operations a child has to perform to produce the apparently simple *The doggy can come in the house, can't he?* First of all, the child has to convert the subject of the declarative sentence (*The doggy*) into a pronoun (*he*)—not just any pronoun but one which is masculine, third person, and in the nominative case. Next, the tag must be made negative by adding *not* or its contraction *n't* to the auxiliary verb *can,* and then be made a question by reversing the order of *he* and *can't.* Finally, the child has to delete from the tag *come in the house*—that is, all of the verb phrases in the declarative sentence except for the auxiliary *can.*

The child continues to refine his speech in this way until about the age of ten, by which time he has internalized all the complicated rules of his native grammar. Children soon outgrow their ability to acquire language with little effort, as is realized by high-school students and adults who try to master a language in addition to their mother tongue. Whether or not a child will speak a foreign language with an accent depends largely upon the age at which he learns the second language. A child who enters a foreign speech community by about the age of three or four learns the new language rapidly and without the trace of an accent. During the next several years, such facility declines slightly. But then, around the age of puberty, an irreversible change takes place, and practically every child loses the ability to learn a second language without an accent.

The unfolding of a child's language is a wondrous thing to listen to, as every parent knows. Working with an extremely limited vocabulary, poorly pronounced, and the meanings only dimly understood, the child produces the grammar of his language. No amount of reward, praise, or punishment makes him do a substantially better or worse job. He of course makes many errors at first, but eventually he puts together a grammar that is equal to the grammar of the people in his

speech community who talked to him and played with
him during the critical years of language acquisition.
As in the development of his personality, the child has
used his innate potential to create something very much
like that of other people in his community, yet also
something uniquely his own.

13

The Spoken Word

Vladimir Nabokov, a contemporary master of the English language, opens his novel *Lolita,* with alliteration, word play—and a brief lesson in speech production:

> Lolita, light of my life, fire of my loins. My sin, my soul. Lo-lee-ta: the tip of the tongue taking a trip of three steps down the palate to tap, at three, on the teeth. Lo. Lee. Ta.

Nabokov's passage demonstrates how euphonious Lolita's name is. To pronounce it, the tongue must move in an arc through all the positions—from back to front and from high to low—used to sound English vowels.

Specialists in the science of speech production were celebrated by George Bernard Shaw in *Pygmalion.* Professor Higgins was modeled upon the linguist Henry Sweet, the author of several volumes about Old English, who was noted for his uncanny talents in discriminating speech sounds. He exhibits his virtuosity in the play by telling people the very streets in London where they were born. Ordinary listeners also have been aware of subtle differences in speech at least as early as Biblical times. The book of Judges tells how the Hebrews used the word *shibboleth,* meaning "stream," as a password during a war with the Ephraimites. Anyone wishing to cross the Jordan River had to utter the password, and since the Ephraimites pronounced the Hebrew *sh* as *s*, their identities were revealed. Speakers and listeners constantly make discriminations of this sort about speech sounds, and they do so quite unconsciously. The human voice can utter thousands of different sounds; human ears can distinguish between almost all of them. Yet, out of the full range of sounds any human being can make and listeners can distinguish, each language limits itself to a meager few, between about a dozen and five dozen, and regards differences between them as significant.

Linguists have given the name "phoneme" (literally, in Greek, "sound unit") to these smallest significant particles of sound. Probably no two languages recognize exactly the same set of phonemes. Miss Fidditch may sing praise to the sounds of the English language —its lilting consonants, its full-bodied consonant clusters, its rich vowels—but these phonemes have no meaning in themselves. They instead function simply as ways to contrast sounds in a language, and thus to signal a difference in meaning between two words that otherwise might sound very much alike. The contrast in English, for example, between *p* and *b* is crucial in discriminating between numerous pairs of similar words, such as *pest* and *best* or *pet* and *bet*. Not all languages recognize this distinction, but in English it is the only way to separate many almost identical utterances. Imagine these sentences spoken by a young woman:

I like to pet.
I like to bet.

The two utterances—and the different kinds of behavior toward her they might evoke—are kept apart solely by a very slight alteration in the vocal organs that speakers of English are in the habit of making.

English speakers are unconsciously aware that they should pronounce *p* and *b* so that no chance of ambiguity exists, and as listeners they learn to detect the minute difference between the two sounds, even when the sounds are uttered by someone with a speech defect. But if a Menominee Indian of Wisconsin pronounces over and over again his word that means "he looks at him," a speaker of English sometimes thinks he hears a *p* in the middle, sometimes a *b,* and sometimes a sound intermediate between the two. This is because the Menominee language does not recognize any contrast between the phonemes *p* and *b,* and so speakers do not pronounce this word in a way that makes clear the distinction between them. To a Menominee, the English words *pet* and *bet* sound exactly alike.

Actually, speakers of English do not pronounce *p* precisely the same way in every word. The *p* of *spin* is not the same as the *p* of *pin.* This is easily proven by holding the palm of the hand in front of the mouth while speaking aloud both words; a very brief puff of air will be felt in the case of *pin* but not of *spin.* Since English does not regard the distinction between the different kinds of *p* as significant, usually only a linguist notices the difference. To most speakers, it is sufficient that what approximates *p* somehow contrasts with the other phonemes of English. A speaker of Hindi, however, immediately notices that English uses different kinds of *p,* because such a discrimination is important in his language.

The fact that speakers of English fussily make two distinct sounds out of Menominee's *p-b* and a single sound out of Hindi's several kinds of *p* explains how so many different languages can be spoken on earth. Out of the thousands of possible sounds that the human tongue can utter, each language selects merely a few— and then it decides that only certain contrasts between them are significant. French, for example, did not select the common English phoneme *jh* as used in *jar, joy,* and other words. Neither French nor English adopted the gargle-like *ch* of German as used in the name of the composer *Bach*. And English, French, and German all lack the five kinds of clicks used as phonemes in the language of the Bushmen of South Africa. The existence of such distinctions explains why the speech of foreigners, even those fluent in English, has a strange quality or "accent." Either foreign speakers fail to make the minor distinctions between sounds that English makes, or they make distinctions called for in their own languages but not in English. A Russian, even though rigorously trained to speak English, will still give himself away by his pronunciation of *t* in English words. Native speakers of English pronounce *t* by making contact between the tongue, just back of its tip, and the upper gum ridge. The Russian *t*, though, is pronounced by contact between the tip of the tongue and the upper teeth.

In addition to vowels and consonants, every language uses other kinds of phonemes—even though they are often overlooked because they are not apparent on the printed page. No one speaks in the perfectly level tone that the straight lines on a page seem to imply, nor does he break up utterances in the way that spaces between words indicate. Stress, pitch, the joining together or separation of syllables, and the rise and fall of the voice are phonemes also—and they are every bit as important in distinguishing messages as is the contrast between *p* and *b*. Stress, for example, is the pronunciation of one syllable with more energy, which usually results in its sounding longer and louder than other syllables in the same word. French largely ignores stress, but English places particular importance on it to distinguish nouns from verbs—as can be seen from the following pairs of words which have the same consonant and vowel phonemes but sound different because of stress (indicated by capitalized syllables):

NOUNS	VERBS
PRESent	preSENT
PERmit	perMIT
CONtract	conTRACT
IMport	imPORT

Stress usually is more complicated than this simple table of nouns and verbs indicates, since sometimes strong and weak stresses alone are insufficient to distinguish words. Speak aloud, for example, the sentence *The surveyors mapped the Kahn tract.* The last two syllables—that is, the tract of land owned by someone named Kahn—clearly are not stressed the same way as the noun *contract.* Nor is that the only difference. The two syllables of *Kahn tract* are uttered with a very brief pause between them, but the two syllables of *contract* are not. Such a pause is known as an "open juncture," and it also is a phoneme of the English language. If open junctures were absent from the English language, no way would exist to distinguish between the following pairs of sentences:

> *That stuff!*
> *That's   tough!*

We're happy to have General Drum right here.
We're happy to have General Drumwright here.

A slight distinction in stress plus an open juncture differentiates *Drum right* from *Drumwright.* This last pair of sentences can also be made to contrast with each other by ending them with the phonemes that are known as "terminal contours." If *We're happy to have General Drumwright here* is spoken so that the voice falls at the end, the sentence is a simple, declarative one. If the voice rises at the end, it indicates surprise that the audience should be pleased that he appeared.

And if the voice remains absolutely level, the listener anticipates that more information is to follow. As with all other phonemes, the pitch level at the end of a sentence has no meaning in itself but merely serves to distinguish between different meanings. English employs pitch to lend expression to the larger utterances of phrases and sentences, but some languages in East Asia and Africa change pitch from syllable to syllable to discriminate between what would otherwise be similar words. In the Mandarin dialect of Chinese, for example, *ma* can mean "hemp," "scold," "mother," or "horse"—depending solely on whether the voice rises, falls, remains level, or dips. Burmese also has a word *ma* with several meanings that are differentiated by pitch changes. It is possible to speak a sentence in Burmese composed completely of *ma* repeated several times with different pitches to mean "Get the horse, a mad dog is coming."

A language is like a game played with a fixed number of pieces—phonemes—each one easily recognized by native speakers. This is true of every language, except that the pieces change from one language game to another. Although linguists occasionally debate the fine points of English phonemes, they generally agree that the language game is played with the following 45 phoneme "pieces":

21 consonants
9 vowels
3 semivowels (*y, w, r*)
4 stresses
4 pitches
1 juncture (pause between words)
3 terminal contours (to end sentences)

These 45 phonemes used in English today represent the total sound resources by which speakers can create an infinity of utterances.

Languages differ from one another not only in their total number of phonemes but also in the varying proportions of phonemes devoted to vowels, consonants, stresses, and so on. Some dialects of Arabic, for example, have twenty-eight consonants but only six vowels. Most African languages are similar to Mandarin and Burmese in that they emphasize pitch and stress to a much greater extent than English does. Twi has five different tones—high, middle, low, rising, and falling—and every syllable of every word is spoken in one of these tones. *Adidi,* when pronounced with the last syllable in a high tone, means "meal"—but when pronounced with the second syllable high and the last syllable in middle tone, the word means "red thread."

Because tone is so important in many languages of Africa, numerous tribes there have been able to make drums serve as surrogates for the human voice. Since various words in these languages are distinguishable solely by their patterns of tone, regardless of their particular vowels and consonants, drums can deliver complete messages by the use of tonal phonemes alone. Nevertheless, drumming out just the tonal pattern in the absence of vowels and consonants could sometimes result in misinterpretation. In the Kele language of the Congo, for example, the four words that mean "above," "forest," and the names of two tropical plants, "manioc" and "plantain," all have the same tonal pattern, even though their vowels and consonants are different. A tonal message sent by drums could not distinguish these four words from one another; but the problem is solved by attaching stock phrases to each of the ambiguous words. Instead of simply sending an ambiguous tonal message for "manioc," the drums beat out the tones for a longer utterance that means "the manioc which remains in the fallow ground"—a message which could never confuse "manioc" with any other word.

The use of stock phrases to prevent ambiguity results

in drum messages that are considerably longer, about eight times on the average, than the spoken versions. A brief spoken message in Kele—"The missionary is coming upriver to our village tomorrow"—would translate as a much longer drum version because of the addition of stock phrases:

> White man spirit from the forest
> of the leaf used for roofs
> comes upriver, comes upriver
> when tomorrow has risen
> on high in the sky
> to the town and the village
> of us
> come, come, come, come.

A single drum message travels no more than six or seven miles, and usually much less than that. But if the news is important, receivers will rebroadcast it from village to village. In addition to important messages, the drums also communicate chitchat, personal messages, poems, and jokes. John F. Carrington, who has pioneered in linguistic studies of drum languages, relates that he once saw a man dash to a drum and beat out a quick message. The man had left his cigarettes in another village and, knowing that a friend would rejoin him later, requested the friend via the drums to bring the cigarettes along. The message was received by his friend, and not by some other person, because everyone has his own drum name. These drum names may be merely an identification of one's parents or a version of the spoken name. But sometimes they are whimsical, as, for example, that of one Lokele man which translates as "Don't laugh at a black skin, because everybody has one."

The talking drums are also an effective channel for broadcasting insults as widely as possible—while at the same time allowing the person who offers the insult to take refuge in the ambiguous meanings of drum talk should the insulted person become angry. One man who aspired to the title of chief received a promise of help from another man, who then failed to honor his promise. So the title-seeker hired a drummer to beat out proverbs which attacked the false friend by innuendo, such as: "A tree which fails to hold up a person when he leans against it will in no way hurt him if it falls upon him." Everyone in his community presumably would know what the title-seeker meant by the proverb—that the false friend had refused to support him and might even actively try to prevent his receiving the title.

The representation of spoken language by surrogate means is actually a world-wide phenomenon, even though the best-known example aside from writing is the talking drum of western and central Africa. In other parts of Africa, gongs and wind instruments are used; the Northern Chin of Burma communicate by means of xylophones; Melanesians bang on the buttress roots of trees; the Chinese of Chekiang use a humming language; and the Swiss yodel. Whistled speech—which has been discovered in Africa, Mexico, and the Canary Islands—is even closer to the spoken language than is the talking drum. On La Gomera in the Canaries, verbal communication is difficult because of the extremely rugged terrain, which limits the distance speech can carry. The Gomeros have solved the problem by whistling to each other, at distances as great as eight miles, across ravines and from valleys to mountaintops. The whistled language is learned effortlessly by Gomero children in the same way that they learn their spoken language, and any child can whistle intelligibly everything he can say in the spoken language.

The Mazateco Indians of the rugged valleys of Oaxaca, Mexico, have also invented a similar sort of whistled language. Its efficiency is attested to by George M. Cowan, who first described it:

Eusebio Martinez was observed one day standing in front of his hut, whistling to a man a considerable distance away. The man was passing on the trail below, going to market to sell a load of corn leaves. The man answered Eusebio's whistle with a whistle. The interchange was repeated several times with different whistles. Finally, the man turned around, retraced his steps a short way and came up the footpath to Eusebio's hut. Without saying a word, he dumped his load on the ground. Eusebio looked the load over, went into his hut, returned with some money and paid the man his price. The man turned and left. Not a word had been spoken. They had talked, bargained over the price, and come to an agreement satisfactory to both parties—using only whistles as a medium of communication.

These few examples should make it apparent that drum and whistle languages are not mere codes equivalent to American Indian smoke signals. Nor are they some quaint folk language. Although they may sound strange to the ears of outsiders, they are no stranger then many spoken languages. In fact, they are clever adaptations to certain physical environments, such as dense forests or mountainous terrain, in which speech cannot carry long distances. The only differences between them and spoken utterances are that they transmit messages by means other than the vocal cords and that they rely upon the tonal phonemes of the language rather than upon the consonants and vowels.

Phonemes are like chemical elements in that they combine only with certain other elements. Combinations of phonemes form syllables, but the kinds of possible syllables vary greatly from one language to another. *Slip* is an English word, but *slin* is not, even though it could be, because it follows the rules for forming English syllables. Nothing in the sound system of English prevents the formation of the word *slin*. Simply as an accident of linguistic history, no such word has ever been put into use, although it may be coined at some future time. On the other hand, *tlip* is not an English word—and it never can be one, because no native English word begins with the combination *tl*, even though this sequence of consonants is common in some other languages. Nor can any English word be formed exclusively of consonants, although in the "L'il Abner" comic strip a character named *Joe Btfsplk* walks around with a perpetual rain cloud over his head. His name is unpronounceable in English, but of course it can be written. English speakers are so accustomed to such rules limiting the formation of words that they do not easily flout them. A manufacturer of a new product might possibly label it *Stug,* since that sequence of phonemes is acceptable in English—but he is not likely to give it the name *Bnug.* Potential purchasers would intuitively realize that *Bnug* is an unacceptable combination in English. Either they would be linguistically deaf to it or they would feel foolish saying it, with the presumable result that sales would suffer.

Combinations of phonemes are not ruled out of languages simply because human speech organs might have difficulty pronouncing them. In fact, almost every combination that speakers of English find strange to their ears or unpronounceable is used by other languages, and the reverse is true as well. Acceptability or nonacceptability depends strictly upon the conventions of individual languages. *Bn* and *tl* are not used at the beginning of English words, but they occur in the middle or at the end of such acceptable words as *hobnob,* and *bottle.* Several additional combinations of sounds—such as *zr, sr, vd,* and *ng*—never appear at the beginning of English words, but they can be found at the beginning of words in other languages. On the other hand, English encourages the clustering of consonants more than many languages do, such as the tongue-twisting *mpsd* in *glimpsed*.

One difficulty in understanding phonemes is that speakers of European languages habitually think of words in terms of the way they are spelled in a dictionary rather than the way they sound in actual speech. The word *tough,* despite its spelling, has the consonant and vowel structure of C(*t*)V(*ou*)C(*gh*)—merely one of the numerous patterns of syllable structure acceptable in English. Each language has its own repertory of permissable structures, and some have more patterns than English, some less. The Cantonese dialect of Chinese has four simple patterns for forming syllables —V, VC, CV, CVC—but no pattern more complex than these. English allows clusters of up to four consonants at the end of a syllable, although a single exception exists in which a five-consonant pattern may occur for those speakers who pronounce the *p* in the obsolete theatrical word *triumphst*—which would give the final syllable the pattern V(*u*)-C(*m*)C(*p*)C(*ph*) C(*s*)C(*t*). Georgian and several other languages of southwestern Russia go even further and allow syllables to end in six consecutive consonants. Speakers unconsciously become used to their language's deep-rooted patterns of forming syllables, and these habits are difficult to change. Whenever nonsense words are uttered or new words are introduced into English by borrowing, these words—strange as they may sound at first—nevertheless conform to the patterns of English phonemes. People may at times speak gibberish, but the gibberish always uses the acceptable sounds for the speaker's own language.

Rules for the creation of a single-syllable English word have been stated in an ingenious formula by Benjamin Lee Whorf. This is only one of several descriptions of the sound system of monosyllabic English words; more recent formulas exist, but I offer this one because it has withstood scrutiny by theoretical linguists for a long time. Forbidding as the formula may appear at first glance, it is among the more simple of those that apply to English words. Every English-speaking child unconsciously learns it by about the age of three, and it so quickly becomes a matter of habit that even nursery nonsense words conform to it. Give the child a word with a sound pattern that is not in accord with the formula and he will have great difficulty pronouncing it. By the age of twelve these formulas are so ingrained that learning a foreign language presents a major problem. The child unconsciously tries to make the words of the foreign language, which of course follow their own formulas, conform to the formulas he is accustomed to in English.

Each of the terms in Whorf's formula is numbered 1 through 15, but it is simplest to begin by looking at the eighth term. This shows a V between two plus signs, which means that every English word must contain a vowel; it may be any vowel in the language, no matter how the word begins or ends. Now go to the beginning of the formula, where the first term shows a zero. The zero indicates that the vowel in a single-syllable English word does not necessarily have to be preceded by a consonant (a rule which would account for a word like *ant*). Such a provision is self-evident to speakers of English, but it is not permissible for speakers of some other languages, such as Polynesian, to begin words with a vowel.

The second term shows a C, which means that a word in English might also begin with a consonant. Note that the C is followed by a minus sign and an *ng*, which indicates the exception that no English word can begin with the consonant pronounced *ng* (even though it may end a word, as in *hang*). The third term consists of two columns of consonants (the Greek theta, θ, is linguistic shorthand for the *th* of *thread*). A word may begin with any of the consonants shown in the first column and be followed by *r*—and *g*, *k*, *f*, and *b*

$$\overbrace{}^{C,C,>C}$$

1	2	3	4	5	6	7	8	9	10	11	12	13	14	15
												l-b,m,f	k	t/d
											mp		ks	st/zd
											sp		n	$\pm$s/z
											s-k	lch	t	⊙₁
												njh	, d	d
						k		w		l,ng	s-t		l n	
				h	k-w	t		y-o			d		n	
	g-1			k	P-l	l					s		f p̣	
k-l h			d	g		n						,	m-pf	
	sh		t	f		p								
		θ		v		m								
	f-l		p	p		w								
	b-l		b	b										
				m										

$$\underbrace{0,\subset ng,\ r,\ w,\ y(u),s{=}t\ r,\ s\ f{+}V{+}(\text{ᵊ})O,\ \pm_r|,C^h,\quad \theta,\ r,}$$

OVERRIDING RESTRICTION

may also be followed by *l*. Therefore, according to this term, *thread* is a possible English word but *thlead* is not. Similarly, the fourth term shows that an English word may begin with still other consonants which may be followed by *w*. The permissible consonant *hw* might at first seem strange, because it does not appear that way in written English, but it is the same consonant usually spelled *wh* or *w*, even though its sound is closer to *hw*. The θ, *th*, followed by a *w* appears in only a handful of English words, such as *thwart*, and the *gw* combination in merely a few archaic words and proper names such as *Gwen*.

The fifth term offers still more possible ways to begin a one-syllable word with a consonant: any of them in this column followed by *y*, but only if the next vowel is *u*. This term provides for the English words that are spelled *hue* and *few*—but whose sounds are more accurately represented by *hyuw* and *fyuw*. The sixth term states that the consonants *k*, *t*, and *p* either may begin a word alone or may be preceded by *s*, but if they are followed by a consonant, that consonant must be *r* (thus forming such words as *crew* and *screw*, *train* and *strain*). The *sk* combination may also be followed by *w* (as in the word spelled *squash*) and the *sp* by *l* (as in *split*). The seventh term suggests still other possibilities: the word might begin with *s* followed by any of the consonants in the long column (*k*, *t*, *l*, and so forth).

Up to this point Whorf's formula has shown that a single-syllable word may begin with any vowel or with particular combinations of consonants. The zero of the ninth term indicates that a vowel may end a word if the vowel is *ah* or the one symbolized by $\supset$ (which sounds like the final vowel in *the* when it is pronounced *thuh*, rather than *thee*). Because writing distorts the actual sounds of English, many people erroneously believe that single-syllable words may also end in other vowels. But the personal pronoun spelled *I* is in reality

sounded *ay;* the word *we* is really *wiy; you* is *yuw.*
Careful attention to the pronunciation of the exclama-
tion *No!* reveals that it does not end the way it is
spelled, with a final *o,* but rather with a clipped *w*
sound.

The rest of the terms show which consonants may
come after the vowels. The tenth term shows that *r,*
w, or *y* may follow the vowel, except when the use of
one of these would result in joining *w* and *y* (indicated
by the zero sign after *y* in the formula). Term eleven
states that a word may end in any single consonant
with the exception of *h* (*hurrah* is spelled as if it ended
with *h,* but it is not pronounced that way). The rules
for terms twelve, thirteen, and fourteen are much the
same as those for terms three, four, and five. Note that
term fourteen represents the pattern of words like
health, width, sixth and others that conclude with the
sound of the θ (which is why it is printed large in the
formula). This term also accounts for the unusual English cluster *mpf,* which appears in the slang word
oomph. The consonants in the fifteenth term may be
added after anything that comes before; this rule allows for forming plurals that end with the sound of *s*
(as in *cats*) or *z* (as in *dogs*).

The formula finally concludes with an "overriding
restriction" which prohibits a one-syllable English word
from ending with the same consonant repeated. (This
formula, remember, applies to spoken and not written
English. *Mutt* is sometimes spelled with a repeated
consonant in final position, but the word is pronounced
as if it ended with only one *t.*) The overriding restriction also prohibits the verb *hit* from being converted
to the past tense *hitt* by the same process that term
fifteen allows the verb *flip* to be converted to its past
tense *flipt.* Such an overriding restriction is by no
means true of all other languages. Arabic, for example,
has words like *hitt,* and the Creek Indian language

permits the same consonant three times in a row, as in *nnn*.

A test of the workability of Whorf's formula is that it has predicted unusual words—product names like *Fab* and slang expressions like *twerp*—which entered the language after he divised it. And the formula explains many of the eccentricities in the English language that are so troublesome to foreigners but are unconsciously observed by native speakers. Many foreigners find *glimpsed* almost impossible to pronounce, but it trips from the English speaker's tongue because the *gl* is allowed by term three, the *i* by eight, and the *mpst* by twelve and fifteen. Native speakers of English have no difficulty in pronouncing the mouthful of consonants *ksθs* (as in sixths), but the simpler cluster *sisths* goes contrary to the formula and therefore sounds strange to them. The formula does not allow for a final *mb* sound, which is why the word spelled *lamb* is pronounced as if it were *lam*.

At the conclusion of his discussion, Whorf commented:

> The way the patterns summarized in this formula control the forms of English words is really extraordinary. A new monosyllable turned out, say by Walter Winchell or by a plugging adman concocting a name for a new breakfast mush, is struck from this mold as surely as if I pulled the lever and the stamp came down on his brain. . . . I can predict, within limits, what Winchell will or won't do. He may coin a word *thrub*, but he will not coin a word *srub*, for the formula cannot produce a *sr*.

Whorf's formula is typical of numerous other ones, often much more complicated, that apply to the sound structure of English. They are unconsciously known by all native speakers of the language, and they are the reason certain words sound either strange or familiar. The nonsense words of Lewis Carroll's "Jabber-wocky" (" 'Twas brillig, and the slithy toves") may indeed be nonsense, but they are *English* nonsense. They conform strictly to rules of English sound structure—and to the grammar also, as will be discussed in the next chapter.

14

Making Combinations

Suppose that Chee, a native speaker of Navaho, and Jack, a native speaker of English, are listening to someone speak Navaho. In an obvious way, Chee and Jack hear exactly the same thing, just as they both might hear the same bird song or the roar of a jet overhead. But at a linguistic level, Chee and Jack "hear" completely different things. Chee has no difficulty in interpreting the utterances as organized phrases and sentences and in judging whether or not they are grammatical. Jack, though, cannot tell whether he hears sentences or nonsentences, gibberish or nongibberish.

If the Navaho speaker says *kintahgoo bil o'ooldloozh* ("He went to town on his horse"), Jack has no way to tell whether or not the fragment *goo bil o* is a structural element in the sentence—any more than Chee can tell whether or not *s ate the bo* is a structural element in the English sentence *The dogs ate the bones*. Chee would not understand why he heard *the* repeated, nor would he know that *dogs* and *bones* are plural nouns but the first is animate and the second is inanimate. Both Chee and Jack are equally unable to make sense of the other's language because each, as a native speaker, possesses information denied to the other. In fact, a good definition of a native speaker is one whose speech conforms to the rules of his language in all their complexity, even though he is unable to explain them.

The rules unconsciously known by native speakers are the language's "grammar"—a forbidding word to those who encountered it, often with considerable trauma, from Miss Fiddich. But the grammar she taught was *prescriptive;* it prescribed how people "ought" to speak and to write. Linguists, on the other hand, are concerned with a much different and considerably more interesting grammar, the *descriptive*. This grammar does not tell anyone how to speak; instead it seeks to describe the knowledge native speakers possess which enables them to make statements they have never before uttered and to understand those they have never before heard. This grammar aims for the total description of a language—and at the same time it offers clues to the way the human mind works and how information is received and understood.

Aristotle made numerous statements about language, one of which was his definition of a word as the smallest meaningful unit of speech, comparable to the atom as the smallest particle of matter. His definition remained unquestioned until this century—though anyone who thought about words should have noticed that it was not true. Most words can be broken down further into smaller meaningful parts, just as atoms can be split into smaller particles. The minimal particles which emerge after a word is split, and which still convey meaning, are known as "morphemes."

A word such as *unhealthy* can immediately be split into three separate and meaningful parts: *health,* plus a prefix *un-* which has the meaning of "not" (as in *unfaithful*), plus a suffix *-y* which indicates the possession of the quality indicated in the root (as in *witty*). *Health,* a word in its own right, can be split further into two morphemes—*heal* plus *-th,* which is a suffix used to form abstract nouns from verbs and adjectives (as in *wide—width* and *weal—wealth*). *Heal,* though, cannot be split any further. (*He-* does, of course, have meaning in English as a personal pronoun, but splitting it off would leave *-al,* which lacks meaning in this context.) *Heal,* therefore, is a minimal particle that still conveys meaning, as are the *un-, -th,* and *-y* morphemes. All languages are similarly built up of morphemes, but many of them differ from those of Europe in their definitions of what constitutes a word. Europeans usually express a single concept by one word, but a "word" in many other languages of the world may express a number of different ideas. In Koryat, spoken in Siberia, the word *nakomajnytamjunnbolamyk* is a complete utterance—composed, of course, of many morphemes—that translates as "They are always lying to us."

English is a particularly vigorous language in which names are constantly being bestowed on new things and new ideas. The average American supermarket that in 1966 stocked eight thousand items, five years later stocked about twelve thousand. These four thousand new items had to be given names—and they were fabricated out of the morphemes of English. Many trade names are obviously modeled upon existing English morphemes that have favorable connotations: *Vel* (from *velvet*), *Lux* (*luxury*), *Brillo* (*brilliant*), and *fab* (*fabulous*). A common supermarket morpheme is *burger,* incorrectly split off from the English word *hamburger,* which was derived from the two morphemes *Hamburg,* the German city, and the suffix *-er.* That derivation is today ignored and most people divide the word into the two morphemes *ham* and *burger.* The *burger* morpheme is now often attached to other morphemes to form such product names as *Gainesburger* and *Burger Chef,* plus of course creations like *cheeseburger, pizzaburger, beefburger,* and *doubleburger.*

Whenever people coin new words out of old morphemes, they unconsciously follow the rules of English grammar, even though they are probably unaware of the existence of such rules. Professor William Whewell, of Cambridge University, told in 1840 exactly how he happened to coin the new word *physicist* to describe a practitioner of what previous centuries called the science of *physic:*

> The terminations *ize, ism,* and *ist* are applied to words of all origins: thus we have to *pulverize,* to *colonize, witticism, heathenism, journalist, tobacconist.* Hence we may make such words when they are wanted. As we cannot use *physician* for a cultivator of *physics,* I have called him a *physicist.*

At first glance, the coining of *physicist* might seem to be merely the union of the two morphemes *physic* and *-ist,* in the same way that *journalist* resulted from the union of the morphemes *journal* and *-ist.* But that is not so, because if *journal* yields *journalist,* then *physic* should have yielded *physikist* (with a hard *k*). Obviously, Whewell unconsciously altered his new word on the basis of other knowledge he possessed about his language. The linguist knows consciously what native speakers know only unconsciously—that in words borrowed from Latin and Greek via French, the *k* sound is changed to an *s* sound before the suffixes *-ist* and *-ism.* Therefore, *physic* had to become *physicist* in the same way that *public* became *publicist* and *cynic* became *cynicism.*

The opportunities to coin new words from morphemes are fewer than the opportunities to use morphemes to manipulate the words already in the English vocabulary. Morphemes allow a speaker to signal relationships, as when *-er* is used to make a comparison between objects or ideas in an utterance like *Jack is older than Jill.* And morphemes also can be used to signal meanings that a language regards as so important that they must be emphasized. The conventions of the English language regard number as very important. English requires its speakers to provide information of this sort by adding one of the three sounds of the plural morpheme: the *-s* of *cats,* the *-z* of *pails,* or the *-ez* of *roses.* A speaker of English is obliged to tell whether Jack carried one pailful of water or more than one, because he is forced to choose between *Jack carried a pail of water* and *Jack carried pails of water.* Because English, like Spanish and French and many other European languages, creates plurals by adding suffixes, speakers of European languages often assume that it is the usual way. Numerous languages, though, employ a variety of alternative methods—among them, not using plural nouns at all. Languages may also indicate plurality by employing prefixes instead of suffixes or by changing an internal vowel (as we occasionally do in English when we create the plurals *men* and *geese* from *man* and *goose*). And some languages, such as ancient Greek, recognize two kinds of plurals, one meaning "two" and another "more than two."

Although English is punctilious in indicating whether a noun is singular or plural, it fails to discriminate between masculine and feminine gender—unless, of course, the gender is part of the definition of the word, as in the feminine *heifer* and the masculine *bull.* English-speaking children are so used to this system from their earliest years that one of the shocks of learning a foreign language is to discover that speakers of other languages find a different system quite natural. Speakers of Spanish, for example, indicate the number and gender of the noun twice—both in the article which agrees with the noun and again in a suffix added to the noun which indicates singular or plural, masculine or feminine. Thus *el caballo* indicates that "the horse" is both singular in number and masculine in gender, and *los cabellos* shows twice that it is plural and masculine.

The string of morphemes *Jack fetch pail water* is not a grammatical sentence because it lacks certain morphemes that English considers essential to signal relationships: *-ed* for the past tense of a verb, *a* to indicate the number of pailfuls, and *of* to express the relation-

ship between *pail* and *water*. When these morphemes
are added, *Jack fetched a pail of water* becomes a
grammatical sentence in English. But other languages
might add different kinds of morphemes—such as those
languages that make it obligatory to indicate Jack's
state of being at the time this event occurred, the size
and shape of the pail, the kind of water, whether the
action being told about dealt with animate or inanimate
things, and so on. For example, the English sentence
I love makes no distinction about whether the thing
being loved is human or nonhuman because the same
utterance can be used to indicate *I love* (my wife) or
I love (mountains). In contrast, the Nahuatl language
of Mexico has a word *nitetlazotla,* "I love," which in-
serts the *te* morpheme to indicate that the object of the
love is human.

Insignificant as the morpheme might appear as the
smallest meaningful particle of a word, it nevertheless
carries a considerable burden of English grammar. The
morpheme *cat,* for example, conveys the information
that it is composed of three phonemes (*k, a, t*) and
that these are arranged in the particular way that produces *cat* rather than *act* or *tack*. Also, the morpheme
cat conveys meaning because English has arbitrarily
made it stand for a kind of animal. Finally, this sequence of phonemes with a particular meaning functions only in a certain way: as an animate noun. If a
speaker wishes to make this morpheme function in
some other way, for example as an adjective, he will
have to attach another morpheme to it, as in *She acted
catty*. The importance of the morpheme, therefore, is
that it ties together three kinds of information: sound,
meaning, and grammar.

When a native speaker hears a sentence, he has an
intuitive feeling for the function of its parts, although
he probably could not satisfy Miss Fiddich's lust for

naming the "parts of speech": noun, pronoun, conjunction, interjection, and so forth. Even if several of these parts are omitted for the sake of brevity, as in a newspaper headline, the native speaker still recognizes the basic structure and he can expand the abbreviated headline into a full grammatical sentence. He can do this because he is presented with an excess of grammatical signals—which Miss Fidditch condemns as the mortal sin of redundancy.

Redundancy, rather than being something that must be extirpated, is an essential property of language. It provides benefits because the repetition of all or part of a message guards against misinterpretation. All human languages, and most animal calls as well, have redundancy built into them. An ape or a monkey continues to emit its food call until the other members of its troop respond. A human speaker says *Let me put that another way* or *in other words,* and he then proceeds to repeat the content of his message all over again. Nearly every sentence in every human language possesses some degree of redundancy. An example in English is the agreement in number between an adjective and the noun it modifies, and the agreement of both of these with the number of the verb, as in *Three boys go.* If I failed to hear part of this sentence—for example, if I heard only *thr-- boy- go*—the redundant grammatical signal in the third person plural verb *go* might allow me to reconstruct the phrase. I could not, however, do that in Chinese so easily because various forms of the verb are often the same—as when *mai* means "buy," "buys," "buying," or "bought"—although the context usually makes the meaning clear. Communication would be extremely precarious if sentences lacked all redundancy, since the loss of merely a sound or two through inattention by the listener, mispronunciation by the speaker, or background noise might make the entire sentence unintelligible.

Find street? is a confusing utterance that a listener

could interpret in a number of ways—in contrast to *Could you please tell me how I might find the main street in this town?* which communicates an excess of instructions but which could never be misunderstood. A fire engine might pass by and blot out nearly any part of the second utterance, yet its message could still be inferred by the listener. This sentence is not only grammatically redundant but its verbal signals would be reinforced also by the redundancy of the speech situation, which gives the listener an indication of the sort of statement he might expect to hear, as well as by the facial expressions and paralanguage of the speaker. If I see someone who is obviously confused standing on a corner and looking at the street signs, who approaches me apologetically and says something with a rise in tone at the end, I can make a guess that he is asking me a question about directions—even though some of his actual words are blotted out by the traffic noises.

Americans visiting a foreign country whose language they speak haltingly often make the mistake of trying to reduce their messages to the bare nouns and verbs instead of adding redundancy to them. An American who says to a Parisian *désire rive gauche* when he desires directions to the Left Bank has reduced the French language to the point of total non-redundancy, with the result that the mispronunciation of almost any sound could make this message incomprehensible. On the other hand, the American who states the complete message *Pardon, monsieur, je désire aller à la rive gauche* has used redundancy to give the Parisian sufficient clues to reconstruct the sentence—even though a portion of it may be so badly pronounced that it cannot be understood.

One linguist has estimated that approximately half of a typical English utterance is redundant because it repeats grammatical instructions, like tense and number, found in the other half—and the same percentage appears to hold true for other languages as well. As a result, people can speak very fast, hesitate, utter ungrammatical sentences—and still be understood. Rather than castigating redundancy, Miss Fidditch should instead sing its praises. It allows an entire utterance to be understood despite the roar of jet planes overhead, mispronunciations, use of words whose exact meanings are not known, and even inadequacies in the structures of the languages themselves.

The multitude of grammatical signals contained in a redundant statement allows a listener to get the drift of intentional nonsense. For example, the "Jabberwocky" poem from Lewis Carroll's *Through the Looking-Glass* begins:

> 'Twas brillig, and the slithy toves
> Did gyre and gimble in the wabe:
> All mimsy were the borogoves,
> And the mome raths outgrabe.

After Alice hears the poem, she renders her judgment: "It seems very pretty, but it's *rather* hard to understand! Somehow it seems to fill my head with ideas—only I don't know exactly what they are!" The ideas that filled Alice's head were of two sorts. On the level of vocabulary, the nonsense words have no precise meaning, yet they ring with overtones because of their similarity to common English words. *Slithy*, for example, could be a blend of *slimy, slithery,* and *lithe; gimble* evokes to some listeners *gambol* and *nimble;* all but one of the words in the entire English vocabulary that begin with *brill* are related to *brilliant.* And on the grammatical level, the ideas that filled Alice's head were the structures of the English language that she unconsciously knew: the rules for forming words, the relationships between words, the functions of the various parts of speech in a sentence, the use of suffixes, and so on. The poem preserves these structures intact—even though its content is inspired nonsense.

"Jabberwocky" demonstrates the important fact about grammar that a listener does not have to understand the exact meaning of a word to know the role it plays in a sentence. This poem is completely understandable in grammatical terms, although not in terms of meaning. For example, here is the skeletal structure of the first two lines, with dashes indicating the nonsense words:

'Twas —, and the —y —s did — and — in the —.

Any native speaker of English could fill in the dashes easily enough in a variety of ways, one of which might be:

'Twas morning, and the happy birds did sing and soar in the meadow.

An English speaker unconsciously knows that the final -y of *slithy* indicates an adjective, and the final -s of *toves* a plural noun; he knows that *did* will be followed by verbs, as in fact it is by *gyre* and *gimble;* and he knows that a noun must come after *in the.* "Jabberwocky" preserves the relatively unimportant functor words (*'Twas, and, the,* and so on) while making the content words, which are supposed to convey meaning, the nonsense. That is a complete reversal of the way in which a telegram or a newspaper headline is written; they eliminate the functors and preserve the content words.

Carroll's poem could not be exactly the same sort of nonsense in any other language because its entire structure, from the way in which individual words are formed to their relationships within sentences, is typically English. The poem has been translated into several foreign languages, but in each case it had to be altered to fit the structure of those languages. Readers with only the scantiest knowledge of French or German can easily enough see how that was done:

"LE JASEROQUE"
Il brilgue: les tôves lubricilleux
Se gyrent en vrillant dans la guave

"DER JAMMERWOCH"
Es brillig war. Die schlichte Toven
Wirrten und wimmelten in Waben

Many languages of the world are true-life jabberwockies that have borrowed their vocabularies from other languages, yet maintain their identity because they preserve their own grammatical structures. One such language is English, which has freely appropriated the major part of its vocabulary from Greek, Latin, French, and dozens of other languages. Even though *The official's automobile functioned erratically* consists entirely of borrowed words, with the single exception of *the,* it is uniquely an English sentence. A more extreme example is Albanian. Scarcely a word in its vocabulary was not derived from Turkish, Latin, Greek, Slavonic, and other languages—yet its underlying grammatical structure remains Albanian.

The method used by Carroll in "Jabberwocky" has also been used in a remarkable novel, *A Clockwork Orange,* by Anthony Burgess. Burgess' nonsense words consist largely of Slavic roots, but he also employs British slang, gypsy words, puns, and sheer fabrications. Yet most readers quickly discover that they can understand the novel perfectly well. That is because their unconscious knowledge of English grammar provides them with the structure of the sentence and therefore allows them to guess at the nonsense words. For example, in a typical sentence—

The gloopy malchicks scatted razdrazily to the mesto.

—*the* alerts the reader that a noun, *malchicks* ("boys"), will follow, whose final -*s* indicates that it is plural. The -*y* ending of *gloopy* ("stupid") signals the adjective that modifies *malchicks*. The -*ed* suffix of *scatted* ("retreated") indicates the past tense of a verb, and the -*ily* of *razdrazily* ("dejectedly") an adverb. *To the* is an English structure that is always followed by a noun, in this case *mesto* ("place"). Burgess has taken great care to position trail markers, in the form of English structure, that allow his readers to find their way through his thicket of nonsense words.

Everyone occasionally speaks a kind of "Jabberwocky" when he makes what are called "slips of the tongue." The interesting thing about such slips is that the speaker, in the very act of twisting the language, nevertheless unconsciously continues to follow the rules of English grammar. The linguist Edgar H. Sturtevant has stated that such slips average about one in every three consecutive sentences, although some speakers rarely can utter a long sentence without several lapses. The Reverend William A. Spooner (1844–1930), of Oxford University, was so noted for his lapses that the name spoonerism has been given to the particular kind on which his tongue tripped. Spooner, for example, once said to a stranger who was occupying his personal pew in the college chapel: "Excuse me, but I think you are occupewing my pie." He began a speech to an audience of farmers: "I have never before addressed so many tons of soil."

An impassioned statement about the way slips of the tongue bedevil language is found in the New Testament book of James (III: 6–8):

And the tongue is a fire, a world of inquity: so is the tongue among our members, that it defileth the whole body, and setteth on fire the course of nature; and it is set on fire of hell.

For every kind of beasts, and of birds, and of serpents, and of things in the sea, is tamed, and hath been tamed of mankind:

But the tongue can no man tame; it is an unruly evil, full of deadly poison.

Even though the most careful speakers cannot completely tame the tongue, at least when it goes wild it does so grammatically.

Native speakers, no matter how minimal their education, have an unconscious awareness of the correctness or incorrectness of an utterance. Such a "sense of grammaticalness," as it has been called, is apparent even in the child of preschool years. He has been exposed to only a limited amount of adult speech, yet he often halts in mid-sentence to revise what he is saying—a clear indication that he is monitoring his own speech against some unconscious notion of what is correct. A typical example of such monitoring is the statement by a three-year-old: *She had a silly putty like me had—like I—like I did.* Three-year-olds are often heard to argue with their playmates about the correctness of utterances, and even to "correct" the speech of their parents when adult speech does not conform to what they think is grammatical.

Self-monitoring continues into the adult world when both speaker and listener cooperate to maintain a conversation. The speaker aids the listener by presenting his message in a grammatical form that can be easily decoded, and the listener in turn cooperates by paying careful attention and attempting to integrate the elements of the message into a meaningful discourse.

Despite the sincere efforts of both speakers and listeners, speech is almost never the "flow of language" it is supposed to be; it is rarely "fluent" or "a flood of words," nor does it "gush," "spout," or "come in a torrent." Instead, about half of a person's speech consists of fragments of three words or less, and three quarters of phrases less than five words long. Actually, more than half of spontaneous speech may consist of pauses and hesitations. Most people talk at about the same speed, but the chatterbox appears to be talking faster simply because he devotes less time to pauses.

The pauses between a speaker's small clusters of words may consist merely of brief periods of silence, but more often the gaps are filled by *uh* sounds, slips of the tongue, repetitions, stuttering, switches in the grammatical structure of the phrase, and various incoherent sounds. Some speakers fill pauses simply by hesitations like *uh* or *rrr*, while others rely on personal speech mannerisms like *you know, I mean, see,* and so on. Many languages also offer more involved ways similar to the English *Mister—whatever-his-name—Smith—or something* and *that—thingamajig—part of the television set.* Instead of the English *uh* or *rrr*, a Russian usually fills a pause with something that sounds like *mm nyuh* and a Japanese with *ah noo*—both of which sound strange to us because they consist of two syllables, a hesitation phenomenon usually not heard in English.

Listeners rarely pay much attention to a speaker's pauses so long as they occur at grammatically significant places. Pauses are almost never apparent before conjunctions like *but* and *therefore,* before pronouns like *who, which, what,* and *why,* or when they occur at the end of a clause or sentence. When speaking carefully and formally, people unconsciously pause at grammatically significant places in their discourse. However, in casual, spontaneous speech, the rate of grammatically correct placement of pauses drops sharply and many hesitations occur at non-grammatical places.

Nevertheless, experiments seem to confirm that native speakers are unconsciously sensitive to the varying degrees of grammaticalness of what they are saying, even when they are making grammatical errors. In one such experiment, test subjects were asked to listen to and then to rate the grammaticalness and meaningfulness of five-word sentences which had been constructed in four quite different ways. The first category consisted of normal grammatical sentences, such as:

> *Furry wildcats fight furious battles.*
> *Respectable jewelers give accurate appraisals.*

The second type of sentence was constructed with words from the first group; these sentences were grammatically correct, but they were meaningless:

> *Furry jewelers create distressed stains.*
> *Respectable cigarettes save greasy battles.*

The third kind consisted of sentences with the grammaticalness destroyed but with a bare hint of meaning retained in that the words in each sentence could conceivably be related in content.

> *Furry fight furious wildcats battle.*
> *Jewelers respectable appraisals accurate give.*

Finally, both grammaticalness and meaning were totally destroyed in such scrambled sentences as:

> *Furry create distressed jewelers stains.*
> *Cigarettes respectable battles greasy save.*

The subjects taking part in the experiment had no trouble with the grammatical and meaningful sentences in the first category. They scored poorly in sentences from the second and third categories—and they found the sentences in the last group incomprehensible. Experiments such as this one have shown the extent to which native speakers are aware of the grammar of their language—and the difficulty they have in repeating even brief sentences that violate the language's grammar.

As was discussed previously, the modern generative-transformational grammar assumes that a speaker learns the rules of grammar rather than a vast collection of specific sentences. These rules allow him to generate a theoretically infinite number of sentences, and also to distinguish the grammatical sentence from the ungrammatical. Generative grammar seeks to make explicit the rules that every native speaker intuitively knows to be true for his own language, rules that characterize every possible sentence that has ever been uttered or ever will be uttered in that language. It differs from other grammars in that it does not merely describe the performance of speakers; more importantly, it probes beneath performance to discover the innate competence that every native speaker unconsciously possesses in his language.

The search for the rules that generate sentences has resulted in an array of formulas and diagrams that often appear forbidding to the layman. Here are several rules that generate just one kind of simple English sentence based on the pattern of subject + predicate + object, as in *The cat will eat the mouse* (the arrow is a shorthand that means "may consist of"):

> Sentence → Noun Phrase + Predicate
> Predicate → Auxiliary + Verb Phrase
> Verb Phrase → Verb + Noun Phrase
> Noun Phrase → Article + Noun
> Article → *the*
> Auxiliary → *will*
> Noun → *cat, mouse*
> Verb → *eat*

These rules can probably be visualized more easily as a tree diagram of branching lines:

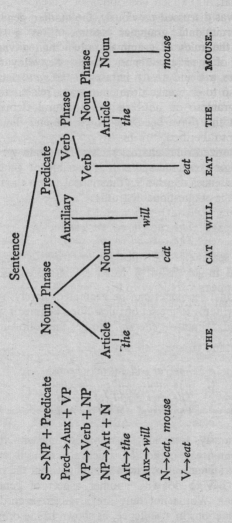

$S \rightarrow NP + Predicate$

$Pred \rightarrow Aux + VP$

$VP \rightarrow Verb + NP$

$NP \rightarrow Art + N$

$Art \rightarrow the$

$Aux \rightarrow will$

$N \rightarrow cat, mouse$

$V \rightarrow eat$

Despite its seeming complexity, the diagram is really a simple and explicit description of sentences like *The cat will eat the mouse.* First of all, this set of rules indicates that the sentence consists of two parts, the noun phrase *the cat* and the predicate *will eat the mouse.* The predicate also consists of two parts, an auxiliary *will* and a verb phrase *eat the mouse. Eat the mouse* further breaks down into parts related to each other—and so on until all the structural elements of the sentence have been accounted for and their relationships described.

This set of rules characterizes only certain very simple English sentences, yet it is capable of generating four sentences which are grammatical (even though the last one is of questionable truth):

> *The cat will eat the mouse.*
> *The cat will eat the cat.*
> *The mouse will eat the mouse.*
> *The mouse will eat the cat.*

Additional sentences can be generated merely by adding new items to the set of rules. For example, if we add the item "Noun → *cheese,*" we get the following new sentences:

> *The cat will eat the cheese.*
> *The mouse will eat the cheese.*
> *The cheese will eat the cat.*
> *The cheese will eat the mouse.*

Obviously, something has gone wrong with the last two sentences, neither of which strikes a listener as being grammatical. An item is missing from the rules—and it has to do with another aspect of generative grammar. Words not only are arranged according to their functions in a sentence, as shown in the branching diagram, but they are also put into classes which possess

"features." The problem with the item "Noun →
cheese" is that the verb *eat* belongs to a class of verbs
that has the feature of taking only animate subjects.
Cheese is not animate, and so the revision of the rules
that added "Noun → *cheese*" is inadequate, because
it fails to take into account that *eat* demands an animate
subject. The solution is to revise the item in the set of
rules about the verb to "Verb → *eat* [+ animate]."
The rules now specify that "Noun → *cheese*" cannot be
added to this sentence because it is inanimate—but a
different noun, like *dog,* may be added because it is
animate.

Rules such as these account for the basic structure
of a language and the apparent relationships between
words in a sentence. Many linguists once hoped that a
complete grammar for English might be constructed
out of such rules, but these rules are inadequate for
at least two reasons. One is that an unwieldy number
of them would be required to describe all the possible
arrangements of words within a sentence. And the second is that such rules would still leave unexplained the
relationship between such pairs of sentences as:

> *The cat will eat the mouse.*
> *The mouse will be eaten by the cat.*

Most native speakers of English intuitively feel that
these two sentences somehow belong together and have
a similar meaning. Yet this feeling cannot be accounted
for by the rules of a simple generative grammar alone.

For such sentences, other rules—known as "transformational"—must be added to the simple generative
rules. In transformational grammar *The cat will eat the
mouse* has the following structure:

Noun Phrase One (*the cat*) + Auxiliary (*will*) +
Verb (*eat*) + Noun Phrase Two (*the mouse*)

A change to the passive *The mouse will be eaten by the cat* demands that the structure be transformed as follows:

> Noun Phrase Two (*the mouse*) + Auxiliary (*will*) + *be* + Verb (*eat*) + *-en* + *by* + Noun Phrase One (*the cat*)

These two sentences were obtained from the same structure, but the opposite might also be true—a single sentence may really correspond to several different structures. The existence of such ambiguous sentences has led Chomsky to state that beneath the surface structure, which can be analyzed by generative-transformational rules like those given in the above examples, lies a deep or underlying structure that is much more abstract than the surface structure. As just one example, think for a moment about the sentence *The man decided on the train*. This sentence might mean that the man decided something while he was on the train—or it might mean that he decided to take a train rather than a bus or an airplane. In the latter meaning, the phrase *on the train* is analyzed to be in close construction with the verb *decided;* on the other hand, in the first meaning *on the train* at a deep level is taken to be a modifier of the entire *The man decided*.

An apparently simple sentence may actually be complex. *A wise man is honest* is analyzed by generative-transformational grammar to establish a surface structure of a noun phrase (*a wise man*) plus a predicate (*is honest*). Deep-structure analysis, however, shows that the sentence is actually composed of two sentences—*A man is wise* and *A man is honest*—which are related in that one of these sentences is embedded in the other to account for the meaning *A wise man is honest* (as is obviously apparent in the synonymous *A man who is wise is honest*).

I hate his shooting is also a deceptively simple sentence. Its surface structure reveals no hidden complexities at all. It consists merely of personal pronoun (*I*) + verb (*hate*) + possessive pronoun (*his*) + noun (*shooting*). Nor does the sentence contain any ambiguous words or morphemes. It is a straightforward English sentence—yet it can mean that I hate the way he shoots, I hate to see him shooting at animals, I hate the fact that he shoots, or I hate his having been shot by someone else. A very simple surface structure is seen to be immensely complicated in its correspondence to deep structures, a basic contradiction that any theory of language has to grapple with.

Chomsky believes that every native speaker's knowledge of his language gives him an intuitive grasp of the relationship between surface and deep structures. He has shown that a native speaker, even a child who has not yet studied "grammar" in school, unconsciously transforms the deep, meaningful structures of sentences into their surface, pronounceable forms. Chomsky uses the following pair of sentences as an example:

> *John is eager to please.*
> *John is easy to please.*

Both sentences look as if they have the same surface structure of noun (*John*) + verb (*is*) + adjective phrase (either *eager to please* or *easy to please*). Yet a native speaker of English immediately recognizes that the two sentences differ profoundly. In the first sentence, *John* is clearly the subject of the verb *to please;* he is the one who is doing the pleasing. But in the case of *John is easy to please,* someone else finds it easy to please John, and so *John* is the direct object of the verb *to please.* Clearly, a basic difference exists between the two sentences—but it is not represented at all in the surface structure. A sequence of complicated transformations is necessary to translate the deep

structure of *John is easy to please* into its surface
structure—yet every native speaker intuitively understands the difference between the two sentences at the
deep level without even thinking about it.

This sort of innate knowledge of the deep structure
of language, apparent even in the speech of a five-
year-old child, is one of the arguments that Chomsky
marshals to maintain that all human beings are born
with a blueprint for language—that at birth they are
adapted to rapid language-learning in the same way that
at birth they are adapted to walking on two legs. The
enormously complicated theory that generative-transformational grammar expounds is what every pre-
school child manages to put together for himself out of
the scattering of sentences, both grammatical and ungrammatical, he has heard in his brief life. And since
a human child can learn any of the thousands of languages spoken in the world with equal ease, depending
solely upon the speech community in which he grows
up, the implication is that languages must have in
common the same deep structure—which is why some
linguists claim a "universal grammar" for all human
beings. Actually, the more we learn about languages,
the more we find they are alike rather than dissimilar.
And the changes that are obvious in a single language
at different periods in its history can often be explained
as the result of universal processes.

V

THE CHANGING GAME

15

Language in Flux

In 1914, Monica Baldwin, the niece of the future British prime minister Stanley Baldwin, entered a convent and remained there in total seclusion for twenty-eight years. When she finally emerged, the map of Europe was scarcely recognizable; technology had dramatically altered everyday life; most of the customs she had been bred to as a young girl had changed greatly. But she was even more puzzled by what she heard. She found it difficult to communicate with other members of her speech community, for not only had words been added or lost in the vocabulary, but the usage of once-familiar words was often different. New idioms had become popular; when people said to her *It's your funeral* or *Believe it or not,* she looked at them befuddled. Seemingly, Monica Baldwin had returned to her own speech community, but in reality it was a different one in time even though it remained the same geographically and in the ethnic composition of its membership.

Miss Baldwin's unsettling experience calls attention to a fact that every speaker unconsciously knows: Language does not stand still. Surprisingly, despite this knowledge, most speakers are fearful of change. The French have for centuries fought against changes in their tongue, and they were generally successful until after the Second World War, when the onslaught of

American English resulted in upward of 35,000 English words (called *franglais* by Frenchmen) entering the French vocabulary. But a commission on terminology, established in 1970 by French president Georges Pompidou, is hard at work eliminating *franglais* from the language. In its initial report the commission purged from government correspondence and speeches, from use on government-controlled broadcasting stations, and from schools some 350 imports like *hit parade, one-man show,* and *zoning*—substituting for them, respectively, *palmares, spectacle solo,* and *zonage.* However, an even larger number of words, mostly of American origin—such as *les blugines* ("blue jeans"), *le weekend, le grand rush,* and *le snacque-barre*—are being endured so long as they are pronounced in the French manner.

Letters to the editors of English and American newspapers often contain expressions of horror about the new terms that creep into the language, and these expressions are usually accompanied by dire predictions about ruination of the mother tongue. Miss Fidditch has dedicated her career to standing rooted as a bastion against change—interposing her massive authority between adverbs and infinitives to prevent the former from "splitting" the latter and insisting upon *Whom did you see?* even though almost every speaker of English nowadays uses *Who.* The question whether or not change is good for a language is irrelevant. The important thing is that all languages inevitably change and nothing can be done about it.

Even so, people continue to complain about change, as did William Caxton, the first English printer, five hundred years ago:

And certaynly our language now used varyeth ferre from that which was used and spoken when I was borne. For we englysshe men ben borne under the domynacyon of the mone, which is never stedfaste, but ever waverynge, wexynge one season, and waneth and decreaseth another season.

The interesting truth that emerges from Caxton's complaint is that language does not change so much as he feared. Despite alterations in spelling conventions since his time, his statement is written in an English comprehensible with slight effort by any reader today.

Although languages change from year to year, it is nevertheless difficult to perceive major shifts during a single lifetime. Such shifts are often the cumulative result of small changes over hundreds of years. An example is the Great Vowel Shift that occurred in English pronunciation between about 1400 and 1600—that is, during the transition from Middle English to Modern English. The stressed long vowels of Old English moved upward in the mouth, with the result that the word formerly pronounced like today's *hay* became the modern personal pronoun *he*. On the other hand, the high vowels moved downward, so that the word formerly pronounced *me* became our modern *my*. Modern English words like *house* and *bite* would have been pronounced by Chaucer during the Middle English period to rhyme respectively with our modern *goose* and *meet*.

Chaucer was one of the Middle English speakers who condemned what he considered haphazard alterations in our language We now know that the seemingly random changes he heard around him were part of a great evolutionary transformation that resulted in the Modern English of Shakespeare's time—just as Chaucer's own speech had evolved out of the Old English. As an example of Old English, here are the opening lines of the Lord's Prayer (whose orthography I have altered slightly to accord with modern spelling):

Faeder ure, thu the eart on heofonum,
si thin nama gehalgod.
("Father our, thou that art on heavens,
be thy name hallowed.")

Most modern readers consider Shakespeare to be more
easily understood than Chaucer and much more so
than Old English writings. That is, of course, true to
some extent, but part of the modern reader's feeling of
difficulty about Old and Middle English stems simply
from the strangeness of outdated spelling conventions.
Nor is Shakespeare as easy to understand as his works
might indicate in their printed versions, which give an
illusion of intelligibility because his spelling conventions are somewhat similar to ours. In fact, had it
been possible to tape record an actual performance of a
Shakespearean play at the Globe Theatre, we would
find it extremely difficult to understand the pronunciation of the actors.

Sound changes often become more marked when a
speech community undergoes disruptions, such as dis-
persal or breaking up into separated communities. At
first these sound changes give rise to dialects, but
later, if the divergence continues, languages evolve that
differ both from each other and from their common
parent language. That happened, for example, with
English and German, both of which evolved from an
ancestral Proto-Germanic. Nevertheless, it is apparent
that the two were the same 1,500 years ago, for sound
correspondences consistently exist between them today.
One such correspondence is that between English *t*
and German *z* at the beginning of words. The English
to, ten, and *tame* correspond, respectively, to the German *zu, zehn,* and *zahm.*

Sound correspondences exist in all closely related
languages, such as the Romance group, which includes
Portuguese, Spanish, French, Italian, Rumanian, and
others. Even if we did not know from historical records

that these languages descended from Latin, linguists would be able to reconstruct a hypothetical language much like Latin on the basis simply of relationships today among the Romance members. Furthermore, on the evidence of other similarities, linguists know that at a much earlier period both Proto-Germanic and Latin were undifferentiated from a large group of languages which today include also Iranian, the Indic languages, Armenian, Greek, Albanian, the Baltic and Slavic tongues, and Celtic—all of which make up the Indo-European family, spoken by approximately a third of the world's population. The Indo-European languages share a word stock similar in form and sound— as can be seen by the English word *three*, which bears an unmistakable resemblance to Sanskrit *tri*, Persian *thri*, Greek *treis*, Latin *tres*, German *drei*, Icelandic *thriu*, and so on. And finally, linguists have drawn inferences about these languages that have enabled them to postulate the Proto-Indo-European ancestral language from which they all derived.

Although historical linguists have achieved wonders in tracing the relationships between languages, they have not been able to agree about the exact causes for change—why French developed out of Latin in one place but Spanish developed in another, or why Proto-German evolved into both English and German in just the way it did. No one knows for sure why the English *t* corresponds to the German *z* with regularity at the beginning of words but not in the middle. Linguists have not been able to arrive at satisfactory explanations of why changes such as these began in the first place and, once precipitated, why they continued. Whereas anthropologists have been successful in formulating theories about the evolution of other aspects of culture—such as the rise of agriculture or the development of complex political organizations— linguists have not been able to agree on equivalent evolutionary sequences in languages.

It was fashionable in the past to place peoples and their tongues on an evolutionary scale from "savage" to "civilized." Such theories usually concluded that one of the European tongues, often the very language spoken by the person enunciating the theory, was "superior" to all the other languages on the scale. But after modern linguists studied the thousands of languages spoken around the world and realized their capacity to express subtle distinctions, they rejected any theory that attempted to show the superiority of certain languages. Modern linguists became virtually unanimous in their judgment that no language is better or worse than any other in its total structure; no language is easier for a child to acquire, less ambiguous, more logical or expressive, more valuable for creative thinking. Modern linguistics emphasizes that every language is efficient for the kind of community in which it is spoken and that it can adapt, when necessary, to changes in other aspects of the culture of that community.

But in their battle against the mistaken, and often racist, evolutionary ideas of the past, linguists may have gone too far in avoiding entirely the subject of the evolution of languages. The facts are self-evident that languages have evolved, that they continue to do so—and that not all languages are equal. As was shown in an earlier chapter, it is difficult to create certain metaphorical place names in the Eskimo language but easy to do so in Kwakiutl, because of the different ways the two languages combine suffixes and stem words. Similarly, when languages are compared in their abilities to meet specific needs, one language may prove more efficient in certain respects than another. Comparing languages in this way does not smack of the superior attitude of European linguists in previous centuries. It is simply a recognition that not all languages possess exactly the same resources. If I wished to create new terms for the study of human anatomy, I would find German more efficient than French because it is very easy to com-

LANGUAGE IN FLUX | 337

pound words in German but extremely difficult to do so in French. A Chinese-American linguist, Yuen Ren Chao, has claimed that Chinese is more congenial than English for discussions about symbolic logic. And I certainly could talk more easily about color in any of the major world languages than in the languages of interior New Guinea.

Although the origin of language itself is forever hidden in the unrecoverable past, sufficient documents exist whereby the beginnings and early history of many modern languages can be traced. English today is the instrument of a remarkable diversity of speech communities around the globe—not only in Great Britain and North America but also in many areas of Southeast Asia and the South Pacific, in the Caribbean, and in former British colonies in Africa. These communities speak their own versions of "English," which may not be mutually intelligible and which certainly differ one from the other in pronunciation, vocabulary, paralanguage, and the strategies of the language game. Yet each kind of "English" can ultimately be traced back to a small geographical area of northern Europe and to the effects of various cultural and historical events.

The origins of English are better known than many other languages because of the number of documents that have survived. When the Roman occupation ended in A.D. 410, Celtic was still the native tongue, though some Latin was spoken in the towns. The Celts might have had a major influence on the future English language, but as a people subjugated first by the Romans, and later by the Jutes, Angles, and Saxons, their effect was negligible. Aside from some British place names (*Thames, Avon, London, York,* and so on), little more than a dozen Celtic words (such as *curse, crag, cross,* and *ass*) survive in today's vocabulary. Soon after the Romans abandoned Britain, a leader of the Celts, who was hard pressed by other tribes, requested military assistance from the Jutes of northern Denmark in exchange for some territory. The Jutes defeated these enemy tribes, the Picts and the Scots—and then turned on the Celts as well, thereby establishing the Teutonic founders of the English language on British soil. Shortly thereafter, in 477, the Saxons, who lived between the Rhine and Elbe rivers, invaded southern Britain, and in the following generation the Angles from southern Denmark established themselves in most of Britain north of the Thames River. During the next three centuries, seven petty kingdoms of Teutonic origins ruled Britain; the Celts, constantly retreating westward before a succession of invaders, finally found sanctuary in Wales and in Cornwall on Britain's southwestern tip.

Despite cultural differences, the Teutonic tribes were linguistically similar; they spoke dialects of Old English that varied only slightly from one to the other. But almost immediately the new English language, which was remarkably like some of the German dialects of today, began to borrow Latin words brought from Ireland by Christian missionaries—words such as *sign, wall, street, mile, cheap, pound, kettle,* and *gem.* The borrowing of Latin words increased during and after the reign of Alfred the Great—who in 878 united all the English-speaking tribes—but the influence at first was largely on the upper class. The mass of the population borrowed from the Scandinavian languages of Danish and Viking invaders. Whereas an English yeoman might have incorporated perhaps a hundred words of Latin origin into his Old English vocabulary, more than two thousand Scandinavian words became part of his speech—simple, everyday words like *birth, law, seat, sky, trust, ugly, crawl, scare, take,* and so on. Even more important was the influence of Scandinavian on the structure of Old English, in the elimination of many frills and grammatical niceties in favor of the clarity and directness so much admired in English today. Among these structural changes was a simplified pronoun system—including the introduction of words like *they, them,* and *their*—which replaced the complex system of Old English.

The English language had been molded into recognizable form, both in its vocabulary and in its grammar, when in 1066 the Normans of France conquered England and crowned William as king. During the next two centuries, the Normans reigned as the total, and often ruthless, masters of England. Aside from the political and social convulsions they caused, they also brought about a lasting split between the Norman-derived vocabulary of English speakers who desired advancement at court and the Anglo-Saxon of the common people. Terms borrowed from Norman were particularly rich in the areas of government (*crown, power, court, minister, council, nation*), the military (*battle, army, war, peace, enemy, soldier, guard, banner*), law (*jury, judge, crime, accuse, justice, defendant, attorney*), and religion and morals (*mercy, pray, preach, angel, religion, baptism, miracle, sermon, virtue, charity*). During the early Middle English period, speakers of both Norman and Anglo-Saxon attempted to heal the linguistic division by using synonyms derived from both speech communities—which is the origin of the numerous parallel expressions still in use, such as *law and order, acknowledge and confess, help and succor, lord and master, love and cherish, ways and means.* But integration of the two languages by parallel construction was an unwieldy device, and the distinction made today between a polite, upper-class vocabulary and a vulgar, lower-class one is traceable to the distinction once made between Norman-derived and Anglo-Saxon-derived words.

The tendency of English speakers to take their vocabulary from wherever they find it has never abated since the formation of the language in the middle of the fifth century. Even the menu for an American breakfast emphasizes that English is a patchwork of words borrowed from other languages. A typical meal might begin with juice or fruit—perhaps *grapefruit* (a compound of two French words first put together on American soil), *melon* (of Greek origin via French), or *cantaloupe* (named after a town in Italy). Or the meal might begin with *an orange,* derived from the Arabic *naranj.* (This word would have been expected to produce the English *narange.* But by an unusual process in English, the *n* has been taken from the noun and added to the article—as happened also with *an adder* and *an apron,* which were originally *a nadder* and *a napron.*) After juice or fruit, the American breakfast usually consists of *cereal* (derived from *Ceres,* the Roman goddess of agriculture) or *bacon* (French) and *eggs* (Old Norse), with *toast* (French), *butter* (Latin), and *marmalade* (Portuguese). The beverage might be *coffee* (Arabic), *tea* (Chinese via Malayan Dutch), or *cocoa* (Nahuatl via Mexican Spanish).

Just this simple meal yields common English words derived from related Germanic and Scandinavian tongues, from the Latin, Greek, and Arabic of the Middle Ages, from the Romance group, and from exotic languages. In fact, everyday English words have been imported from languages in all parts of the world:

LOANING LANGUAGE	EXAMPLE OF A BORROWED WORD
Algonkian Indian	*skunk*
Arabic	*alcohol*
Arawak	*barbecue*
Bantu	*zebra*
Canadian French	*rapids*
Celtic	*vassal*
Chinese	*yen* ("craving")
Croatian	*cravat*
Czech	*robot*
Dutch	*boss*
Eskimo	*kayak*

LOANING LANGUAGE	EXAMPLE OF A BORROWED WORD
French	*emotion*
German	*delicatessen*
Greek	*astronomy*
Hawaiian	*ukulele*
Hebrew	*amen*
Hindi	*punch*
Irish	*smithereens*
Italian	*rocket*
Japanese	*tycoon*
Latin	*focus*
Mexican Spanish	*hoosegow*
Nahuatl	*tomato*
Ojibway Indian	*mackinaw*
Old Norse	*salt*
Persian	*lilac*
Portuguese	*cuspidor*
Quechua Indian	*quinine*
Russian	*sputnik*
Sanskrit	*jute*
Tongan	*taboo*
Tupi Indian	*jaguar*
Turkish	*yoghurt*
West Indian	*mahogany*
Yiddish	*kibitzer*

This list could easily enough have been extended beyond these three dozen, but the point is obvious that English has been a verbally acquisitive language from its beginnings.

All languages, of course, borrow to some extent, and for various reasons. Prestige was an important factor for those Englishmen who wanted to advance in government, the military, or the clergy and who therefore larded their speech with Norman terms. Another reason is that a speech community expanding beyond its borders finds it easier to borrow an existing word from the indigenous language than to coin a new word. The settlers of North America were quick to extirpate the Indians they found on the land—but quick also to preserve the Indian vocabulary for rivers, settlements, plants, animals, and various native inventions (*Mississippi, Chicago, squash, woodchuck, moccasin,* and so on). Finally, borrowings also reflect the routes of cultural imports—science from the Arabs during the Middle Ages (*zero, alchemy, algebra, alkali, elixir*) and music from Italy (*opera, soprano, piano, virtuoso*).

The real test, though, of the impact of one language upon another is not in the number of borrowed nouns but in the extent to which verbs and grammatical structures have been appropriated. The American colonists borrowed hundreds of words for places and material objects from the Indians, yet only four verbs in English stem from Indian influence and even these were ultimately derived from nouns: *to caucus, to powwow, to tomahawk,* and *to skunk.* Not a single phoneme, verb ending, pronoun, or new method of word order passed into the English language from the dozens of Indian language families the settlers encountered. Much the same thing occurred with words the American colonists borrowed from the French in the New World. *Pumpkin, chowder, butte, levee, prairie, shanty, carryall,* and *dime* were readily incorporated from French into American English—but only four verbs were borrowed (*to toboggan, to cache, to portage,* and *to sashay*).

Borrowing is rarely the simple transaction of appropriating a term from someone else's language. Numerous influences in the appropriating language assure that the borrowed item will not be admitted unchanged, whether it be in sound, in meaning, or in grammar. For example, almost all the French words admitted to English since the Norman Conquest have been forced to obey the English sound system. The English *r* was substituted for the rolled French *r;* nasalized French vowels, such as the -on of nation, lost their strong nasalization after adoption into English; the patterns of stress and tone in the original words were almost always altered. The reason for such changes is obvious. Borrowers know how to pronounce their own language but not the language from which they are borrowing. Occasionally, though, sounds as well as words are borrowed. Both v and z were rare in English before the Norman Conquest, but loan words from the French (such as very, valley, zeal, and zest) resulted in the establishment of these sounds in English. And once they had been admitted as sounds, the way was open for English to borrow words from other languages that used them.

English speakers of today will inform those in the future exactly how each word is now pronounced, for they will leave behind them libraries of electronic recordings. Previous generations have not endowed today's linguists with recordings, but rather with a different guide to pronunciation: the rhymes of poetry. For example, in the eighteenth century Alexander Pope rhymed a couplet this way:

> Yet write, O write me all, that I may join
> Griefs to my griefs, and echo sights to thine

Obviously, to produce a rhyme, either join or thine had to be pronounced differently in the eighteenth century than it is in the twentieth. This couplet, as well as other poetry dating from that period, shows that join was pronounced as if it were spelled jine, a pronunciation which has been preserved to this day in southern Appalachian mountain speech. Actually, the oi vowel entered English through borrowings from French and was but slowly accepted as an everyday vowel in the language. Even in the twentieth century some speakers persist in pronouncing oil as if it were spelled ile (which is the title of a one-act play by Eugene O'Neill).

By a similar process the consonant cluster *sch*—as in *schmaltz, schlemiel, schmuck,* and *schnauzer*—has in recent decades been borrowed from German and Yiddish and no doubt will soon be combined with native sounds to produce new combinations in English. During the few decades, primarily 1920 to 1940, in which Yiddish was an important minority language in America, it enriched English out of all proportion to the number of its speakers. In addition to endowing American English with such words as *schnook, mazuma, shamus* ("detective"), and *bagel,* Yiddish also contributed numerous idioms which are merely literal translations of Yiddish expressions: *I should worry, I should live so long, Get lost, Pardon the expression, He doesn't know from nothing, Give a look, I need it like a hole in the head,* and so on. The grammatical device popular nowadays of adding an intensifier to the end of a phrase—as in *He asked for five dollars yet!*—was taken from a similar structure in Yiddish which places *noch* at the end of a sentence. And derived from Yiddish also is today's rhyming slang, often used to lend a note of deprecation: *Oedipus-schmoedipus, so long as he loves his mother.*

The meanings of words, also, are in constant flux during a language's history. When Shakespeare wrote in *King Lear* about "mice, and rats, and such small deer," he obviously was not giving *deer* its modern meaning but rather was using it as a general word to signify "animals." Such a change from a general to a more restricted meaning is common in the history of any language. In English, for example, *meat* meant "any kind of food" until about five hundred years ago, when it began to lose its general meaning and to refer specifically to the flesh of animals, driving out the previous word *flesh.* A new general word was therefore needed to fill the place of the original meaning of *meat,* so *food* came into more widespread use. *Meat* is still undergoing restriction in meaning, since increasingly it refers only to certain kinds of animal flesh, usually that from cattle and sheep. The opposite process is, of course, also at work as certain words expand from a restricted to a very general meaning. *Dog* once referred only to a powerful breed of hunting dog, but nowadays it applies to any breed at all, from a chihuahua to a St. Bernard.

Finally, languages undergo changes in their grammatical structures. Miss Fidditch enunciates the commandment that thou shalt not use two negatives in the same sentence, as in *He didn't find nobody home.* But double negatives never troubled Shakespeare, who, to give just one example, wrote in *Romeo and Juliet:* "I will not budge for no man's pleasure." And even earlier Chaucer wrote in *Canterbury Tales:*

> He nevere yet no vilenye ne seyde
> In al his lyf unto no maner wight.

Chaucer's sentence translates into Modern English as: "He never did not say no harm to no kind of creature in all his life"—an appalling use, by Miss Fidditch's standards, of four negatives. Shakespeare, Chaucer, and numerous other authors have piled up negatives as a way to emphasize negation—but, unfortunately, Miss Fidditch's logic that two negatives cancel each other out and produce an affirmative is resulting in the disappearance of this device.

Modern speakers of English often regard as exalted "poetry" some of the strange grammatical devices they encounter in Shakespeare. They are likely to attribute unusual sentence structure, word order, or phraseology to the inspired tongue of the divine bard of Stratford—whereas in many cases Shakespeare was merely recording accurately the way the people of his time spoke. *What say you?* might sound "poetic" to modern ears, but it was simply the word order common in Shakespeare's time for posing the question equivalent in today's speech to *What do you say?* And Shakespeare's line from *The Taming of the Shrew*—"Villain, knock me at the gate"—is not so much poetic inspiration as a grammatical device of the Elizabethans which was more emphatic than today's *Villain, knock at the gate for me.*

Such changes in the structure of English grammar resulted from the internal evolution of the language itself, but other changes sometimes were the result of borrowing grammatical principles from other languages. Scandinavian, for example, gave English the principle of strong stress on the preposition—which might at first seem to be a modest gift, but which actually was the key by which English has been able to form idiomatic verbs and, in turn, idiomatic nouns from them. In the sentence *Let's goof OFF this job,* an idiomatic verb has been formed by stressing the preposition *off.* This idiomatic verb is then easily converted into an idiomatic noun merely by moving the stress forward: *He's a GOOF-off.*

Latin, too, endowed English with new words and also with new ways to form them: by attaching prefixes and suffixes like *ab-, bi-, com-, contra-, dis-, -ation,* and *-able* to root words. Many of these Latin prefixes and suffixes entered English attached to Norman words, such as *amiable,* but they soon were separated from their foreign roots and tacked on to native ones to form words like *eatable* and *lovable.* English today vigorously forms new words by the same process, because speakers feel free to attach affixes to familiar root words—and thus produce unfamiliar new combinations like *de-escalate, rethink, disinflation, nonpriority, miniaturize, evacuee,* and *circuitry.*

Previous to the Latin influence of creating new words by affixing, Old English commonly formed words by the process of compounding. This was the way *wisdom,* for example, was created out of *wise* and *dom.* But compounding as a process of word formation was swamped by Latin affixing—until borrowings from Greek later revived the ancient Anglo-Saxon tradition, with the result that *telephone* and *astrology,* both compounded from Greek roots, could enter the language. In this century compounding has once again become a common process of word formation. *Stardom* was produced in the same way as the Old English *wisdom,* and so were *breakdown, bobby-soxer,* and *teen-ager.*

If borrowing were the only influence on language change, then all the languages of the world would grow increasingly homogenized and eventually merge on some common ground—but obviously that has not happened. It is true that many languages—among them Sumerian, Chaldean, Etruscan, Gothic, Pict, and Cornish—disappeared long ago and that numerous aboriginal New World and Pacific languages have become extinct in modern times. But the cause of extinction was not homogenization so much as military conquest of the territories of their speakers, and sometimes the physical extermination of all the speakers as well.

The history of the Romance languages after the fall of the Roman Empire illustrates the counteracting mechanism to homogenization—what is known as language diversification. At the height of Rome's power, Latin either replaced most of the local languages of western Europe or became so mixed with them that differences between these languages were minimized. But with the decline of Rome, new local variants derived from Latin arose. And when Roman influence disappeared altogether, differences between the languages deepened and eventually produced the Romance tongues. The Romance group illustrates a surprising fact about change: the dialects in the center of the area of a language's influence are apt to change more than those isolated at the fringes. French and Italian arose in the very heart of Roman influence, yet they changed more from Latin than did isolated Spanish and Rumanian—even though the mother tongue of all four, Latin, had been preserved through the influence of the Roman Catholic Church and continued to serve as a model:

LATIN	SPANISH	RUMANIAN	FRENCH	ITALIAN
tum ("then")	*entonces*	*atunci*	*alors*	*allora*
dies ("day")	*día*	*zi*	*jour*	*giorno*
magis ("more")	*más*	*mai*	*plus*	*più*

People sometimes assume that internal changes in a language are attributable to the influence of great orators and authors like Demosthenes, Shakespeare, and Winston Churchill, but great men do not make for great changes in a language. Most societies do place a high value on the speaker who displays creativeness in style, but the influence of such a stylist often disappears or becomes much diminished after his death. Instead, changes are brought about by unconscious processes that occur in the entire population of speakers. A close look at speech today does not allow us to predict which pronunciations, dialects, styles, or grammatical usages will surely be accepted over others in future decades and centuries. Yet the basic processes at work now have undoubtedly caused diversification in the past, and some will continue to do so in the future. Listed below are a few examples of these processes; although taken from English, they are undoubtedly similar in most other languages.

Loss. Speakers tend to telescope syllables or to drop unstressed parts of a word or phrase, which is why many English words exist in both a strong form and a weak form. Read aloud the previous sentence and you will probably pronounce the word *and* in its strong form; its weak form occurs in an unstressed context such as *Put away the pens 'n' pencils.* Adding -*ing* to a verb like *tickle* results not in *tickle-ing* but in the loss of a weak syllable to produce *tickling*. Most speakers refuse to be burdened by excess syllables, and so in American speech today *laboratory* is being reduced to *labratory* and *cabinet* to *cabnet*. As yet unacceptable to many speakers, except in very informal speech, are the fusions *Wyncha come?* for *Why didn't you come?* and *Tsawright* for *It's all right*—but such a reduction of weak syllables may forecast more widespread changes in the future.

Assimilation. This is a process by which one sound is altered by the influence of a neighboring sound to the extent that it becomes more like the sound that exerts the influence. The assimilation process has been at work since the beginnings of the English language. The word *scant* was adopted from the Scandinavian *skammt,* but the *m* was soon changed to an *n* because in English the nasal *n* precedes stops like *t* and *d*. An attentive listener today can hear assimilation at work in the speech around him. *Grandpa* first became *granpa* through the process of loss. Next, the *n* was assimilated to form *m,* resulting in the widespread pronunciation, *grampa*. This assimilation occurred because it is easier to make two succeeding sounds with the lips (*m* and *p*) than to make one with the tongue (*n*) and the next (*p*) with the lips. A similar sequence of losses and assimilations has resulted in *government* being pronounced *goverment,* then *guvment,* and finally *gubment*.

Metathesis. This process, somewhat akin to the slips of the tongue discussed on pages 318–319 as the spoonerism, results in the switching of sounds inside a word or phrase. An utterance like the Reverend Spooner's *occupewing my pie* is only a humorous lapse, but some changes in the sequences of sounds endure because they are adopted by many speakers.

A modern speaker often pronounces *uncomfortable* in such a way that *-or-* jumps to the next syllable, producing *uncomftorble.*

Addition. Speakers often deal with a difficult cluster of consonants in a very logical way: they simply insert another sound into the midst of the cluster. That is how English words ending in *-mble* acquired their *b.* Originally, the *m* was in direct contact with the *l*—but to go from *m* to *l* the speech organs had to pass from a sound made with the lips to one made with the tongue and teeth. Speakers eventually found it easier to insert a *b* between *m* and *l,* resulting in such words as *humble* and *grumble.* The same process can be heard at work today as increasing numbers of speakers pronounce *athlete as athalete.*

Spelling Pronunciations. A standardized system of spelling can sometimes be a conservative force that prevents pronunciation from going too far astray—but it may also have the opposite effect and itself create changes in speech. That is because increased literacy during the past few centuries caused people to learn new words by reading them rather than by hearing them spoken in their speech community. One might think that spelling should have adapted itself to actual speech, but the surprising thing is that in many cases pronunciation has accommodated itself to the inexactness and occasional pretensions of the dictionary makers. Words that had traditionally been pronounced with a simple *t* sound became standardized in spelling as *th*—among them *theater, author,* and *Catholic*—with the result that they are now pronounced with the *th* they did not originally possess in speech. And nowadays the pronunciation of *often* almost always includes the *t,* which was not the case before people began encountering this word on the printed page.

Spelling pronunciations are grotesque because they are based on the imperfect spelling practices of our language, which have been called by John Nist, a specialist in the structural history of English, "the worst of any major language of the world." In one well-known condemnation of English spelling, it has been shown that the hypothetical word *ghoti* could logically be pronounced *fish*—because it consists of the *gh* of *rough*, the *o* of *women*, and the *ti* of *nation*. In some dialects of English today we spell the sound *sh* in fourteen different ways: *shoe, sugar, issue, mansion, mission, nation, suspicion, ocean, nauseous, conscious, chaperon, schist, fuchsia*, and *pshaw*. Spelling reform has long been supported by many notable figures—among them Charles Darwin, Alfred Lord Tennyson, Andrew Carnegie, George Bernard Shaw, and Theodore Roosevelt (whose own first name suffered from the process of spelling pronunciation, although his nickname *Teddy* has survived in its correct form). Despite a few modern improvements, today's written form of English is as poor an approximation of the spoken language as it ever was.

Blends. Time magazine and theatrical columnists are well known for the technique of intentionally combining two words to form a new blend: *slanguage, sextraordinary*, and *alcoholidays*. Most such blends soon disappear from use—but many of today's common words originally entered our language as blends, though few speakers are aware of it. Some blends are extremely old, as can be seen by the following sampling, which gives the dates of earliest occurrence of the two combining words and of the resulting blend:

bat (1205) plus *mash* (1000) yielded *bash* (1641)
clap (1375) plus *crash* (1400) yielded *clash* (1500)

flame (1377) plus *glare* (1400) yielded *flare* (1632)
gleam (1000) plus *shimmer* (1100) yielded *glimmer* (1440)
smack (1746) plus *mash* (1000) yielded *smash* (1778)

More recent examples are *smog* from *smoke* and *fog; sparsity* from *sparseness* and *scarcity;* and *rarely ever* from *rarely* and *hardly ever.*

Malapropisms. This word is derived from the name of Mrs. Malaprop, a character in Richard Brinsley Sheridan's comedy *The Rivals* (1775) who blundered magnificently in her use of words. More recently, Mayor Richard Daley of Chicago has contributed such daleyisms as *harassing the atom* and *rising to higher platitudes of achievement.* Such blunders by a single speaker rarely have any lasting effect upon a language, but sometimes the same mistake is committed by numerous speakers because of a similarity between two words. When that happens, the confused word often replaces the correct one, as was the case with *The car careened down the street* instead of the correct *careered.*

Popular Etymology. People who hear an unfamiliar word or phrase often assume that something else was meant, and they make a "correction" where no correction was necessary, thereby becoming self-appointed etymologists. Sometimes so many speakers make the same correction that the change becomes entrenched—and occasionally the new forms are logical improvements over the original ones. The Old English *scam-faest,* which meant "confirmed in shame" and therefore "modest," became the Modern English *shame-fast*—but popular etymology changed it to *shame-faced,* which perhaps better suggests the blushes of modesty. Similarly, the modern *crayfish* seems much more apt for the water-dwelling crustacean it describes than the Middle English *crevice*, "crab." *Helpmate* originally had nothing to do with a *mate* in marriage but rather was formed from *help* plus *meet*, "fitting." Popular etymology is an ongoing process, as can be heard in the current status of the piece of furniture used for lounging and correctly termed a *chaise longue*, "long chair" in French—but which is now rapidly undergoing change to *chaise lounge*.

Popular etymology and the other processes discussed in this chapter are some of the ways in which blundering speakers have changed and are continuing to change the English language—processes which no doubt can be demonstrated for many other languages as well. A point to be emphasized is that we can discuss these changes in terms of "processes," but it is not processes that are in daily contact with other processes in speech communities. It is human beings who speak to other human beings—and all of them are fallible, misunderstand and misinterpret, and are endlessly creative in playing with their language. Human beings, and not "processes," produce changes in languages—which is sufficient explanation for why even unlimited borrowing can never render a language bland and homogenized.

16

Repairing Babel

Attempts to account for the diversity of languages—
such as the story of the Tower of Babel, where Je-
hovah confounded the universal tongue of humankind
into separate languages—appear again and again in
widely scattered speech communities. Here is a version
told by the Choctaw Indians, who in primeval times
lived in what are now southern Louisiana and Mississippi:

Many generations ago, Aba, the good spirit above,
created many men, all Choctaw, who spoke the
language of the Choctaw, and understood one another. These came from the bosom of the earth, being formed of yellow clay, and no men had ever lived
before them. One day all came together and, looking
upward, wondered what the clouds and the blue
expanse above might be. They continued to wonder
and talk among themselves and at last determined to
reach the sky. So they brought many rocks and began
building a mound that was to have touched the
heavens. That night, however, the wind blew strong
from above and the rocks fell from the mound. . . .
The men were not killed, but when daylight came and
they made their way from beneath the rocks and began to speak to one another, all were astonished as
well as alarmed—they spoke various languages and
could not understand one another. Some continued
thenceforward to speak the original tongue, the lan-

guage of the Choctaw, and from these sprung the Choctaw tribe. The others, who could not understand this language, began to fight among themselves. Finally, they separated. The Choctaw remained the original people.

Myths such as these from speech communities around the world offer evidence of two facts. The first is that human beings are conscious of the problems caused by a multiplicity of languages, and they often view these problems as a punishment. The second is that people regard a common tongue not only as desirable but actually as the natural state of humankind before its fall from grace.

To repair the damage done to mutual understanding at the Tower of Babel or at the Choctaw mound, about seven hundred artificial languages have been constructed since Francis Bacon first suggested the idea in the seventeenth century. These languages have usually been promoted in the hope that nations no longer would misinterpret what their neighbors were saying, that suspicion, quarrels, and wars between speakers of different languages would end.

No other artificial tongue has equaled the popularity and widespread acceptance (for a time) of Esperanto, which means "a person who hopes" in this language. Esperanto was devised in 1887 by a Polish physician who borrowed its vocabulary and grammar, both in greatly simplified form, largely from Latin and the Romance languages. As part of the simplification process, all nouns end in *-o* (plural *-oj*), adjectives in *-a* (plural *-aj*), adverbs in *-e,* and infinitives in *-i.* For verbs, the present tense always ends in *-as,* the past in *-is,* the future in *-os.* The Lord's Prayer, for example, thus begins: *Pato nia, kiu estas en la chielo, sankta estu via nomo.* The response to the new language was enthusiastic. An estimated 100,000 people around the world soon became fluent speakers, and many times that number learned at least a smattering of the language. Esperanto produced a flourishing literature of thousands of works, both original and in translation, and scores of periodicals were published in it in many countries. But after a few decades Esperanto went into a decline, and today it survives largely as the preoccupation of die-hards who are trying to promote its use in tourism and science instead of as the universal tongue for Everyman.

Neither Esperanto nor any other artificial language has achieved lasting acceptance—owing to a number of drawbacks that go to the heart of how languages work. As soon as an artificial language wins a large number of adherents, it begins to change in the same way that natural languages are constantly changing. Despite the widespread acceptance of Esperanto, its speakers had little chance to use it in everyday speech. Questions of usage arose that could not be settled because Esperanto was not the property of a speech community with its own rules and conventions. And the lack of concentrations of native speakers made it impossible to employ the strategies of the language game. I cannot duel verbally in Esperanto, nor can I accompany my utterances with a gestural system exclusive to that language. Were I to say in Esperanto *Kien li iras?* ("Where's he going to?"), I would have no paralinguistic way to express by tone, pitch, or stress my annoyance, impatience, anxiety, wonderment, or whatever to another Esperanto speaker.

Even greater obstacles to widespread acceptance exist. Esperanto and the other artificial languages so far proposed are simplified and made universal only in trivial ways. They remain European in their underlying vocabulary, sound pattern, grammar, and categories of meaning. A Javanese would probably find it little easier to learn Esperanto than to learn any of the world languages. Another very important consideration is that artificial languages ignore the reality of linguistic nationalism. Many speech communities—such as the Choctaw Indians, the Chamulas of Mexico, the Rundi of Africa, and others I have discussed—feel that their language is the best or the original one. But basing an artificial language on the Indo-European family implies linguistic chauvinism, a judgment that this family is superior to Afro-Asiatic, Niger-Congo, Finno-Ugric, Malayo-Polynesian, Sino-Tibetan, and the other language families of the world.

After the difficulties of establishing an artificial language became apparent in recent years, enthusiasm switched to another possibility: cybernetics or computer technology. Various projects have been proposed, among them one to program computers so they can decode speech and then translate it immediately into other languages. The hope was expressed that eventually a person might travel the world with a miniature computer, have speakers of foreign languages talk into it, and then immediately hear a translation in his own language. The miniaturization of computers, increasing their speed and storage capacity, and other problems are minuscule in comparison with the enormous difficulty of programming the computer to interpret utterances. In fact, it is as yet impossible to develop a program, because linguists still know very little about the way the human mind is structured with respect to language. And, of course, the computer would need to store an encyclopedic knowledge of the world as it is categorized in all speech communities as well as linguistic rules, such as those for deep structures, which are only imperfectly understood. The pessimism of many specialists in computer technology was summarized recently by Yehoshua Bar-Hillel:

The shotgun marriage of Cybernetics and Linguistics should be dissolved by mutual consent, though there is no reason why they should not remain, after the divorce, "good friends" ever after. Let them continue to join forces in the study of linguistic performance in speech (and communication, in general), but let the study of linguistic competence in language be given into the exclusive custody of Linguistics, with Cybernetics entitled to visit this offspring and follow its growth only during one afternoon each month.

A different kind of solution to the Babel problem has been to encourage the world-wide use of one of the languages already spoken in the world—in much the same way that Latin was spread throughout western Europe by intellectuals during the Middle Ages. Strictly speaking, this language was not the living Latin of the Roman speech community; it was more like a code or an artificial language that had been kept alive by generations of scholars. Only because Latin possessed a literature, an intellectual tradition, highly trained users, and the sponsorship of the Roman Catholic Church could it be artificially preserved long after it had evolved into the Romance languages. But as soon as poets like Dante and philosophers and theologians began to write in the vulgar tongues, Latin, which had long been dead as a living language, died again as an artificial one. After the double death of Latin, various living languages came into vogue one after the other as universal tongues: Italian, Portuguese, Spanish, French, and English. The rise of these languages was not due to linguistic considerations or to any intrinsic merits they possessed in comparison with other languages. The "virtues" of the Italian language for statecraft and of French for intellectual clarity are imaginary virtues that were discovered only after the nations that spoke these languages had already become dominant in the political and economic sphere.

For the past hundred years or so, world events have been dominated by two nations, Great Britain and the United States, which speak approximately the same language—and once again we see an example of a language that has risen to prominence because of the political and economic influence of its speakers. The spread of English began about three centuries ago when British explorers, missionaries, traders, and colonizers carried it to the far places of the world. The two world wars in this century sent millions of English-speaking soldiers and civilian bureaucrats around the globe in one of the great language exportations in history. No longer was English the exclusive property of the native speaker or of the educated and wealthy foreigner. It quickly became the lingua franca of the world as people learned that it represented the passkey to American and European wealth and technology.

English is today the most widely spoken language on earth. About 350 million people use it in their daily speech and probably an additional 400 million know it as a second language, which means that at least one out of every five people on earth can speak it fluently or haltingly. In comparison, the second most widely spoken language, the Mandarin dialect of Chinese, has about 450 million speakers. Not only do more people speak English but they are also distributed throughout the world on every continent and they include people of all races, nationalities, and religions. On the other hand, almost no one speaks Mandarin Chinese outside western and northern China and Taiwan. English today accounts for the major part of the world's communication by mail, telegraph, radio, and television. Most of the capital cities of Asian and African nations publish English-language newspapers, and all around the world people play *beisbol,* wear *blue djins,* chew *gomma americana,* and dance the *buki-wuki.*

English flourishes today not because it is indisputably the best language for all kinds of communication but because of influences that have nothing to do with linguistics at all: the wealth and military power of the United States, the traditional prestige of British culture, the status of many nations of the world as former colonies or present Commonwealth associates of Great Britain. These things aside, though, English *does* possess certain characteristics that have aided its growth as the world's major language. It has traditionally been receptive to borrowing vocabulary and even grammatical structures from all language families of the world. It is amazingly succinct and direct, as was shown in a meticulous count of the number of syllables needed to translate the Gospel According to St. Mark into various languages:

LANGUAGE	NUMBER OF SYLLABLES
English	29,000
Teutonic languages	32,650 (average)
French	36,500
Slavic languages	36,500 (average)
Romance languages	40,200 (average)
Indo-Iranian languages	43,100 (average)

And its grammatical apparatus is quite simple and orderly—in contrast, for example, to a language like Russian with its three genders, six cases, and confusing pronoun system. If some accident of history had made Celtic rather than English the language of Great Britain and if Britain had similarly risen to prominence, the peoples of the world would have had to learn an extremely difficult language, judging from present-day Welsh. The Welsh system of noun changes, for example, would pose great problems because of the phenomenon known as mutation. In Welsh "a garden" is simply *gardd,* but "the garden" changes the noun to *ardd*. "Horse" in Welsh is *ceffyl*—but it mutates to *ei geffyl* for "his horse," to *ei cheffyl* for "her horse," and to *fy ngheffyl* for "my horse."

No wonder, then, that some people believe English is the answer to the need for a universal tongue. And even better, they feel, would be a simplified version that foreigners could learn in a few months: the Basic

English that was promoted by Winston Churchill and Franklin Roosevelt, among others. Basic English consists of a mere 850 words—600 things (nouns), 150 qualities (adjectives), and 100 operators (verbs and structural words). Such a small vocabulary would not necessarily limit Basic English, since, as was seen in the discussion of pidgin languages, words can be manipulated to serve a variety of functions. This book is not the place to enter into an extended analysis of what is wrong with Basic English, but its flaws and limitations are numerous. Its vocabulary of 850 words is extremely arbitrary. Important words are overlooked and many of those included are useless to speakers in non-European communities. It does not pay sufficient attention to the different ways its vocabulary might be categorized by non-English speakers, many of whom would find it impossible to understand metaphors like *"mouth" of a river* or *family "tree."* And the inclusion of certain operator verbs (such as *be, get,* and *do*) makes the task of learning English harder instead of easier, because these verbs are among the most difficult ones to handle in the language. Symptomatic of the flaws is that it has failed miserably in rendering into Basic English the very words with which Winston Churchill promoted it as the world language.

All of the solutions for repairing Babel that have been offered—an artificial language like Esperanto, the revival of a dead language like Latin, computer translation, or the intentional spread of a modern language like English—have serious linguistic or sociological drawbacks. And we should also acknowledge the possibility that the search for linguistic uniformity has been carried on with the wrong assumptions. Even if speakers around the world could somehow be brought to put aside their national prejudices—which might mean that Russians and Chinese acknowledged English to be the world language, or that Americans were persuaded to learn some artificial tongue—the remaining problems would be almost insurmountable. The thousands of speech communities of the world would have to agree to accept the same rigid rules about spelling, phonemes, the meaning of morphemes, and the grammatical structures of utterances. To prevent another Babel, they would have to solemnly vow to keep the world language free from change of any kind—even though it is a fact of language history that as soon as speakers become separated socially, economically, or politically their language breaks up into dialects and sometimes into separate languages. The greatest problem, though, would be to convince the speakers of the world that the chosen language is the best one. That is because language is more than merely correct spelling, usage, or sets of grammatical rules. It is a way of perceiving the world, of organizing experiences, of interacting with other people—and for these purposes all languages presently used in their own speech communities would be superior to the chosen world language.

A better solution would be to understand the languages we already have—to work with, rather than against, the natural processes by which languages arise, spread, change, and are used by communities of living speakers. In fact, the thousands of languages of the world are a lot closer to each other already, without introducing any artificial manipulations, than most people realize. It is understandable that the idiosyncrasies of languages should fascinate us, but in the process we have gotten into the habit of exaggerating the differences while ignoring the uniformities. Out of the multitudes of possible language systems, human beings communicate with one another in an extraordinarily limited number of ways. Despite apparent differences, languages are very much alike. They are, in fact, but variations on a common structural theme.

I realize that this statement encounters the ingrained prejudices of everyone who has attempted to learn a foreign language. Yet children everywhere, who are just beginning to speak their own language, employ very similar strategies. They usually condense multisyllable words and pronounce only the end of them, as when an English-speaking child says *key* to stand for *monkey*. Very young children avoid exceptions to the basic rules in their language, preferring to say *Daddy comed* instead of *Daddy came*—and they avoid rearranging words, preferring to pose a question as *Doggy can go?* instead of *Can doggy go?* Not long ago, the speech patterns of very young children speaking thirty languages from ten different language families were compared, and the astounding fact emerged that the children produced sentences with almost identical grammatical features regardless of the language they spoke. A mere eighteen grammatical relationships accounted for nearly every utterance they made in language families as diverse as Indo-European (English), Japanese, and Malayo-Polynesian (Samoan). Among the relationships found to be universally expressed were the nominative (*that tree*), expressions of recurrence (*more tree*) or of disappearance (*tree gone*), the possessive (*daddy chair*), and the attributive (*big chair*). For example, the English-speaking child's possessive *mommy's hat* finds an equivalent structure in the German child's *mammas hut,* the Russian child's *chashka mami* ("mama's cup"), and the Samoan's *paluni mama* ("balloon mama"). Even more surprising, the children constructed the same sort of declarative sentences by the same combinations of an agent (*daddy*), an action (*sit*), and an object (*chair*)—as in agent-action (*daddy sit*), action-object (*sit chair*), and agent-object (*daddy chair*). The children, of course, expressed these grammatical relationships by using the vocabularies of their own languages, but the amazing discovery is that they selected only eighteen relationships out of the hundreds or even thousands that are theoretically possible.

The world's adult speakers have similarly ignored a

tremendous range of possibilities and have unanimously chosen instead only one kind of human language. On a very obvious level, all human beings have constructed their languages out of only a comparatively few sounds while they rejected the thousands of other grunts, gurgles, rumbles, snorts, bleats, whistles, and croaks the vocal apparatus is capable of making. More than that, every language has rigid rules about how the few chosen sounds will be used in combination with other sounds—and these combinations are very much the same in all languages. On the grammatical level, all languages insert a meaningless morpheme in one place or another in a sentence, such as the *that* in *John said that he will come.* I could possibly make a case for the value of doubling the meaningless morpheme to create *John said that that*—but no language does it. Nor does any language insist that speakers use an odd or an even number of morphemes, or that the only grammatical category is nounlike words, thereby producing strings of nouns that result in no actions. I am certain that misunderstandings would be considerably reduced if each word were repeated, as in *John John said said that that he he will will come come*—but no language does that either. Other systems which I might also logically devise to prevent misunderstanding have already been rejected by the languages of the world, usually because they show an excess of redundancy. In fact, it is remarkable that all languages have approximately the same rate of redundancy, close to 50 per cent. Speakers of every language twist and turn sentences in transformations, but they are severely limited in the ways in which they can do so. I can transform *John said that he will come* into a question (*Did John say that he will come?*), a negative (*John didn't say that he will come*), and so on. But neither English nor any other language permits me to transform the sentence by reciting it backward, by skipping every other word, or by lumping the nouns at the beginning and the verbs at the end.

A clear fact emerges from an examination of the languages of the world: They universally prohibit certain kinds of utterances—and they universally agree about other kinds. All languages have strict rules about the number of phonemes, the contrasts that speakers must make between them, their relationships to morphemes, the way morphemes combine to produce wordlike elements, and the way these elements are further structured into sentences. Sentences possess certain elements that function like nouns and some that function like verbs; they use other kinds of words to modify their nouns, as English does with its adjectives, and a different class of words to modify their verbs, as English does with its adverbs. Languages have rules to convert verblike words into nounlike words, such as forming the noun *bakery* from the verb *to bake*—or to convert their verblike words into those that function like adjectives, as when *the man who walks* becomes *the walking man.* All languages express quantity, time, distance, and states of feeling and have proper names and pronouns. They offer their speakers a dummy element to use as a substitute for an utterance, like the *so do* in *Jack wants to go up the hill for water, and so do I.* A list of such similarities could go on and on— and, in fact, at a conference on language universals one linguist suggested sixty ways in which the thousands of languages of the world are alike, and another linguist offered an additional forty-five.

It is customary to conclude a book about language behavior with a pat assurance to the reader that mutual intelligibility will bring peace and understanding to our splintered world. In all honesty, I can do no such thing. The question might well be asked: Is not our preoccupation with developing an international tongue based on false premises? The fact is that no one has yet proven that a world language will bring either peace or understanding. Indeed, the people of linguistically diverse little Switzerland—who speak French, German, Italian, and Romansch, as well as several dialects—have managed to get along quite well for centuries without a common tongue.

The more likely truth is that an inability to communicate has little to do with international friction—as is seen in the special ferocity of wars fought between people who speak the same language. During the time I wrote this book the inhabitants of Northern Ireland and of Vietnam were killing brother speakers at will. And similar examples can be found throughout history: civil wars in almost every country on earth; the fratricidal religious wars that plagued the nations of Europe in the sixteenth and seventeenth centuries; the numerous wars between Spanish-speaking countries in Latin America and between various Arab sheikdoms and states. People who speak the same language can hate one another as easily as can people who speak unrelated languages—which emphasizes a point made over and over again in this book. It is impossible to abstract language from its environment of speakers—with their diverse and often conflicting political, economic, and religious concerns—and to claim that language will cure some ill or other in the body politic.

Language cannot be separated from the totality of human behavior. It stems first of all from the unique kind of animal we are, an animal that talks. Since language is learned so early in life and so effortlessly by all human children, it forms the core of all our other cultural concerns: our arts, sciences, customs, and institutions. Within each speech community, the language spoken mirrors human life—the personalities of the speakers, their attitudes and beliefs, their styles of thought and expression, their interactions with one another. More important, language categorizes the totality of human experience and makes an infinite number of unrelated events around us understandable. In fact, language so interpenetrates the experience of being human that neither language nor behavior can be understood without knowledge of both.

REFERENCES AND BIBLIOGRAPHY

REFERENCES

Introduction: The Play and the Players

As stated in the introductory chapter, this book aims to blend two approaches to language that have often been in conflict. One is the recent generative-transformational grammar, which seeks to explain the ability of native speakers to produce well-formed sentences; the other, the sociolinguistic, is interested in the strategies of language interaction in social contexts. Eventually the two views will probably be reconciled, and at this time efforts to do just that can be detected in both camps. The grammarians known as generative semanticists, for example, insist more and more on examining language in a social context. A discussion of ways in which the two points of view might come together can be found in J. Sherzer (In Press B).

The *Hamlet* quotation is from Act 3, Scene 2. Doctor Poussaint's exchange with the policeman in Jackson, Mississippi, is reported at greater length in his article in *The New York Times Magazine,* August 20, 1967; see also Ervin-Tripp (1972) for comments about this interaction. A discussion of rules, and many other wise things, can be found in Searle (1969). The Minor White quote is from *Light* 7, Aperture, 1971, p. 72. Material on the language of the Aranda is from

Strehlow (1947) and that on American Indian languages is from Farb (1968).

1. The Ecology of Language

The metaphor of the "ecology" of language was proposed by Haugen (1971). An important paper on the interaction of language and the social environment is Hymes (1972). An excellent discussion of the social environment in which grammatical rules operate is Lakoff (1972). More information about Apache warpath language can be found in Opler and Hoijer (1940). The detailed study of Burundi speech is in Albert (1972). Functions of speech are more fully discussed in Jakobson (1960) and phatic communication in Malinowski (1923), pp. 313–316. Numerous books have been written about the Marx Brothers, but one which examines their behavior from the viewpoint of communications is Eyles (1969). The *Gulliver's Travels* quote is from part 3, chapter 5. The Hausa tale is quoted by Finnegan (1970); I have modified it somewhat. Finnegan's book is a searching analysis of oral literature with particular reference to Africa; much of my discussion here and elsewhere is indebted to points she originally raised. The analysis of the code word S–P–E–A–K–I–N–G is from Hymes (1972).

2. Speech Situations

The speech situations in which *you must, you should,* and *you may* are used are discussed by Lakoff (1972). The Subanun material is from Frake (1964). The discussion of Javanese is derived from C. Geertz (1960); readers interested in knowing more about the social attitudes expressed by the Javanese language are urged to read H. Geertz (1961). An excellent discussion of

American forms of address is Ervin-Tripp (1972); an earlier but still valuable study is Brown and Ford (1961).

Exceedingly little has been written on the subject of male and female speech. The most recent discussion, and also one of the best, is Key (1972). See also Haas (1944) and Furfey (1944); Jespersen (1964), originally published in 1921, devotes his chapter 13 to the subject. Some of the ideas in my discussion are from Crystal (1971). The Madagascar example is from a paper by Elinor Keenan read at the University of Texas 1972 Conference on the Ethnography of Speaking. The data from Norwich, England, are from Trudgill (1972).

The French-English experiment in Canada is from Lambert *et al.* (1960). This technique has subsequently been used with other ethnic groups; see Anisfeld, Bogo, and Lambert (1962) and Lambert, Anisfeld, and Yeni-Komshian (1965). The study of the variable pronunciations of *going* and *goin'* is by Fischer (1958). All of the New York City and Martha's Vineyard material is indebted to the studies by Labov (1972, 1969, 1968, 1967, 1966, 1963).

3. Words and Deeds

The Princeton experiments are reported in Krauss (1968) and Glucksberg and Krauss (1967), the auditory illusion experiments in Warren and Warren (1970). The fascinating analysis of a five-minute conversation is by Pittinger, Hockett, and Danehy (1960). Glossolalia has been examined in depth by Samarin (1973, 1972, 1969, 1968, among others); see also Goodman (1972). Speech acts around the world that are possibly related to glossolalia are discussed by May (1956). The Minnesota study of the speaker as prophet is by Festinger, Riecken, and Schachter (1956).

4. The Speakable and the Unspeakable

A delightful account of Miss Fidditch is given by Joos (1967). Labov (1969) is the source of the typology of different categories of rules. Much of the Zuñi material is from Newman (1955). I first read the Robert Graves story in Sagarin (1962), where I also learned about the original name of the Alcott family. For the Nupe, see Nadel (1954). Euphemisms about death can be found in Jessica Mitford's *The American Way of Death,* Simon and Schuster, 1963. A paper by Thomas L. Bernard, Mount Holyoke College, on the division between Norman and Anglo-Saxon is in press. One of the very few studies of the language of menstruation is Joffe (1948). My information on taboo words among the Creek and Nootka Indians is from Haas (1957).

The examination of animal terms of abuse is in Leach (1964). The children's name-calling categories are from Winslow (1969). My discussion of obscenity was influenced by Sagarin (1962), La Barre (1955), Stone (1954), and Read (1934). The best analysis of sexual humor is Legman (1968) and I am indebted to it for several ideas in this chapter. The Legman quotation appears on his page 15 and the Sagarin on his page 136. The Freud quotation is from (1938), p. 696. The Nupe pun is abridged from Nadel (1954). An interesting discussion of the two-element structure of puns is by Dundes and Georges (1962). The closing quotation of the chapter is from Read (1934).

5. Verbal Dueling

Conversation openers are discussed by Ervin-Tripp (1964). Rules that govern taking turns in conversations are found in Duncan (1972) and Jaffe and Feldstein (1970). I came across the story about the conversation on the Lublin train in Schegloff (1972); he quotes it from *A Treasury of Jewish Folklore,* edited by Nathan Ausubel, Crown Publishers, 1948. An extended analysis of the conventions of a telephone conversation, and also of conversation openers, is in Schegloff (1972).

Wolfenstein (1954) discusses children's riddles. The Alexander the Great anecdote is from Huizinga (1955), p. 111. Examples of African riddles are from Finnegan (1970), pp. 426–432. Abrahams (1972), Maranda (1971), and Georges and Dundes (1963) present excellent analyses of the riddle form. Social aspects of the riddle are examined by Roberts and Forman (1972) and Blacking (1960). My discussion is indebted to all of the above. Other important studies of the riddle are Du Toit (1966), Scott (1965), Hart (1964), and Taylor (1951). I appropriated the term "gnomic expressions" from D. Sherzer (In Press), who was kind enough to send me her paper in advance of publication. The Yoruba proverb is from Arewa and Dundes (1964).

The Japanese and Arabic examples of disguised speech are from Burling (1970), pp. 135–136, and the Cuna and French examples are from J. Sherzer (In Press A). My discussion is indebted to J. Sherzer, who allowed me to see his paper prior to publication, and also to Burling's excellent discussion in his (1970).

I based my discussion of playing the dozens on Labov (1972 B), Mitchell-Kernan (1972), Abrahams (1970, 1962), and Kochman (1969). The example of Turkish dueling is from Dundes, Leach, and Ozkok (1972) and the Eskimo one is from Farb (1968). The material on Chamula dueling is based on a paper read at the 1971 American Anthropological Association meetings by Gary H. Gossen; I am indebted to Gossen for sending me a draft of his forthcoming paper on the subject.

6. Playing with Language

The Frost quotation is from *Robert Frost: The Years of Triumph* by Lawrance Thompson, Holt, Rinehart & Winston, 1970. An excellent discussion of sound symbolism is Brown (1968), pp. 110–131. Some other studies of interest are Johnson (1967), Johnson, Suzuki, and Olds (1964), Taylor (1963), and Miron (1961). The quotation by Brooks and Warren is from *Understanding Poetry*, Holt, Rinehart & Winston, 1960, p. 1. The Huizinga quotation is from his (1955), p. 119. Almost all of the material on children's rhymes is derived from the fascinating study by Burling (1966), from which the quotation was also taken. The analysis of the lines from E. E. Cummings and Dylan Thomas is partly derived from Levin (1962 A); another of his publications of interest is Levin (1962 B). A further comment on these discussions is Thorne (1965). See also the collection of essays in Chatman and Levin (1967).

The Big Con was published by Bobbs-Merrill, 1940. Aerospace English is discussed by Sears and Smith (1969) and McNeill (1966). The examples of the Anang, Iroquois, and Paliyans first came to my notice in Hymes (1972). My brief mention of the Quakers is from a much longer discussion in a paper by Richard Bauman read at the University of Texas 1972 Conference on the Ethnography of Speaking; Bauman further examines Quaker speech habits in his (1970). Pyles (1959) is the source for my discussion of the Bible Belt style of child-naming. I am indebted to Richard Ohmann for some of the points I abstracted from his (1964) about literary style; another study by him of related interest is (1966). The Twain quotation is from the Harper & Row edition, 1966, p. xxiii. An important collection of studies about the linguistic interest in style is Sebeok (1960).

The Swift quotation is from *Gulliver's Travels,* part 4, chapter 4. The Antinomy of the Liar is discussed by Tarski (1969), Stroll (1954), and Koyré (1946), among others. I came across the Lucian quotation in *Travelers and Travel Liars* by Percy G. Adams, University of California Press, 1962, which I also relied on for my discussion of travel lies. The Twain quotation is from *The Complete Humorous Sketches and Tales of Mark Twain* edited by Charles Neider, Doubleday, 1961, pp. 507–508. The game aspects of lying are presented in much greater detail in Goffman (1969), particularly pp. 102–113.

7. Linguistic Chauvinism

The anecdote about Queen Isabella is told by Lewis Hanke in *Aristotle and the American Indian,* Indiana University Press, 1970, p. 8. Sexist language is discussed in Key (1972) and also in "One Small Step for Genkind," by Casey Miller and Kate Swift, *The New York Times Magazine,* April 16, 1972. (See the reply by Ms. Sandy Whiteley in the issue of May 7, 1972.) An exchange of letters on the subject has appeared in the *Newsletter of the American Anthropological Association,* vol. 13 (1972), nos. 4, 6, 7.

Russian kinship terminology is discussed by Friedrich (1967). The literature on pidginization and creolization is extensive. Two very valuable studies, which touch on almost every conceivable aspect and many controversial points, are Hymes (1971) and Hall (1966); both volumes were major sources for my discussion. The Hymes volume also contains an up-to-date bibliography. Non-European pidgins are discussed by Nida and Fehderau (1970) and the importance of Portuguese pidgin is maintained by Tonkin (1971).

"Diglossia" was coined by Ferguson (1959), originally to refer to a speech community that recognizes two or more languages for communication inside that community; but nowadays its use has expanded to include any situation in which varieties of language are spoken. The Paraguay example is based on research by Rubin (1968 A, 1968 B, 1962). The Pima Indian interviews were carried out by Miller (1970). Unfortunately, space limitations prohibited a fuller analysis of the bilingual process, but it is discussed by Kolers (1968, 1966) and Lambert (1969). The literature on bilingualism and diglossia is vast. See, among others, the papers collected in Haugen (1972), Gumperz (1971), Fishman, Ferguson, and Das Gupta (1968), Macnamara (1967), and Rice (1962). Articles of interest are Blom and Gumperz (1972) and Fishman (1972).

Black English is discussed at length by Dillard (1972); his point of view is a controversial one. For a linguistic analysis of the dialect, see also the chapters by Fasold and Shuy (1970). Excellent discussions of the strategy of speaking Black English, its structure, its history, and its status as a stigmatized dialect can be found in Fasold (1970), Stewart (1970), Fasold and Shuy (1970), and Wolfram (1969). Black speech behavior is examined in depth by Abrahams (1970, as well as in several forthcoming publications). In addition, I have found valuable almost every issue of *The Florida FL Reporter*, an excellent source for information about minority languages; the anecdote about Stewart and "The Night Before Christmas" is from p. 14 of the Spring–Summer 1969 issue. The classic work on languages in contact is Weinreich (1953). The role of minority languages is discussed at great length and with a view toward their preservation in Fishman *et al.* (1966). Important studies are Barth

(1972), Fishman (1971 A), Fishman, Ferguson, and Das Gupta (1968), and Rice (1962).

8. Man at the Mercy of Language

The Wittgenstein quote is from (1963), p. 115. I hope that readers familiar with the richness of Wittgenstein's thoughts will forgive my cursory summary. Those who have not yet read him will surely be rewarded by his *Tractatus* and *Philosophical Investigations*. The Sartre quotation is from (1959), p. 169.

The chart showing how English, Shona, and Bassa divide the color spectrum is adapted from Gleason (1961), p. 4. The classic experiment in color codability is Brown and Lenneberg (1954); Fridja and Van de Geer (1961) used this technique for codability of facial expressions. The study of basic color terms is by Berlin and Kay (1969); some of this research has been challenged by Heider (1972 A, 1972 B), Nickerson (1971), and others, but it has been supported in general by the research of Hays *et al.* (1972). In the past decade or so linguists have shown an increasing interest in the evolution of language, but it is still a subject most of them shy away from because it might be missed by racists attempting to prove the "superiority" of certain language families. An evolutionary approach was proposed by Hymes (1961), but few linguists have answered his call. The evolution of language was a life-long concern of Swadesh (1971); see also Ferguson (1968).

The way speech communities round off numbers is discussed by Lotz (1964). The Greek and German examples are from Menninger (1969), a fascinating account of the relationships between numbers and language. The California examples are from Heizer and Whipple (1951), pp. 63–67. Boas' comparison of Kwakiutl and Eskimo place names can be found in Hymes (1964), pp. 171–176.

The Sapir quote is from (1929), p. 209. Whorf's writings are collected in his (1956); a valuable discussion of his theories is Hoijer (1954). The experiment with bilingual Japanese women is described in Ervin-Tripp (1964). The Western Apache system for classifying parts of the automobile is from Basso (1967).

9. How to Talk about the World

An excellent source for more information about how languages categorize phenomena is Tyler (1969), which reprints several papers I list below. Other important studies, which I could not discuss because of space limitations, are: Witherspoon (1971) and Kluckhohn (1960) on Navaho categories; Pospisil (1965) for Papuan laws of inheritance; Lounsbury (1965) and Wallace and Atkins (1960) on kinship; Frake (1961) for an interesting analysis of the way a Philippines tribe categorizes disease; Haugen (1957) for categories of Icelandic navigation. An irreverent view of many such studies is Burling (1964). Ways to categorize livestock was inspired by Lamb (1964), whose discussion I have enlarged upon.

My description of the American kinship system is abridged from Goodenough (1965); a somewhat different system is Romney and D'Andrade (1964). See also a critique by Schneider, reprinted along with the Goodenough paper in Tyler (1969). A fuller discussion of Jinghpaw is in Leach (1966).

The quotation is from Carroll (1960), p. 269. An intriguing essay on *Alice in Wonderland* in relation to language is by Warren Shibles in his *Wittgenstein, Language & Philosphy,* Dubuque, Iowa: Kendall/Hunt Publishing, 1969. A brief, but excellent, summary of some specific flaws readers will find in dictionaries is in

Bolinger (1968), pp. 286–292. The Mark Twain translations are from *The Complete Humorous Sketches and
Tales of Mark Twain,* edited by Charles Neider, Doubleday, 1961, pp. 261–276. My Russian examples
were inspired by Jakobson (1959). The Nida quotation and examples of Biblical translation problems are
from his (1959). Material on the Yokuts language is
from Gayton and Newman (1940). Important papers
about many aspects of translation can be found in
Brower (1959).

10. In Other Words

The Goffman quotation is from his (1963), p. 35;
other works by him of particular interest are (1971,
1969, 1967). An important collection of papers about
nonverbal communication is Birdwhistell (1970), from
which I took the Mayor La Guardia anecdote. A comparison of the gestural systems of immigrant Jews and
Italians can be found in Efron (1941). Turn-taking
experiments are discussed by Duncan (1972). An interesting description of American Indian sign language
is Kroeber (1958). Kakumasu (1968) reports on the
Urubu sign language. The story of Clever Hans is told
in Pfungst (1911). The experiments with experimenters
are described in Rosenthal and Jacobson (1968).

11. Man the Talker

The Sapir quote is from his (1921), p. 234. An excellent discussion of the theoretical infinity of utterances
is "Grammar and Meaning," by Richard Ohmann, in
*The American Heritage Dictionary of the English Lan-
guage,* Houghton Mifflin, 1969, pp. xxxi–xxxiv. A very
clear, and also sympathetic, statement of Chomsky's
theories is Lyons (1970). The most accessible work by

Chomsky for the general reader is (1972). An elaborate attack on Chomsky's theories is Hockett (1968).

I came across the Alexander Graham Bell anecdote in Barnett (1967), p. 55, which also furnished the Bertrand Russell quotation. The extent of the difference between the vocal apparatus of human beings and non-human primates is described by Lieberman (1968). A controversial view that only *Homo sapiens*—and none of his antecedents, such as Neanderthal—possesses the apparatus for speech is Lieberman, Crelin, and Klatt (1972). The Washoe research has been reported by Gardner and Gardner, particularly in their (1969) paper and also at the 1972 meeting of the American Anthropological Association, and by Bronowski and Bellugi (1970). Premack's experiments with Sarah are reported in (1972, 1971). I am indebted to Irven De-Vore, of Harvard, for the anecdote about Washoe's meeting with a human child. For primate communication in general, see also various papers in Altmann (1967) and DeVore (1965). Speculations about the language capacity of nonhuman primates and early man are Peters (1972) and Russell and Russell (1971). S. L. Washburn, R. W. Wescott, and others discussed the subject at the 1972 meeting of the American Anthropological Association. Research on honeybee communication is reported in detail by Von Frisch (1967). The fact that animal communication is only peripherally related to human communication prohibited inclusion of many fascinating details about mammals, birds, and lower animals; see the papers in Hinde (1972) and Sebeok (1968), among others.

12. The Language of Children

The story of Victor is told by Itard (1962) and that of the Ohio girl by Davis (1947). Casagrande (1948) is the source for Comanche baby talk.

Much of my material on the innateness of language is from Lenneberg (1969); see also his (1967), pp. 135–139. Chomsky's argument with the behaviorists is clearly stated in his (1959). Hockett (1968) and Steiner (1971) present detailed criticisms of Chomsky's theories. A valuable discussion of how children acquire social skills in the use of language at the same time that they acquire their grammar is Ervin-Tripp (1971). The path of normal language development in the child is abridged from Lenneberg (1967), pp. 125–135, with some valuable insights taken from Eimas *et al.* (1971). Tag questions and the example of *hisself* are discussed by Brown (1973 B) in an important paper on recent trends in the study of language acquisition. The literature about the way children acquire language is immense and fascinating; unfortunately, space limitations allowed only major themes to be presented in this book. The papers in Bellugi and Brown (1964) are valuable, as are those by Smith and Miller (1966) and Lenneberg (1970, 1969, 1967, 1964 A, 1964 B). See also King (1969), pp. 66–78, Carol Chomsky (1969), Ervin and Miller (1968), Ervin (1964), and Brown and Bellugi (1964). Technical discussions of many aspects of language acquisition are in Huxley and Ingram (1971). A very important book, Brown (1973 A), on the subject appeared just as this book was going to press.

13. The Spoken Word

Excellent discussions of phonemes, as well as other points touched on in the first half of this chapter, are Lehmann (1972), Chomsky and Halle (1968), Abercrombie (1967), Gleason (1961), and Hockett (1958). Much of my material about stress, juncture, and pitch is based on Dineen (1967). The example of a Burmese sentence made up solely of *ma* is from La Barre (1954), p. 181.

Most of my drum talk material is from Finnegan (1970), pp. 481–499. She gives primary sources, among them the pioneering work of Carrington, summarized in his (1971). The drummed insult is described by Arewa and Dundes (1964). Cowan's report on Mazateco whistled speech is from his (1948). Other discussions of whistled languages are Stern (1957) and Classe (1957).

Whorf's formula for creating one-syllable English words is from his (1956), pp. 220–232.

14. Making Combinations

I learned about the coining of the word *physicist* from Sturtevant (1947), p. 120. Alice's comments about "Jabberwocky" and the two translations of the poem are from Carroll (1960), pp. 191, 193, 197. *A Clockwork Orange* was originally published in 1962; the Ballantine Books edition, 1965, contains an afterword about the jabberwocky words. An entertaining paper on Spooner is Robbins (1966). Some interesting discussions of slips of the tongue and related phenomena are Goldstein (1968), Hockett (1967), Brown and McNeill (1966), and Sturtevant (1947), pp. 85–109.

Hesitations are discussed by Houston (1972), Goldman-Eisler (1968, 1958), Tannenbaum, Williams, and Hillier (1965), Maclay and Osgood (1959), among others; Rochester (1973) offers a summary of the literature about pauses. Experiments on the sense of grammaticalness are reported in Danks and Glucksberg (1970), Stoltz (1969), Marks (1967 A, 1967 B), Coleman (1965), Marks and Miller (1964), and Miller and Isard (1963).

Chomsky's theories are explained very clearly in Lyons (1970). Other works about generative-transformational grammar are Lester (1970), Jacobs and Rosenbaum (1968), and, of course, Chomsky's titles listed in my Bibliography. My book has been written largely from the viewpoint of Chomsky's grammar, yet it would be unfair not to point out that other important theories also exist. Among them is the "stratificational grammar" of Sydney Lamb (1966), of Yale, which states that Chomsky's two levels of surface and deep structures are insufficient—that there are, in fact, numerous levels or strata, each with its own kind of structure, and all connected in a network of sounds, morphemes, and meanings. The "tagmemic theory" of Kenneth L. Pike (1967), of the University of Michigan, views language as just one form of human behavior; Pike attempts a single general theory to explain language and all other forms of human behavior, including football games and church services.

15. Language in Flux

This chapter owes a debt to a wide variety of sources; it would be impractical to attempt to cite them individually for every statement made or for every example given. Let me instead call attention to those that were particularly valuable: Pyles (1971), Laird (1970), Bolinger (1968), Nist (1966), Bloomfield and Newmark (1963), Baugh (1957), and Alexander (1940). An essential reference book about American English is, of course, Mencken (1963, or in the original three-volume edition published 1919–1948). The subject of historical linguistics in its many fascinating aspects is explained well by King (1969) and Lehmann (1962). Interesting studies of recent changes in English are Foster (1968) and Barber (1964).

The story of Monica Baldwin is told in her *I Leap Over the Wall*, London: Hamish Hamilton, 1949, which I first learned about in Foster (1968). Caxton is quoted by Alexander (1940), p. 22. The paucity of recent writings on the evolution of language is referred to in my notes to Chapter 8. Excellent discussions of Yiddish are Maurice Samuels' *In Praise of Yiddish*, Cowles Book Co., 1971, and Joshua Fishman's "Yiddish in America," *International Journal of American Linguistics*, vol. 31 (1965), no. 2.

16. Repairing Babel

The Choctaw myth is from *The Choctaw of Bayou Lacomb*, by David I. Bushnell, Jr., Bureau of American Ethnology Bulletin 48 (1909), p. 30. For the section on artificial languages, I am in part indebted to some interesting thoughts of Robert A. Hall in his readable (1960). The Bar-Hillel quote is from his (1970), p. 300. My facts and figures on the status of English today are from a variety of sources, among them Barnett (1967), Nist (1966), and Baugh (1957). The count of the number of syllables necessary to translate Mark is from Nist (1966), p. 379. My Welsh example is from Burgess (1964). Readers interested in knowing more about Basic English can consult *Basic English: International Second Language* by C. K. Ogden, edited by E. C. Graham, Harcourt Brace Jovanovich, 1968. Pei (1958) is a readable history of efforts to find a world language. Greenberg (1966) is an important volume for the views of many specialists about language universals; another excellent collection of papers is Bach and Harms (1968).

BIBLIOGRAPHY

Abercrombie, David. 1967. *Elements of General Phonetics.* Aldine.

Abrahams, Roger D. 1972. "The Literary Study of the Riddle." *Texas Studies in Literature and Language,* vol. 14, pp. 177–197.

——. 1970. *Deep Down in the Jungle.* Aldine, revised edition.

——. 1962. "Playing the Dozens." *Journal of American Folklore,* vol. 75, pp. 209–220.

Albert, Ethel M. 1972. "Culture Patterning of Speech Behavior in Burundi." In Gumperz and Hymes (1972), pp. 72–105.

Alexander, Henry. 1940. *The Story of Our Language.* Nelson.

Altmann, Stuart A., editor. 1967. *Social Communication among Primates.* University of Chicago Press.

Anisfeld, M., Bogo, N., and Lambert, W. E. 1962. "Evaluational Reactions to Accented English Speech." *Journal of Abnormal and Social Psychology,* vol. 65, pp. 223–231.

Ardener. E., editor. 1971. *Social Anthropology and Language.* London: Tavistock Press.

Arewa, E. O., and Dundes, Alan. 1964. "Proverbs and the Ethnography of Speaking Folklore." In Gumperz and Hymes (1964), pp. 70–85.

Bach, Emmon, and Harms, Robert, editors. 1968. *Universals in Linguistic Theory.* Holt, Rinehart & Winston.

Bar-Adon, Aaron, and Leopold, Werner F. 1971. *Child Language.* Prentice-Hall.

Barber, Charles. 1964. *Linguistic Change in Present-Day English.* University of Alabama Press.

Bar-Hillel, Yehoshua. 1970. *Aspects of Language.* Jerusalem: Magnes Press.

Barnett, Lincoln. 1967. *The Treasure of Our Tongue.* Mentor Books edition.

Barth, Fredrik. 1972. "Ethnic Processes on the Pathan-Baluch Boundary." In Gumperz and Hymes (1972), pp. 454–464.

Basso, Keith H. 1967. "Semantic Aspects of Linguistic Acculturation." *American Anthropologist,* vol. 69, pp. 471–477.

Baugh, Albert C. 1957. *A History of the English Language.* Appleton-Century-Crofts.

Bauman, Richard. 1970. "Aspects of Quaker Rhetoric." *Quarterly Journal of Speech,* vol. 56, pp. 67–74.

Bellugi, Ursula, and Brown, Roger. 1964. *The Acquisition of Language.* Monograph of the Society for Research in Child Development.

Berlin, Brent, and Kay, Paul. 1969. *Basic Color Terms: Their Universality and Evolution.* University of California Press.

Birdwhistell, Ray L. 1970. *Kinesics and Context: Essays on Body Motion Communication.* University of Pennsylvania Press.

Black, Max. 1968. *The Labyrinth of Language.* Praeger.

Blacking, John. 1960. "The Social Value of Venda Riddles." *African Studies,* vol. 20, pp. 1–32.

Blom, Jan-Petter, and Gumperz, John J. 1972. "Code Switching in Norway." In Gumperz and Hymes (1972), pp. 407–434.

Bloomfield, Morton W., and Newmark, Leonard. 1963. *A Linguistic Introduction to the History of English*. Knopf.

Bolinger, Dwight. 1968. *Aspects of Language*. Harcourt Brace Jovanovich.

Bright, William, editor. 1966. *Sociolinguistics*. The Hague: Mouton.

Bronowski, J., and Bellugi, Ursula. 1970. "Language, Name, and Concept," *Science*, vol. 168, pp. 669–673.

Brower, R. A., editor. 1959. *On Translation*. Harvard University Press.

Brown, Roger. 1973 A. *A First Language*. Harvard University Press.

——. 1973 B. "Development of the First Language in the Human Species." *American Psychologist*, vol. 28, pp. 97–106.

——. 1968. *Words and Things*. The Free Press.

—— and Bellugi, Ursula. 1964. "Three Processes in the Child's Acquisition of Syntax." In Lenneberg (1964 B), pp. 131–162.

—— and Ford, Marguerite. 1961. "Address in American English." *Journal of Abnormal and Social Psychology*, vol. 62, pp. 375–385.

—— and Lenneberg, Eric H. 1954. "A Study in Language and Cognition." *Journal of Abnormal and Social Psychology*, vol. 49, pp. 454–462.

—— and McNeill, David. 1966. "The 'Tip of the Tongue' Phenomenon." *Journal of Verbal Learning and Verbal Behavior*, vol. 5, pp. 325–337.

Burgess, Anthony. 1964. *Language Made Plain*. Crowell.

Burling, Robbins. 1970. *Man's Many Voices*. Holt, Rinehart & Winston.

——. 1966. "The Metrics of Children's Verse: A Cross-Linguistic Study." *American Anthropologist*, vol. 68, pp. 1418–1441.

——. 1964. "Cognition and Componential Analysis: God's Truth or Hocus-Pocus?" *American Anthropologist,* vol. 66, pp. 20–28. (See also further discussions of this paper in the same publication, vol. 66, pp. 116–121.)

Carrington, John F. 1971. "The Talking Drums of Africa." *Scientific American,* vol. 225, pp. 90–94.

Carroll, Lewis. 1960. *The Annotated Alice,* edited by Martin Gardner. Clarkson Potter.

Casagrande, Joseph B. 1948. "Comanche Baby Language." *International Journal of American Linguistics,* vol. 14, pp. 11–14.

Chao, Yuen Ren. 1968. *Language and Symbolic Systems.* Cambridge University Press.

Chatman, Seymour, and Levin, Samuel R., editors. 1967. *Essays on the Language of Literature.* Houghton Mifflin.

Chomsky, Carol. 1969. *The Acquisition of Syntax in Children from 5 to 10.* M.I.T. Press.

Chomsky, Noam. 1972. *Language and Mind.* Harcourt Brace Jovanovich, revised edition.

——. 1965. *Aspects of the Theory of Syntax.* M.I.T. Press.

——. 1959. "Review of B. F. Skinner's *Verbal Behavior.*" *Language,* vol. 35, pp. 26–58.

——. 1957. *Syntactic Structures.* The Hague: Mouton.

—— and Halle, Morris. 1968. *The Sound Pattern of English.* Harper & Row.

Classe, André. 1957. "The Whistled Language of La Gomera." *Scientific American,* vol. 196, pp. 111–120.

Coleman, E. B. 1965. "Responses to a Scale of Grammaticalness." *Journal of Verbal Learning and Verbal Behavior,* vol. 4, pp. 521–527.

Cowan, George M. 1948. "Mazateco Whistled Speech." *Language,* vol. 24, pp. 280–286.

Crystal, David. 1971. "Prosodic and Paralinguistic Correlates of Social Categories." In Ardener (1971), pp. 185–205.

Danks, Joseph H., and Glucksberg, Sam. 1970. "Psychological Scaling of Linguistic Properties." *Language and Speech,* vol. 13, pp. 118–138.

Davis, K. 1947. "Final Note on a Case of Extreme Social Isolation." *American Journal of Sociology,* vol. 52, pp. 432–437.

DeVore, Irven, editor. 1965. *Primate Behavior.* Holt, Rinehart & Winston.

Dillard, J. L. 1972. *Black English.* Random House.

Dineen, Francis P. 1967. *An Introduction to General Linguistics.* Holt, Rinehart & Winston.

Duncan, Starkey. 1972. "Some Signals and Rules for Taking Speaking Turns in Conversations." *Journal of Personality and Social Psychology,* vol. 23, pp. 283–292.

Dundes, Alan, and Georges, Robert A. 1962. "Some Minor Genres of Obscene Folklore." *Journal of American Folklore,* vol. 75, pp. 221–226.

——, Leach, J. W., and Ozkok, B. 1972. "The Strategy of Turkish Boys' Verbal Dueling Rhymes." In Gumperz and Hymes (1972), pp. 130–160.

Du Toit, Brian M. 1966. "Riddling Traditions in an Isolated South African Community." *Journal of American Folklore,* vol. 79, pp. 471–475.

Efron, David, 1941. *Gesture and Environment.* New York: King's Crown Press.

Eimas, Peter D., *et al.* 1971. "Speech Perception in Infants." *Science,* vol. 171, pp. 303–306.

Ervin, Susan M. 1964. "Imitation and Structural

Change in Children's Language." In Lenneberg (1964 B), pp. 163–189.

—— and Miller, W. R. 1968. "Language Development." In Fishman (1968), pp. 68–98.

Ervin-Tripp, Susan. 1972. "On Sociolinguistic Rules: Alternation and Co-occurrance." In Gumperz and Hymes (1972), pp. 213–250.

——. 1971. "Social Backgrounds and Verbal Skills." In Huxley and Ingram (1971), pp. 29–39.

——. 1964. "Interaction of Language, Topic and Listener." *American Anthropologist,* vol. 66, pp. 86–102.

Eyles, Allen. 1969. *The Marx Brothers: Their World of Comedy.* A. S. Barnes, second edition.

Farb, Peter. 1968. *Man's Rise to Civilization as Shown by the Indians of North America from Primeval Times to the Coming of the Industrial State.* E. P. Dutton.

Fasold, Ralph W. 1970. "Distinctive Characteristics of Black English." *Report of the 20th Annual Round Table on Linguistics and Language Studies,* edited by James E. Alatis. Georgetown University Press, pp. 233–238.

—— and Shuy, Roger W. 1970. *Teaching Standard English in the Inner City.* Washington, D. C.: Center for Applied Linguistics.

Ferguson, Charles A. 1968. "Language Development." In Fishman, Ferguson, and Das Gupta (1968), pp. 27–35.

——. 1964. "Baby Talk in Six Languages." In Gumperz and Hymes (1964), pp. 103–114.

——. 1959. "Diglossia." *Word,* vol. 15, pp. 325–340.

Festinger, L., Riecken, H. W., and Schachter, S. 1956. *When Prophecy Fails.* University of Minnesota Press.

Finnegan, Ruth. 1970. *Oral Literature in Africa.* Oxford University Press.

Fischer, John L. 1958. "Social Influences on the Choice of a Linguistic Variant." *Word,* vol. 14, pp. 47–56.

Fishman, Joshua A. 1972. "Domains and the Relationships Between Micro- and Macrosociolinguistics." In Gumperz and Hymes (1972), pp. 435–453.

——. 1971 A. "The Sociology of Language: An Interdisciplinary Social Science Approach to Language in Society." In Fishman (1971 B), pp. 217–404.

——, editor. 1971 B. *Advances in the Sociology of Language.* The Hague: Mouton, 2 volumes.

——, editor. 1968. *Readings in the Sociology of Language.* The Hague: Mouton.

——, Ferguson, C. A., and Das Gupta, J., editors. 1968. *Language Problems of Developing Nations.* Wiley.

—— et al. 1966. *Language Loyalty in the United States.* The Hague: Mouton.

Fodor, Jerry A., and Katz, Jerrold J. 1964. *The Structure of Language.* Prentice-Hall.

Foster, Brian. 1968. *The Changing English Language.* St. Martin's Press.

Frake, Charles O. 1964. "How to Ask for a Drink in Subanun." In Gumperz and Hymes (1964), pp. 127–132.

——. 1961. "The Diagnosis of Disease among the Subanum of Mindanao." *American Anthropologist,* vol. 63, pp. 113–132.

Freud, Sigmund. 1938. *The Basic Writings.* Modern Library.

Fridja, N. H., and Van de Geer, J. P. 1961. "Codeability and Facial Expressions." *Acta Psychologica,* vol. 18, pp. 360–367.

Friedrich, Paul. 1967. "The Linguistic Reflex of Social Change: From Tsarist to Russian Kinship." In Lieberson (1967), pp. 31–57.

Furfey, Paul H. 1944. "Men's and Women's Language." *The American Catholic Sociological Review,* vol. 5, pp. 218–223.

Gardner, R. A., and Gardner, B. T. 1969. "Teaching Sign Language to a Chimpanzee." *Science,* vol. 165, pp. 664–672.

Gayton, Ann H., and Newman, Stanley S. 1940. *Yokuts and Western Mono Myths.* University of California Publications, Anthropological Records, vol. 5.

Geertz, Clifford. 1960. *The Religion of Java.* The Free Press.

Geertz, Hildreth. 1961. *Javanese Family.* The Free Press.

Georges, Robert A. 1969. "Toward an Understanding of Storytelling Events." *Journal of American Folklore,* vol. 82, pp. 313–328.

—— and Dundes, Alan. 1963. "Toward a Structural Definition of the Riddle." *Journal of American Folklore,* vol. 76, pp. 111–118.

Gleason, Henry A., Jr. 1961. *An Introduction to Descriptive Linguistics.* Holt, Rinehart & Winston, revised edition.

Glucksberg, Sam, and Krauss, Robert M. 1967. "What Do People Say After They Have Learned How To Talk? Studies of the Development of Referential Communications." *Merrill-Palmer Quarterly,* vol. 13, pp. 309–316.

Goffman, Erving. 1971. *Relations in Public.* Basic Books.

——. 1969. *Strategic Interaction.* University of Pennsylvania Press.

——. 1967. *Interaction Ritual.* Doubleday Anchor.

——. 1963. *Behavior in Public Places.* The Free Press.

Goldman-Eisler, F. 1968. *Psycholinguistics: Experiments in Spontaneous Speech.* Academic Press.

——. 1958. "The Predictability of Words in Context and the Length of Pauses in Speech." *Language and Speech*, vol. 1, pp. 226–231.

Goldstein, Myron. 1968. "Some Slips of the Tongue." *Psychological Reports*, vol. 22, pp. 1009–1013.

Goodenough, Ward H. 1965. "Yankee Kinship Terminology: A Problem in Componential Analysis." In Hammel (1965), pp. 259–287.

Goodman, Felicitas D. 1972. *Speaking in Tongues: A Cross-Cultural Study of Glossolalia*. University of Chicago Press.

Greenberg, Joseph H. 1971. *Language, Culture, and Communication*. Stanford University Press.

——. 1969. "Language Universals: A Research Frontier." *Science*, vol. 166, pp. 473–478.

——. 1968. *Anthropological Linguistics*. Random House.

——, editor. 1966. *Universals of Language*. M.I.T. Press, second edition.

Gumperz, John J. 1971. *Language in Social Groups*. Stanford University Press.

—— and Hymes, D., editors. 1972. *Directions in Sociolinguistics*. Holt, Rinehart & Winston.

—— and Hymes, D., editors. 1964. *The Ethnography of Communication*. American Anthropological Association Special Publication, vol. 66.

Haas, Mary R. 1957. "Interlingual Word Taboos." *American Anthropologist*, vol. 53, pp. 338–341.

——. 1944. "Men's and Women's Speech in Koasati." *Language*, vol. 20, pp. 142–149.

Hall, Robert A., Jr. 1966. *Pidgin and Creole Languages*. Cornell University Press.

——. 1960. *Linguistics and Your Language*. Doubleday Anchor, revised edition.

Hammel, E. A., editor. 1965. *Formal Semantic Analysis*. American Anthropological Asssociation Special Publication, vol. 67.

Hart, Donn V. 1964. *Riddles in Filipino Folklore*. Syracuse University Press.

Haugen, Einar. 1972. *The Ecology of Language*. Stanford University Press.

——. 1971. "The Ecology of Language." *The Linguistics Reporter,* supplement 25, pp. 19–26.

——. 1957. "The Semantics of Icelandic Orientation." *Word,* vol. 13, pp. 447–459.

Hays, David G., *et al.* 1972. "Color Term Salience." *American Anthropologist,* vol. 74, pp. 1107–1121.

Heider, Eleanor R. 1972 A. "Universals in Color Naming and Memory." *Journal of Experimental Psychology,* vol. 93, pp. 10–20.

——. 1972 B. "The Structure of the Color Space in Naming and Memory for Two Languages." *Cognitive Psychology,* vol. 3, pp. 337–354.

Heizer, R. F., and Whipple, M. A. 1951. *The California Indians*. University of California Press.

Hill, Archibald A., editor. 1969. *Linguistics Today*. Basic Books.

Hinde, R. A., editor. 1972. *Non-Verbal Communication*. Cambridge University Press.

Hockett, Charles F. 1968. *The State of the Art*. The Hague: Mouton.

——. 1967. "Where the Tongue Slips, There Slip I." In *To Honor Roman Jakobson* (1967), vol. 2, pp. 910–936. The Hague: Mouton.

——. 1958. *A Course in Modern Linguistics*. Macmillan.

Hoenigswald, H. M. 1960. *Language Change and Linguistic Reconstruction*. University of Chicago Press.

Hoijer, Harry, editor. 1954. *Language in Culture*. University of Chicago Press.

Houston, Susan H. 1972. *A Survey of Psycholinguistics*. The Hague: Mouton.

Huizinga, Johan. 1955. *Homo Ludens*. Beacon Press.

Huxley, Renira, and Ingram, Elisabeth, editors. 1971. *Language Acquisition: Models and Methods*. Academic Press.

Hymes, Dell H. 1972. "Models of the Interaction of Language and Social Life." In Gumperz and Hymes (1972), pp. 35–71.

——. 1961. "Functions of Speech: An Evolutionary Approach." In *Anthropology and Education*, edited by Frederick C. Gruber (1961), pp. 55–83. University of Pennsylvania Press.

——, editor. 1971. *Pidginization and Creolization of Languages*. Cambridge University Press.

——, editor. 1964. *Language in Culture and Society: A Reader in Linguistics and Anthropology*. Harper & Row.

Itard, J. M. G. 1962. *The Wild Boy of Aveyron*. Appleton-Century-Crofts.

Jacobs, R. A., and Rosenbaum, P. S. 1968. *English Transformational Grammar*. Waltham, Mass.: Blaisdell.

Jaffe, Joseph, and Feldstein, Stanley. 1970. *Rhythms of Dialogue*. Academic Press.

Jakobson, Roman. 1960. "Linguistics and Poetics." In Sebeok (1960).

——. 1959. "On Linguistic Aspects of Translation." In Brower (1959), pp. 232–239.

Jespersen, Otto. 1964 (originally published 1921). *Language*. Norton.

Joffe, Natalie F. 1948. "The Vernacular of Menstruation." *Word*, vol. 4, pp. 181–186.

Johnson, Ronald C. 1967. "Magnitude Symbolism of English Words." *Journal of Verbal Learning and Verbal Behavior*, vol. 6, pp. 508–511.

——, Suzuki, N. S., and Olds. W. K. 1964. "Phonetic Symbolism in an Artificial Language." *Journal of Abnormal and Social Psychology*, vol. 69, pp. 233–236.

Joos, Martin. 1967. *The Five Clocks*. Harcourt Brace Jovanovich.

Kakumasu, Jim. 1968. "Urubu Sign Language." *International Journal of American Linguistics*, vol. 34, pp. 275–281.

Key, Mary R. 1972. "Linguistic Behavior of Male and Female." *Linguistics*, no. 88, pp. 15–31.

King, Robert D. 1969. *Historical Linguistics and Generative Grammar*. Prentice-Hall.

Kirshenblatt-Gimblett, Barbara, editor. In Press. *Speech Play on Display*. The Hague: Mouton.

Kluckhohn, Clyde. 1960. "Navaho Categories." In *Culture and History*, edited by Stanley A. Diamond (1960), pp. 65–98. Columbia University Press.

Kochman, Thomas. 1969. "Toward an Ethnography of Black American Speech Behavior." *Trans-Action*, vol. 6, pp. 26–34.

Kolers, Paul A. 1968. "Bilingualism and Information Processing." *Scientific American*, vol. 218, pp. 78-86.

———. 1966. "Reading and Talking Bilingually." *American Journal of Psychology*, vol. 74, pp. 357–376.

Koyré, Alexandre. 1946. "The Liar." *Philosophy and Phenomenological Research*, vol. 6, pp. 344–362.

Krauss, Robert M. 1968. "Language as Symbolic Process in Communication." *American Scientist*, vol. 56, pp. 265–278.

Kroeber, A. L. 1958. "Sign Language Inquiry." *International Journal of American Linguistics*, vol. 24, pp. 1–19.

La Barre, Weston. 1955. "Obscenity: An Anthropological Appraisal." *Law and Contemporary Problems,* vol. 20, pp. 533–543.

——. 1954. *The Human Animal.* University of Chicago Press.

Labov, William. 1972 A. "On the Mechanism of Linguistic Change." In Gumperz and Hymes (1972), pp. 512–538.

——. 1972 B. "Rules for Ritual Insults." In Sudnow (1972), pp. 120–169.

——. 1969. *The Study of Nonstandard English.* Washington, D.C.: Center for Applied Linguistics.

——. 1968. "The Reflection of Social Processes in Linguistic Structures." In Fishman (1968), pp. 240–251.

——. 1967. "The Effect of Social Mobility on Linguistic Behavior." In Lieberson (1967), pp. 58–75.

——. 1966. *The Social Stratification of English in New York City.* Washington, D.C.: Center for Applied Linguistics.

——. 1963. "The Social Motivation of a Sound Change." *Word,* vol. 19, pp. 273–309.

Laird, Charlton. 1970. *Language in America.* Prentice-Hall.

Lakoff, Robin. 1972. "Language in Context." *Language,* vol. 48, pp. 907–927.

Lamb, Sydney. 1966. *Outline of Stratificational Grammar.* Georgetown University Press.

Lamb, Sydney. 1964. "The Sememic Approach to Structural Semantics." In Romney and D'Andrade (1964), pp. 57–78.

Lambert, Wallace E. 1972. *Language, Psychology, and Culture.* Stanford University Press.

——. 1969. "Psychological Studies of the Interdependencies of the Bilingual's Two Languages." In Puhvel (1969), pp. 99–126.

——, Anisfeld, M., and Yeni-Komshian, G. 1965. "Evaluational Reactions of Jewish and Arab Adolescents to Dialect and Language Variations." *Journal of Personality and Social Psychology,* vol. 2, pp. 84–90.

——, Hodgson, R. C., Gardner, R. C., and Fillenbaum, S. 1960. "Evaluational Reactions to Spoken Languages." *Journal of Abnormal and Social Psychology,* vol. 60, pp. 44–51.

Landar, Herbert. 1966. *Language and Culture.* Oxford University Press.

Langacker, Ronald W. 1968. *Language and Its Structure.* Harcourt Brace Jovanovich.

Leach, Edmund. 1966. *Rethinking Anthropology.* Humanities Press.

——. 1964. "Anthropological Aspects of Language: Animal Categories and Verbal Abuse." In Lenneberg (1964 B) pp. 23–63.

Legman, G. 1968. *Rationale of the Dirty Joke.* Grove Press.

Lehmann, Winfred P. 1972. *Descriptive Linguistics.* Random House.

——. 1962. *Historical Linguistics,* Holt, Rinehart & Winston.

—— and Malkiel, Yakov, editors. 1968. *Directions for Historical Linguistics.* University of Texas Press.

Lenneberg, Eric H. 1970. "The Biological Foundations of Language." In Lester (1970), pp. 3–20.

——. 1969. "On Explaining Language." *Science,* vol. 164, pp. 635–643.

——. 1967. *Biological Foundations of Language.* Wiley.

——. 1964 A. "A Biological Perspective of Language." In Lenneberg (1964 B), pp. 65–88.

——, editor. 1964 B. *New Directions in the Study of Language.* M.I.T. Press.

Lester, Mark, editor. 1970. *Readings in Applied Transformational Grammar*. Holt, Rinehart & Winston.

Levin, Samuel R. 1962. A. "Poetry and Grammaticalness." *Proceedings of the Ninth International Congress of Linguists,* edited by H. Lunt. The Hague: Mouton.

——. 1962 B. *Linguistic Structures in Poetry*. The Hague: Mouton.

Lévi-Strauss, Claude. 1962. *The Savage Mind*. University of Chicago Press.

Lieberman, Philip. 1968. "Primate Vocalizations and Human Linguistic Ability." *Journal of Acoustical Society of America,* vol. 44, pp. 1574–1584.

——, Crelin, E. S., and Klatt, D. H. 1972. "Phonetic Ability and Related Anatomy of the Newborn and Adult Human, Neanderthal Man, and the Chimpanzee." *American Anthropologist,* vol. 74, pp. 287–307.

Lieberson, Stanley, editor. 1967. *Explorations in Sociolinguistics*. Indiana University Press.

Loflin, Marvin D. 1967. "A Teaching Problem in Nonstandard Negro English." *English Journal,* vol. 56, pp. 1312–1314.

Lotz, John. 1964. "On Language and Culture." In Hymes (1964), pp. 182–183.

Lounsbury, F. G. 1965. "Another View of the Trobriand Kinship Categories." American Anthropological Association Special Publication, vol. 67, pp. 142–186.

Lyons, John. 1970. *Chomsky*. Viking.

——. 1968. *Introduction to Theoretical Linguistics*. Cambridge University Press.

——, editor. 1970. *New Horizons in Linguistics*. Penguin Books.

Maclay, Howard, and Osgood, Charles E. 1959. "Hesitation Phenomena in Spontaneous English Speech." *Word,* vol. 15, pp. 19–44.

Macnamara, John, editor. 1967. *Bilingualism in the Modern World*. Special Issue of *Journal of Social Issues,* vol. 23.

Malinowski, Bronislaw. 1923. "The Problem of Meaning in Primitive Languages." In Ogden and Richards (1923), pp. 296–336.

Maranda, Elli K. 1971. "Theory and Practice of Riddle Analysis." *Journal of American Folklore,* vol. 84, pp. 51–61.

Marks, Lawrence E. 1967 A. "Judgements of Grammaticalness of Some English Sentences and Non-Sentences." *American Journal of Psychology,* vol. 80, pp. 196–204.

——. 1967 B. "Some Structural and Sequential Factors in the Processing of Sentences." *Journal of Verbal Learning and Verbal Behavior,* vol. 6, pp. 707–713.

—— and Miller, G. A. 1964. "The Role of Semantic and Syntactic Constraints in the Memorization of English Sentences." *Journal of Verbal Learning and Verbal Behavior,* vol. 3, pp. 1–5.

May, L. Carlyle. 1956. "A Survey of Glossolalia and Related Phenomena in Non-Christian Religions." *American Anthropologist,* vol. 58, pp. 75–96.

McNeill, David. 1966. "Speaking of Space." *Science,* vol. 152, pp. 875–880.

Mencken, H. L. 1963. *The American Language*. (Abridged edition, by Raven I. McDavid, Jr.) Knopf.

Menninger, Karl. 1969. *Number Words and Number Symbols*. M.I.T. Press.

Miller, G. A., and Isard, S. 1963. "Some Perceptual Consequences of Linguistic Rules." *Journal of Verbal Learning and Verbal Behavior,* vol. 2, pp. 217–228.

Miller, Mary R. 1970. "The Language and Language Beliefs of Indian Children." *Anthropological Linguistics*, vol. 12, pp. 51–61.

Minnis, Noel, editor. 1971. *Linguistics at Large*. Viking.

Miron, Murray S. 1961. "A Cross-Linguistic Investigation of Phonetic Symbolism." *Journal of Abnormal and Social Psychology*, vol. 62, pp. 623–630.

Mitchell-Kernan, Claudia. 1972. "Signifying and Marking." In Gumperz and Hymes (1972), pp. 161–179.

Nadel, S. F. 1954. "Morality and Language among the Nupe." *Man*, vol. 54, pp. 55–57.

Newman, Stanley. 1955. "Zuñi Sacred and Slang Usage." *Southwestern Journal of Anthropology*, vol. 11, pp. 345–354.

Nickerson, Nancy P. 1971. "Review of *Basic Color Terms*." *International Journal of American Linguistics*, vol. 37, pp. 257–270.

Nida, Eugene A. 1959. "Principles of Translation as Exemplified by Bible Translating." In Brower (1959), pp. 11–31.

—— and Fehderau, Harold W. 1970. "Indigenous Pidgins and Koinés." *International Journal of American Linguistics*, vol. 36, pp. 146–155.

Nist, John. 1966. *A Structural History of English*. St. Martin's Press.

Ogden, C. K., and Richards, I. A. 1923. *The Meaning of Meaning*. Harcourt Brace Jovanovich.

Ohmann, Richard. 1966. "Literature as Sentences." *College English*, vol. 27, pp. 261–267.

——. 1964. "Generative Grammar and the Concept of Literary Style." *Word*, vol. 20, pp. 423–439.

Oldfield, R. C., and Marshall, J. C., editors. 1968. *Language: Selected Readings*. Penguin Books.

Opler, Morris, and Hoijer, Harry. 1940. "The Raid and War-Path Language of the Chiricahua Apache." *American Anthropologist,* vol. 42, pp. 617–634.

Osgood, Charles E., and Sebeok, Thomas A., editors. 1965. *Psycholinguistics.* Indiana University Press.

Pei, Mario. 1958. *One Language for the World.* Devin-Adair.

Peters, Charles R. 1972. "Evolution of the Capacity for Language." *Man,* vol. 7, pp. 33–49.

Pfungst, O. 1911 (reissued 1965). *Clever Hans.* Holt, Rinehart & Winston.

Pike, Kenneth L. 1967. *Language in Relation to a Unified Theory of the Structure of Human Behavior.* The Hague: Mouton.

Pittinger, R. E., Hockett, C. F., and Danehy, J. J. 1960. *The First Five Minutes.* Ithaca, N.Y.: Martineau.

Pospisil, Leopold. 1965. "A Formal Analysis of Substantive Law: Kapauku Papuan Laws of Inheritance." American Anthropological Association Special Publication, vol. 67, pp. 166–185.

Premack, David. 1972. "Teaching Language to an Ape." *Scientific American,* vol. 227, pp. 92–99.

——. 1971. "Language in Chimpanzee?" *Science,* vol. 172, pp. 808–822.

Puhvel, Jaan, editor. 1969. *Substance and Structure of Language.* University of California Press.

Pyles, Thomas. 1971. *The Origins and Development of the English Language.* Harcourt Brace Jovanovich, revised edition.

——. 1959. "Bible Belt Onomastics or Some Curiosities of Anti-Pedobaptist Nomenclature." *Names,* vol. 7, pp. 84–100.

Read, Allen W. 1934. "An Obscenity Symbol." *American Speech,* vol. 9, pp. 264–278.

Rice, Frank A. 1962. *Study of the Role of Second Languages*. Washington, D.C.: Center for Applied Linguistics.

Robbins, Rossell H. 1966. "The Warden's Wordplay: Toward a Redefinition of the Spoonerism." *The Dalhousie Review,* vol. 46, pp. 457–465.

Roberts, John M., and Forman, Michael L. 1972. "Riddles: Expressive Models of Interrogation." In Gumperz and Hymes (1972), pp. 180–209.

Rochester, S. R. 1973. "The Significance of Pauses in Spontaneous Speech." *Journal of Psycholinguistic Research,* vol. 2, pp. 51–81.

Romney, A. K., and D'Andrade, R. G., editors. 1964. *Transcultural Studies in Cognition*. American Anthropological Association Special Publication, vol. 66.

Rosenthal, Robert. 1967. "Covert Communication in the Psychological Experiment." *Psychological Bulletin,* vol. 67, pp. 356–367.

——. 1966. *Experimenter Effects in Behavioral Research*. Appleton-Century-Crofts.

Rosenthal, Robert, and Jacobson, Lenore. 1968. *Pygmalion in the Classroom*. Holt, Rinehart & Winston.

Rubin, Joan. 1968 A. *National Bilingualism in Paraguay*. The Hague: Mouton.

——. 1968 B. "Language and Education in Paraguay." In Fishman, Ferguson, and Das Gupta (1968), pp. 477–488.

——. 1962. "Bilingualism in Paraguay." *Anthropological Linguistics,* vol. 4, pp. 52–58.

Russell, Claire, and Russell, W. M. S. 1971. "Language and Animal Signals." In Minnis (1971), pp. 159–194.

Sagarin, Edward. 1962. *The Anatomy of Dirty Words*. Lyle Stuart.

Samarin, William J. 1973. *Tongues of Men and Angels*. Macmillan.

——. 1972. "Variation and Variables in Religious Glossolalia." *Language in Society*, vol. 1, pp. 121–130.

——. 1969. "The Forms and Functions of Nonsense Languages." *Linguistics*, vol. 50, pp. 70–74.

——. 1968. "Linguisticality of Glossolalia." *Hartford Quarterly*, vol. 8, pp. 49–75.

Sapir, Edward. 1949. *Selected Writings*, edited by D. G. Mandelbaum. University of California Press.

——. 1929. "The Status of Linguistics as a Science." *Language*, vol. 5, pp. 207–214.

——. 1921. *Language: An Introduction to the Study of Speech*. Harcourt Brace Jovanovich.

Sartre, Jean-Paul. 1959. *Nausea*. New Directions.

Schegloff, Emanuel A. 1972. "Sequencing in Conversational Openings." In Gumperz and Hymes (1972), pp. 346–380.

Schneider, David M. 1965. "American Kin Terms and Terms for Kinsmen." In Hammel (1965), pp. 288–308.

Scott, Charles T. 1965. "Persian and Arabic Riddles." *International Journal of American Linguistics*, vol. 31, pp. 1–135.

Searle, John R. 1969. *Speech Acts*. Cambridge University Press.

Sears, Donald A., and Smith, Henry A. 1969. "A Linguistic Look at Aerospace English." In *Aspects of American English*, by Elizabeth M. Kerr and Ralph M. Aderman (1971), pp. 128–138. Harcourt Brace Jovanovich.

Sebeok, Thomas A., editor. 1968. *Animal Communication*. University of Indiana Press.

——. 1964. *Approaches to Semiotics*. The Hague: Mouton.

——, editor. 1960. *Style in Language*. M.I.T. Press.

Sherzer, Dina. In Press. "Saying Is Inventing: Gnomic

Expressions in *Molloy*." In Kirshenblatt-Gimblett (In Press).

Sherzer, Joel. In Press A. "Linguistic Games: Implications for (Socio) Linguistics." In Kirshenblatt-Gimblett (In Press).

———. In Press B. "Some Current Issues in Linguistic Theory—A Sociolinguistic Perspective."

Slobin, Dan I. 1971. *Psycholinguistics*. Scott, Foresman.

Smith, Frank, and Miller, George A. 1966. *The Genesis of Language*. M.I.T. Press.

Steiner, George. 1971. *Extraterritorial: Papers on Literature and the Language Revolution*. Atheneum.

Stern, Theodore. 1957. "Drum and Whistle 'Languages.'" *American Anthropologist*, vol. 59, pp. 487–506.

Stewart, William A. 1970. "Historical and Structural Bases for the Recognition of Negro Dialect." *Report of the 20th Annual Round Table on Linguistics and Language Studies*, edited by James E. Alatis (1970), pp. 239–247. Georgetown University Press.

Stoltz, Walter S. 1969. "Some Experiments with Queer Sentences." *Language and Speech*, vol. 12, pp. 203–219.

Stone, Leo. 1954. "On the Principal Obscene Word of the English Language." *International Journal of Psycho-Analysis*, vol. 35, pp. 30–56.

Strehlow, T. G. H. 1947. *Aranda Traditions*. Melbourne University Press.

Stroll, Avrum. 1954. "Is Everyday Language Inconsistent?" *Mind*, vol. 63, pp. 219–225.

Sturtevant, Edgar H. 1947. *An Introduction to Linguistic Science*. Yale University Press.

Sudnow, David, editor. 1972. *Studies in Social Interaction*. The Free Press.

Swadesh, Morris. 1971. *The Origin and Diversification*

of Language, edited by Joel Sherzer, Aldine-Atherton.

Tannenbaum, P. H., Williams, F., and Hillier, C. S. 1965. "Word Predictability in the Environments of Hesitations." *Journal of Verbal Learning and Verbal Behavior,* vol. 4, pp. 134–140.

Tarski, Alfred. 1969. "Truth and Proof." *Scientific American,* vol. 220, pp. 63–77.

Taylor, Archer. 1951. *English Riddles from Oral Tradition.* University of California Press.

Taylor, Insup K. 1963. "Phonetic Symbolism Re-examined." *Psychological Bulletin,* vol. 60, pp. 200–209.

Thorne, James P. 1965. "Stylistics and Generative Grammars." *Journal of Linguistics,* vol. 1, pp. 49–59.

Tonkin, Elizabeth. 1971. "Some Coastal Pidgins of West Africa." In Ardener (1971), pp. 129–155.

Trudgill, Peter. 1972. "Sex, Covert Prestige and Linguistic Change in the Urban British English of Norwich." *Language in Society,* vol. 1, pp. 179–195.

Turner, Lorenzo D. 1949. *Africanisms in the Gullah Dialect.* University of Chicago Press.

Tyler, Stephen A., editor. 1969. *Cognitive Anthropology.* Holt, Rinehart & Winston.

Ullmann, Stephen. 1962. *Semantics.* Oxford: Basil Blackwell.

Von Frisch, K. 1967. *The Dance Language and Orientation of Bees.* Harvard University Press.

Wallace, A. F. C., and Atkins, John. 1960. "The Meaning of Kinship Terms." *American Anthropologist,* vol. 62, pp. 58–80.

Warren, Richard M., and Warren, Roslyn P. 1970. "Auditory Illusions and Confusions." *Scientific American,* vol. 223, pp. 30–36.

Weinreich, Uriel. 1953. *Languages in Contact.* Linguistic Circle of New York.

——, Labov, W., and Herzog, M. 1968. "Empirical Foundations for a Theory of Language Change." In Lehmann and Malkiel (1968), pp. 95–188.

Whorf, Benjamin L. 1956. *Language, Thought and Reality.* M.I.T. Press.

Winslow, David J. 1969. "Children's Derogatory Epithets." *Journal of American Folklore,* vol. 82, pp. 255–263.

Witherspoon, Gary, 1971. "Navajo Categories of Objects at Rest." *American Anthropologist,* vol. 73, pp. 110–127.

Wittgenstein, Ludwig. 1963. *Tractatus Logico-Philosophicus.* Humanities Press, second edition.

——. 1958. *Philosophical Investigations.* Oxford: Basil Blackwell, second edition.

Wolfenstein, Martha. 1954. *Children's Humor: A Psychological Analysis.* The Free Press.

Wolfram, Walter A. 1969. *A Sociolinguistic Description of Detroit Negro Speech.* Washington, D.C.: Center for Applied Linguistics.

Index to Languages and Cultures

Index to Subjects and Names

ABOUT THE AUTHOR

PETER FARB'S deep interest in language and how people use it dates back to one of his fields of concentration during his undergraduate years at Vanderbilt University: the comparative study of Mediterranean languages. He was also employed on a research project to collect folk ballads and various styles of English speech in isolated communities in the South. Later, in graduate school at Columbia, his study of anthropological linguistics gave him a new perspective on remote, non-European languages. He became familiar with a wide variety of American Indian languages—in North America as well as in Mexico, Central America and Brazil—in the course of his travels to research two of his bestselling books, *Man's Rise to Civilization as Shown by the Indians of North America* and *Face of North America*. Mr. Farb has served as Consultant to the Smithsonian Institution in Washington, D.C., as Curator of American Indian Cultures at the Riverside Museum in New York City and most recently as Visiting Lecturer in English at Yale, where he is a fellow of Calhoun College. He lives in Amherst, Massachusetts.